AF375466

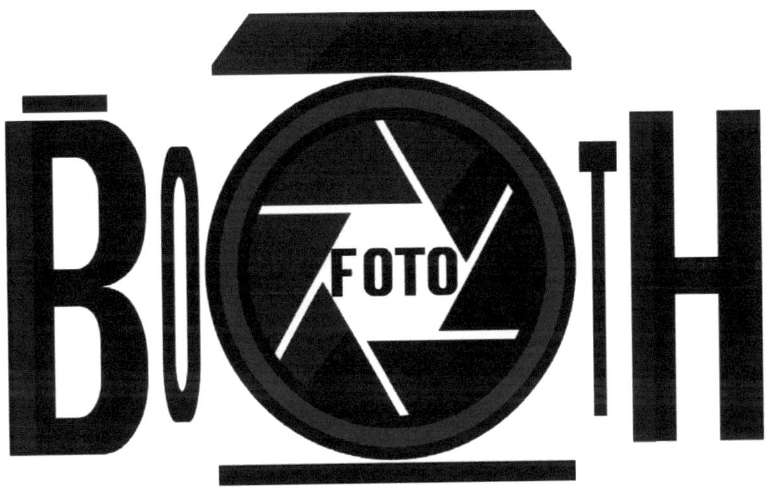
BOOTH
FOTO

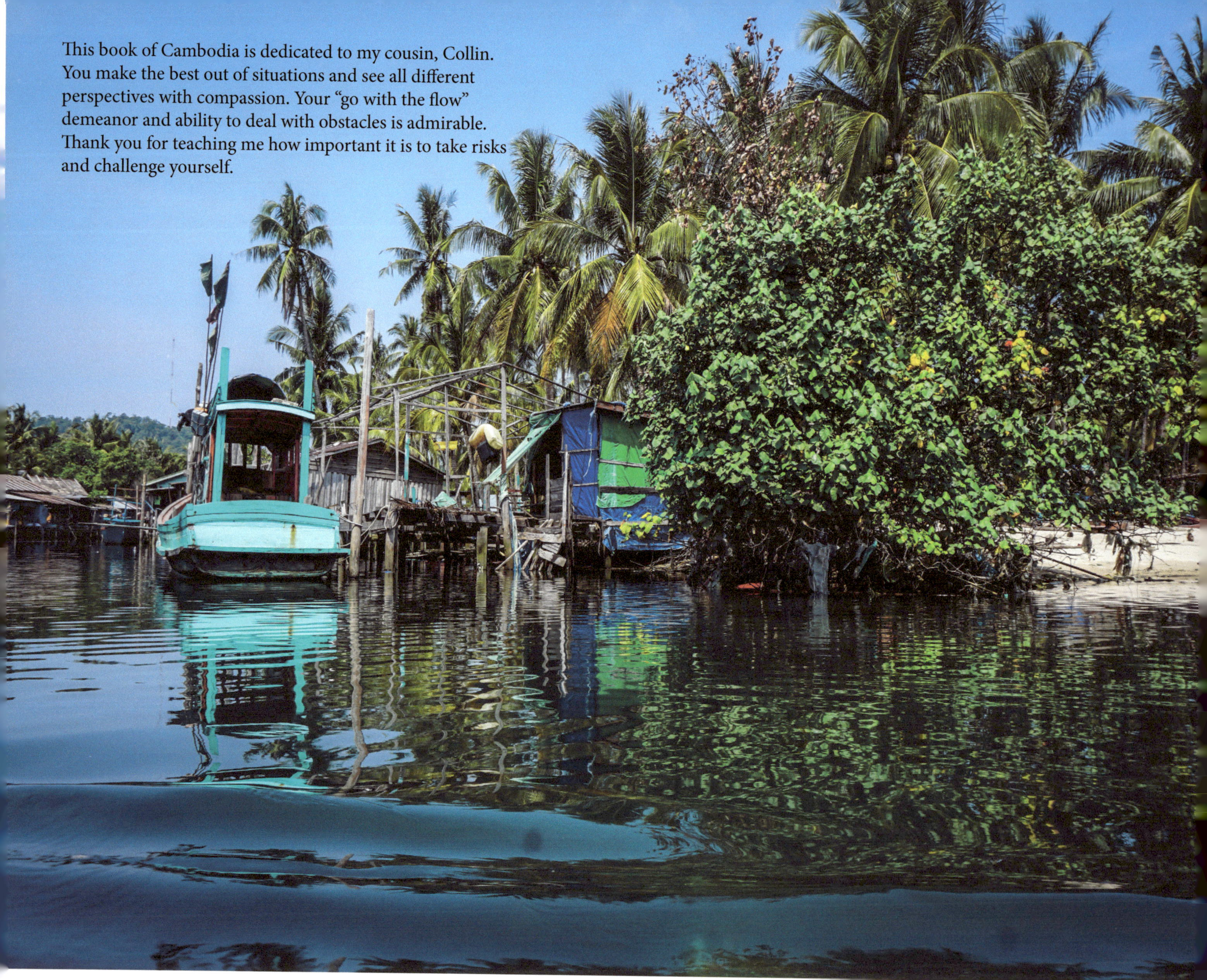

This book of Cambodia is dedicated to my cousin, Collin. You make the best out of situations and see all different perspectives with compassion. Your "go with the flow" demeanor and ability to deal with obstacles is admirable. Thank you for teaching me how important it is to take risks and challenge yourself.

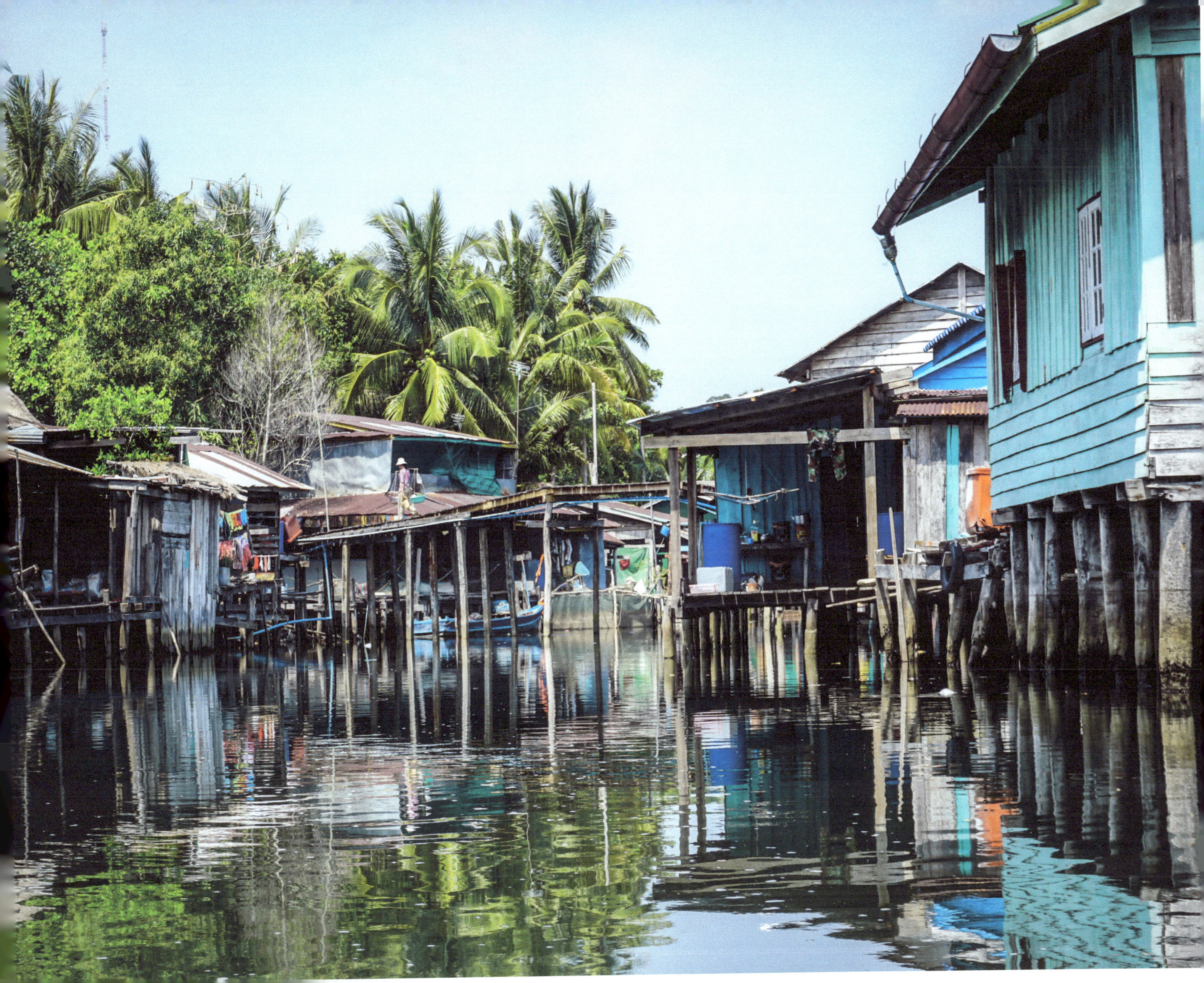

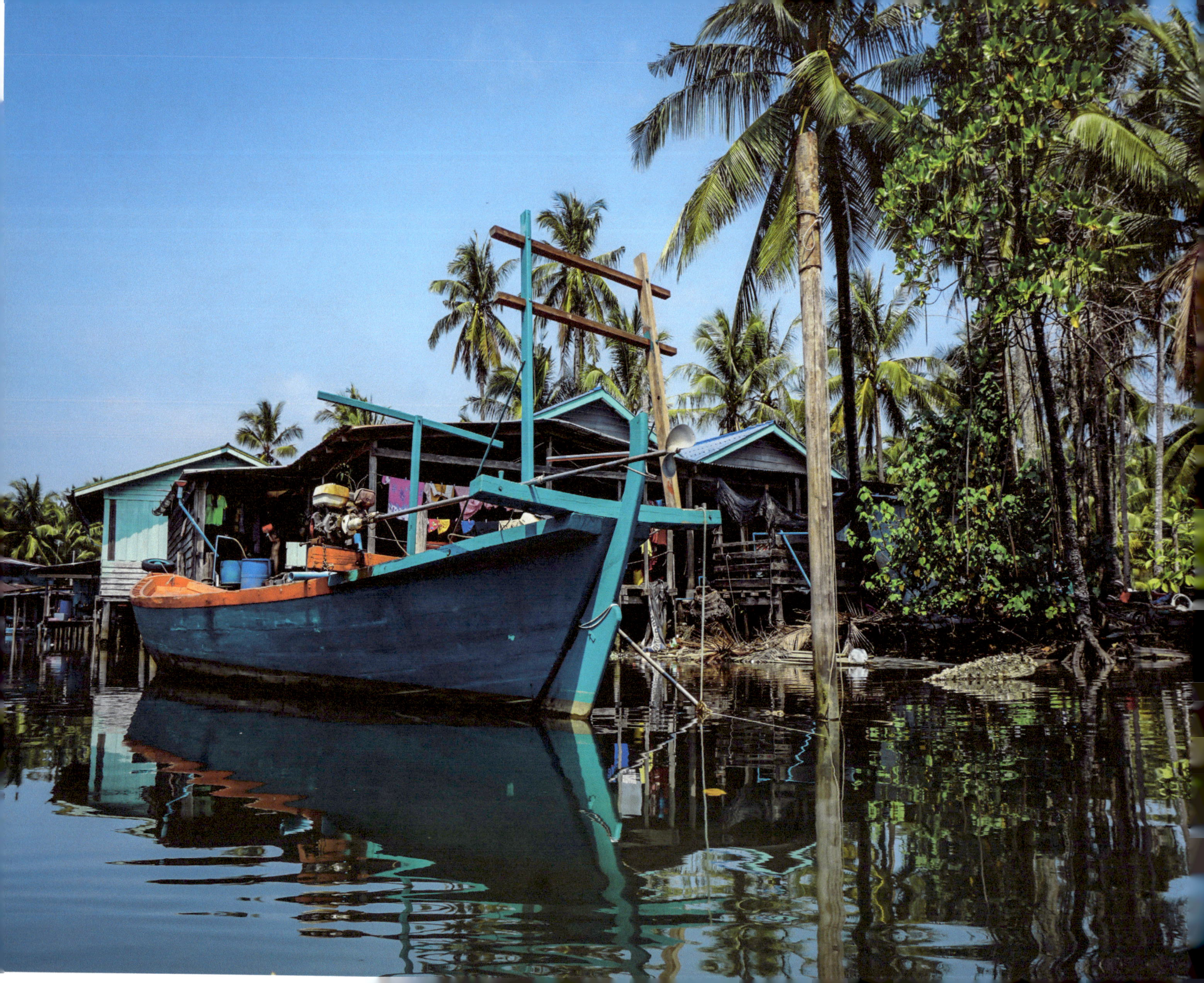

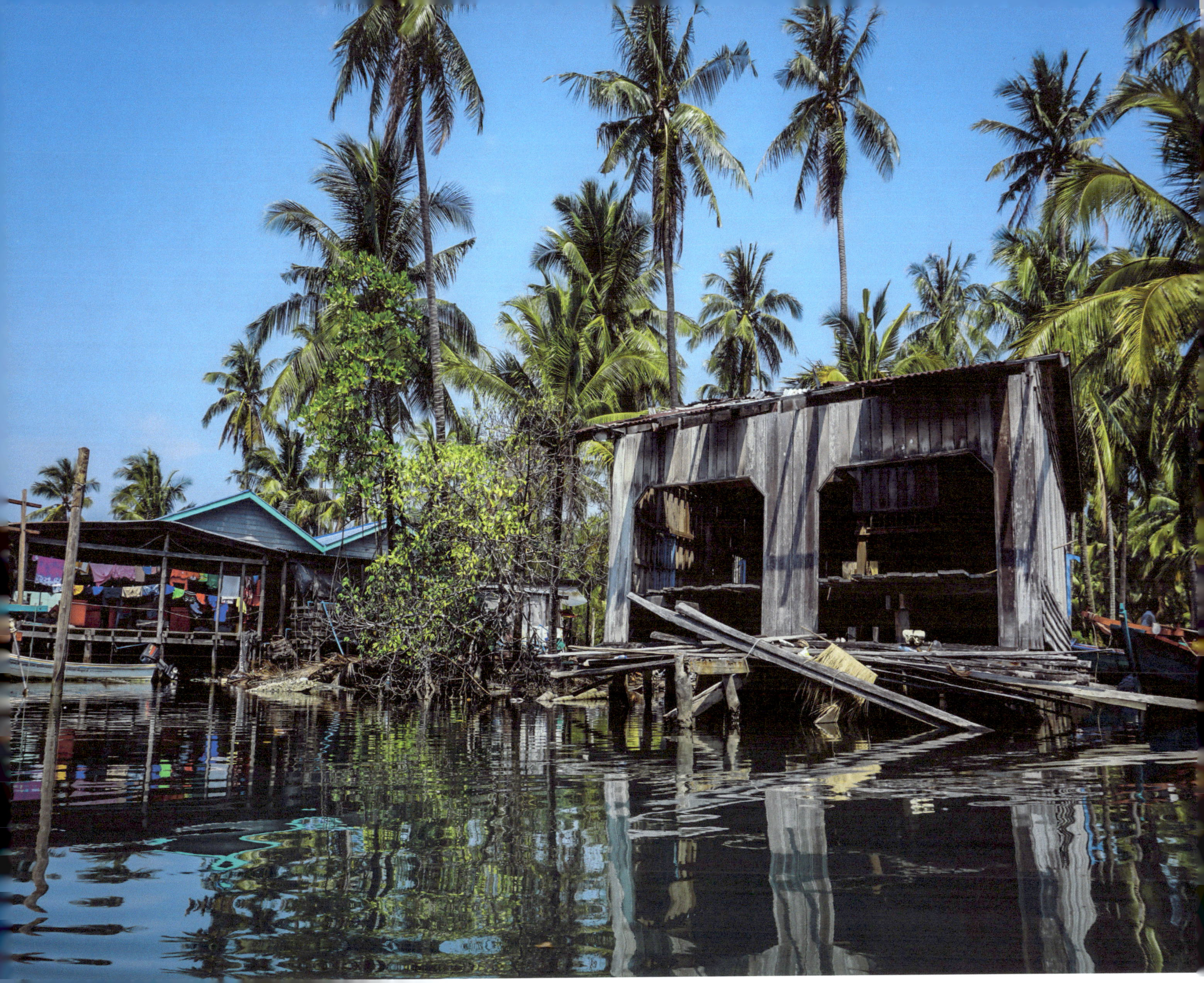

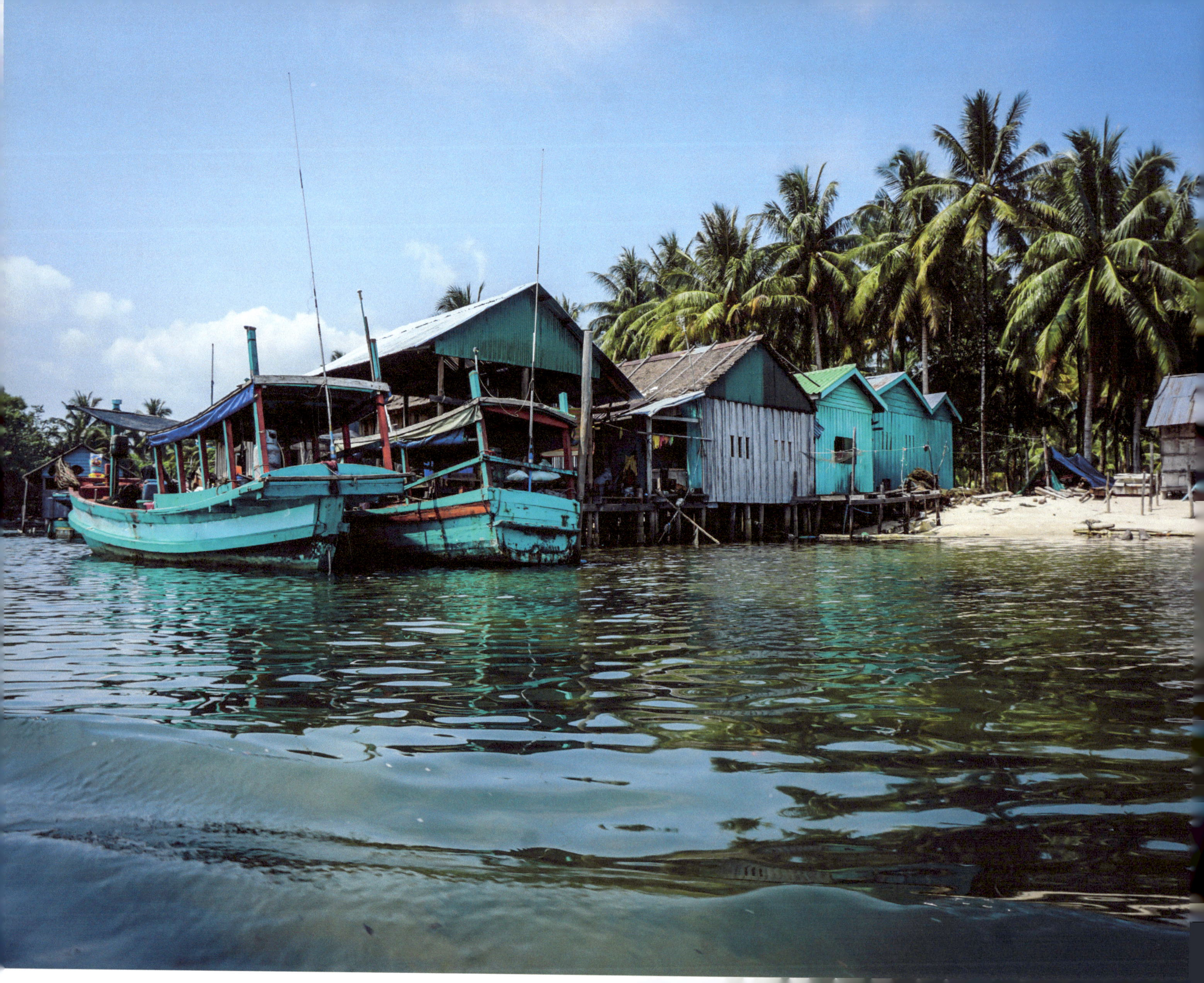

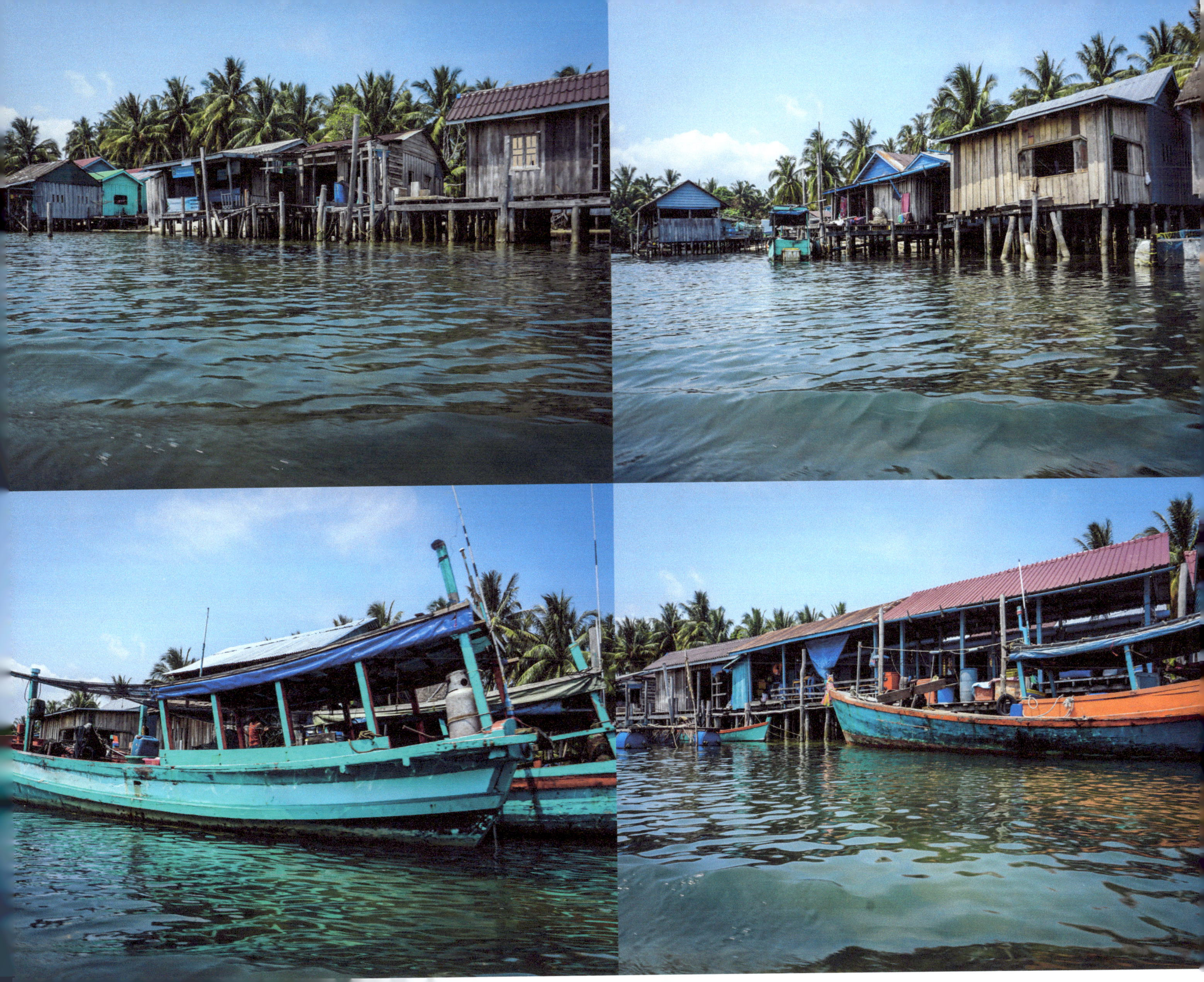

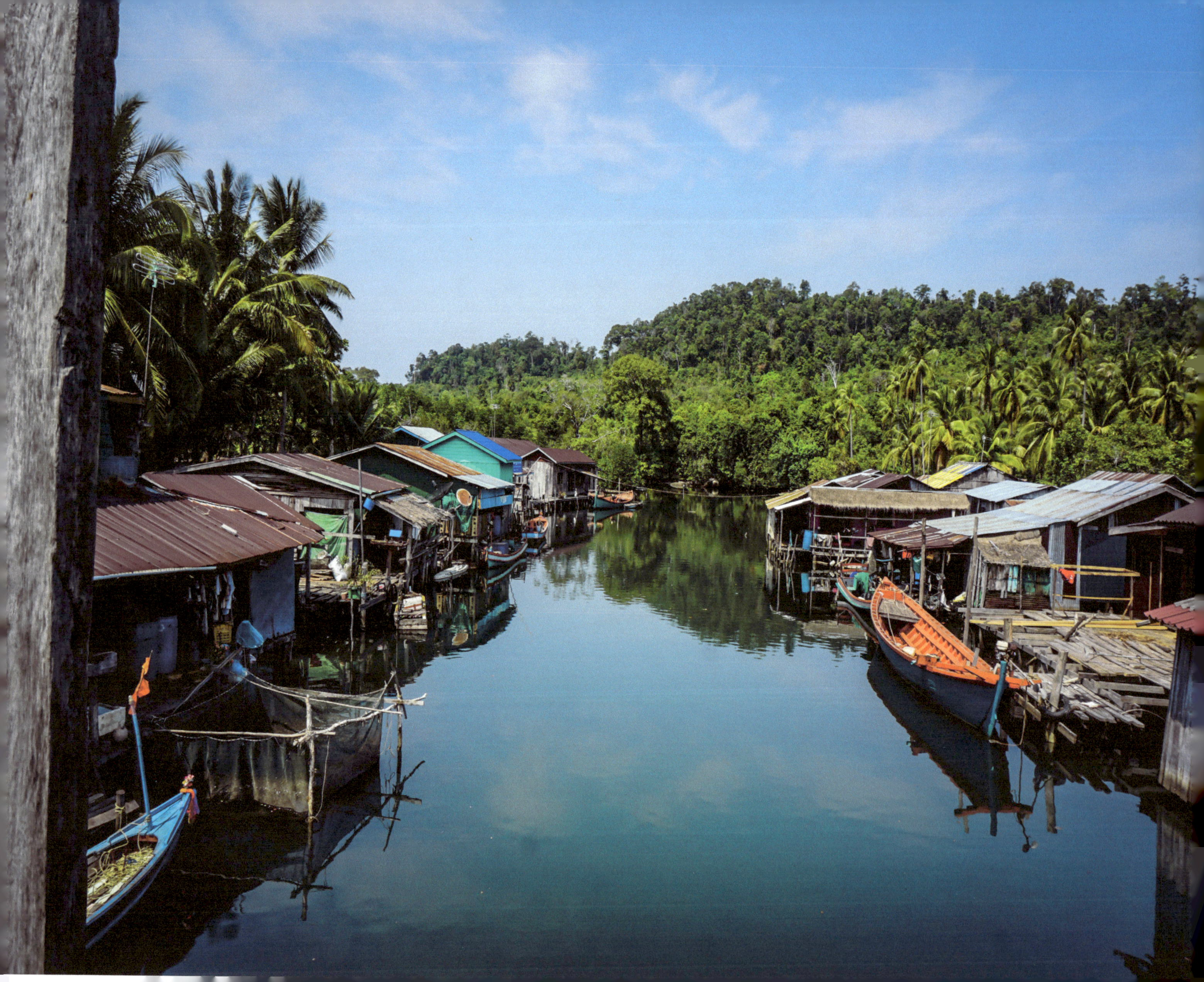

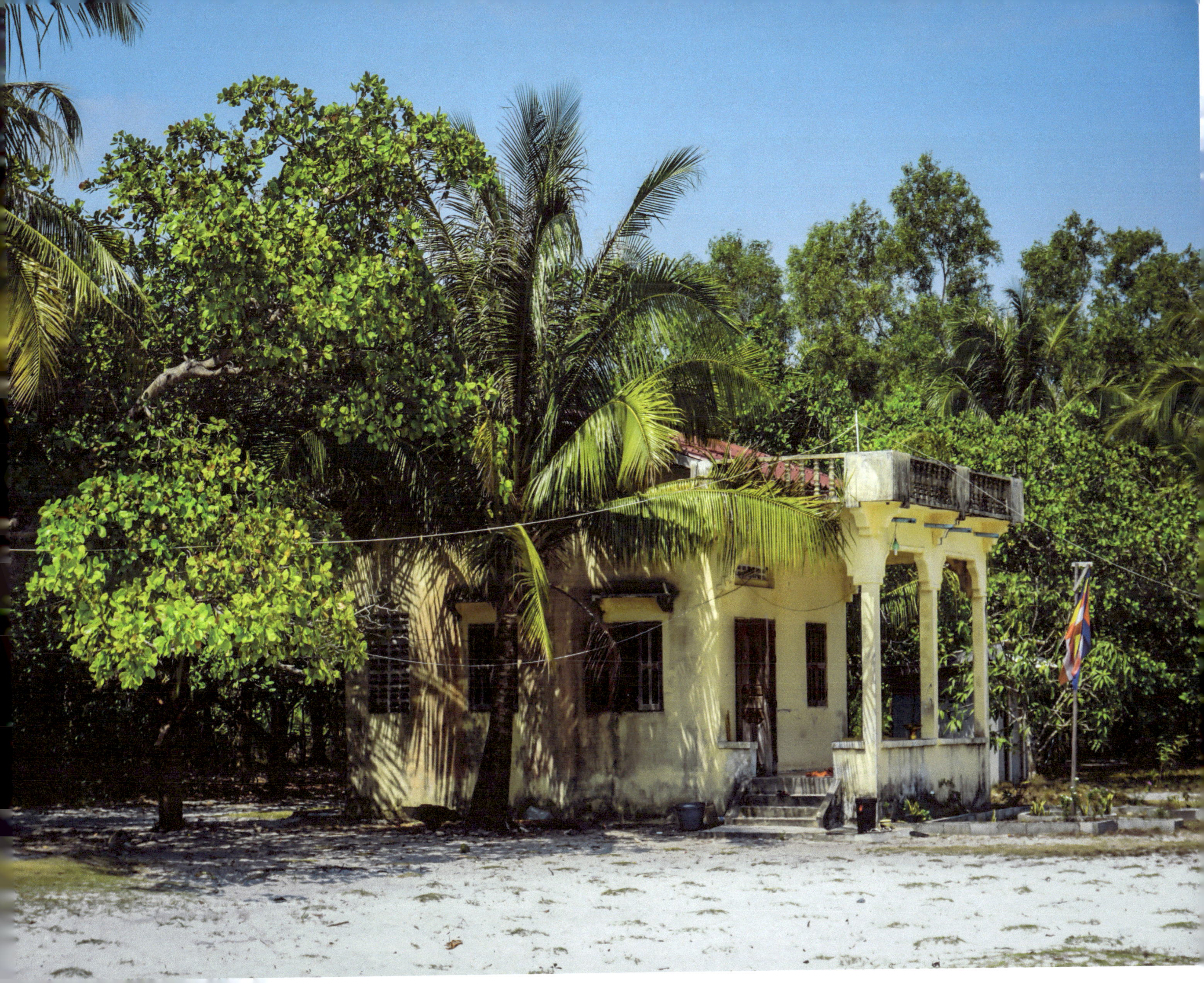

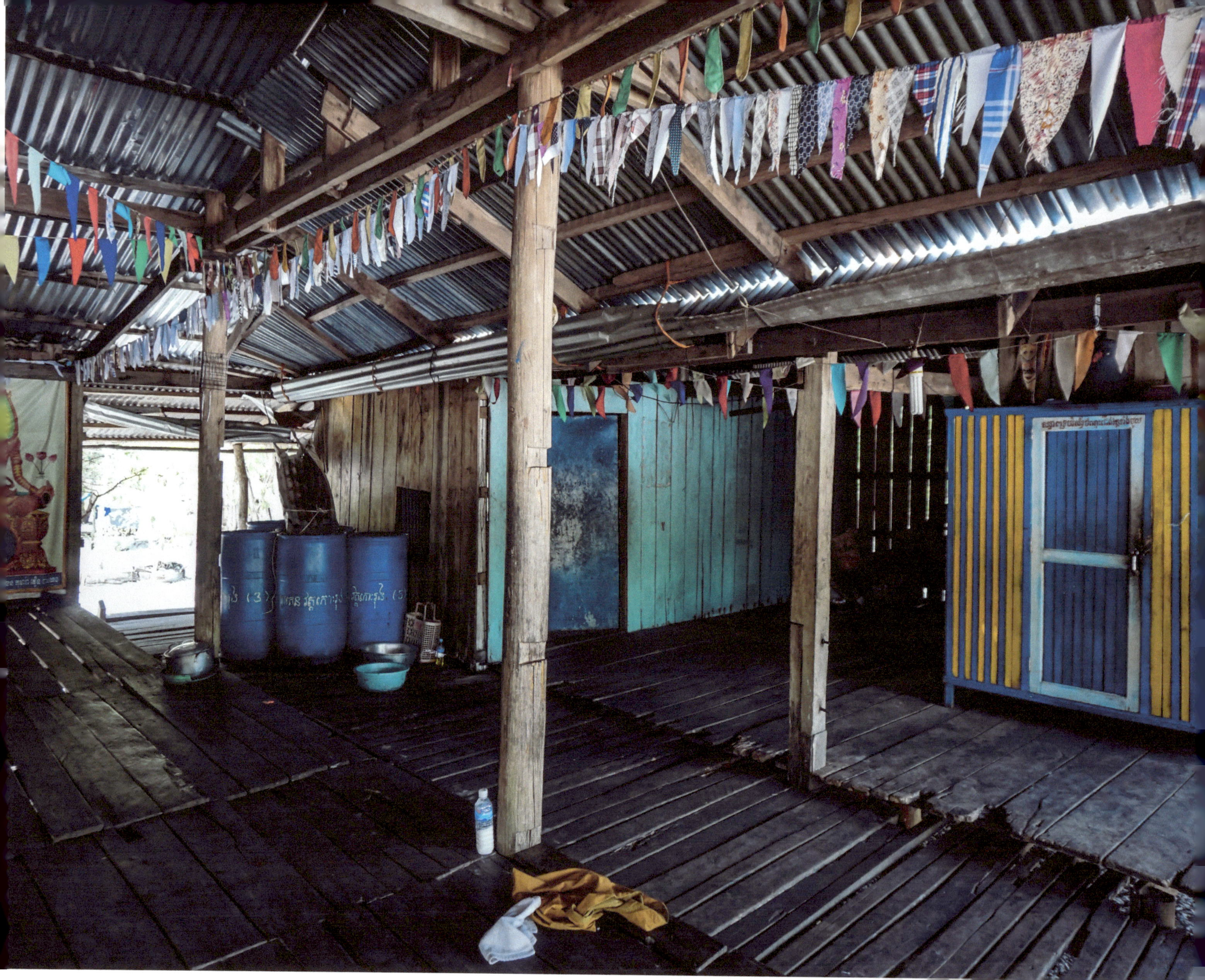

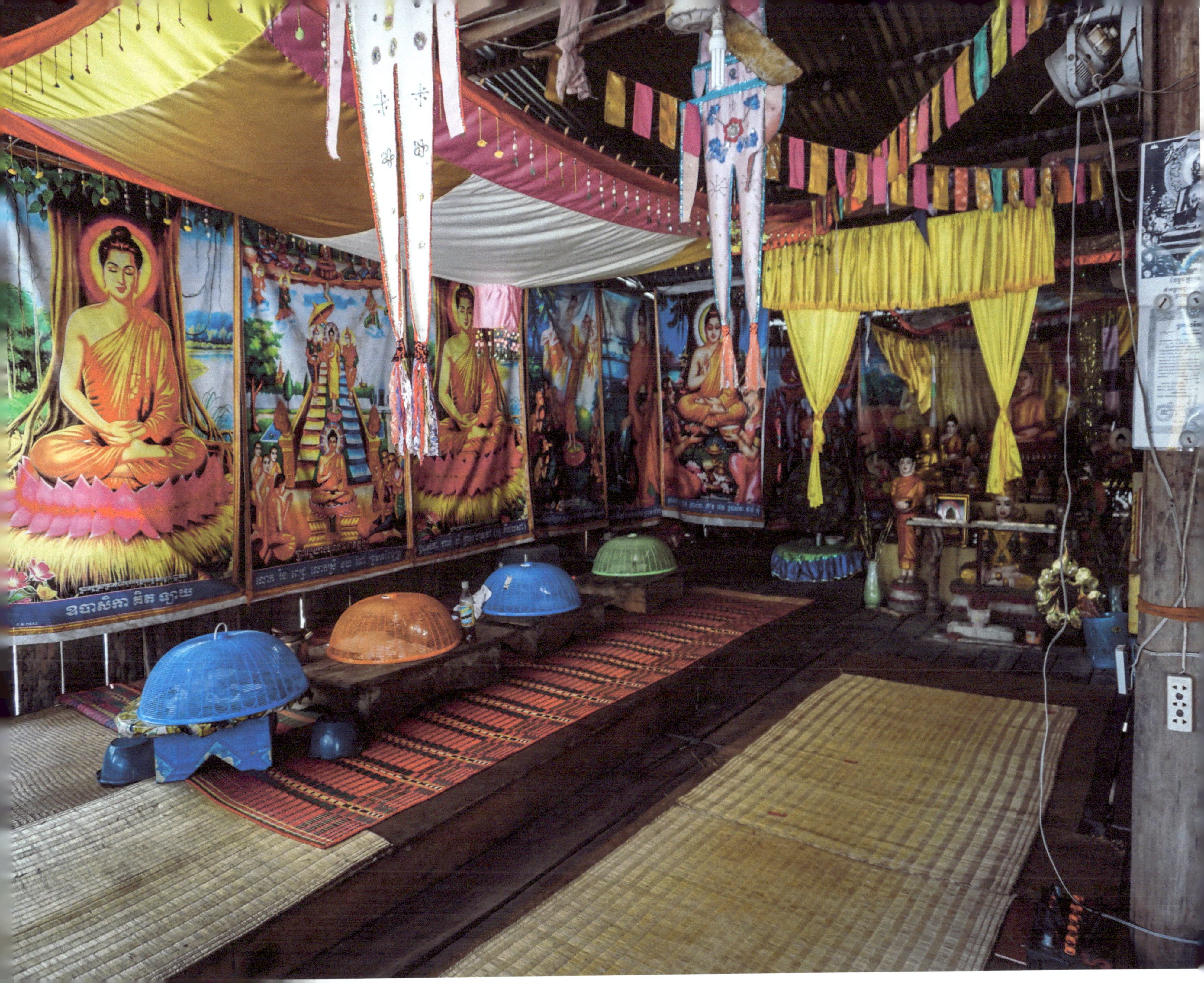

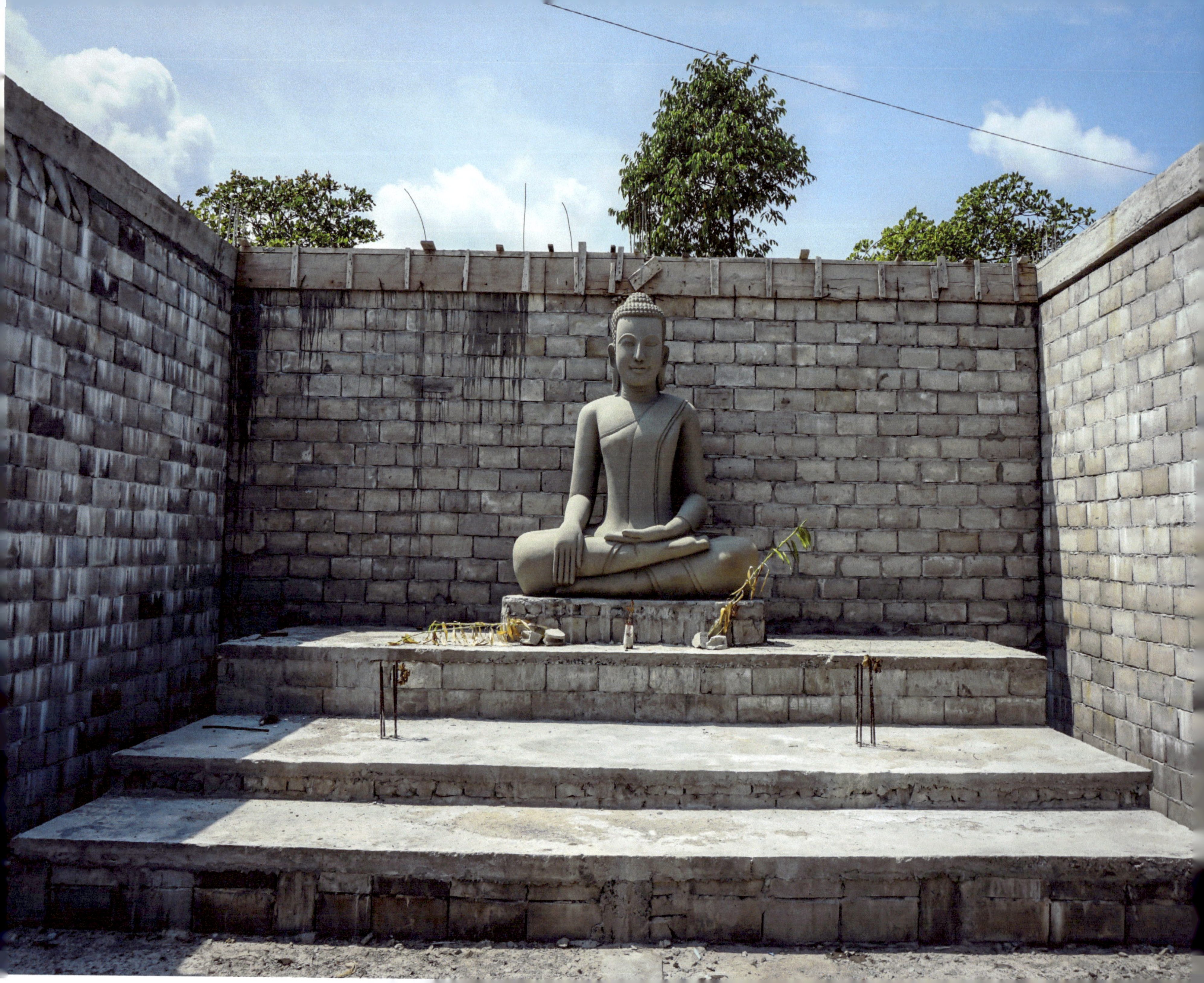

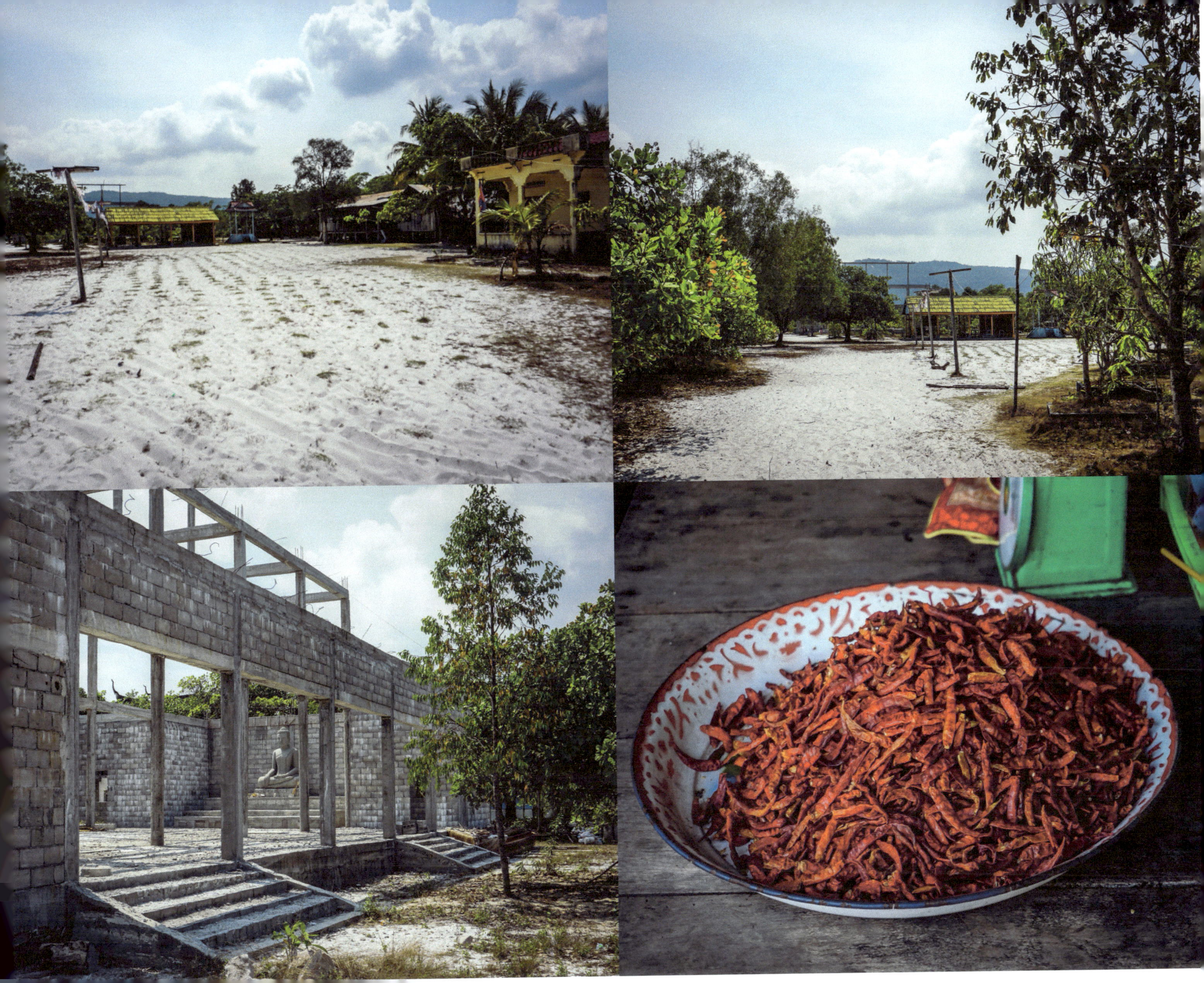

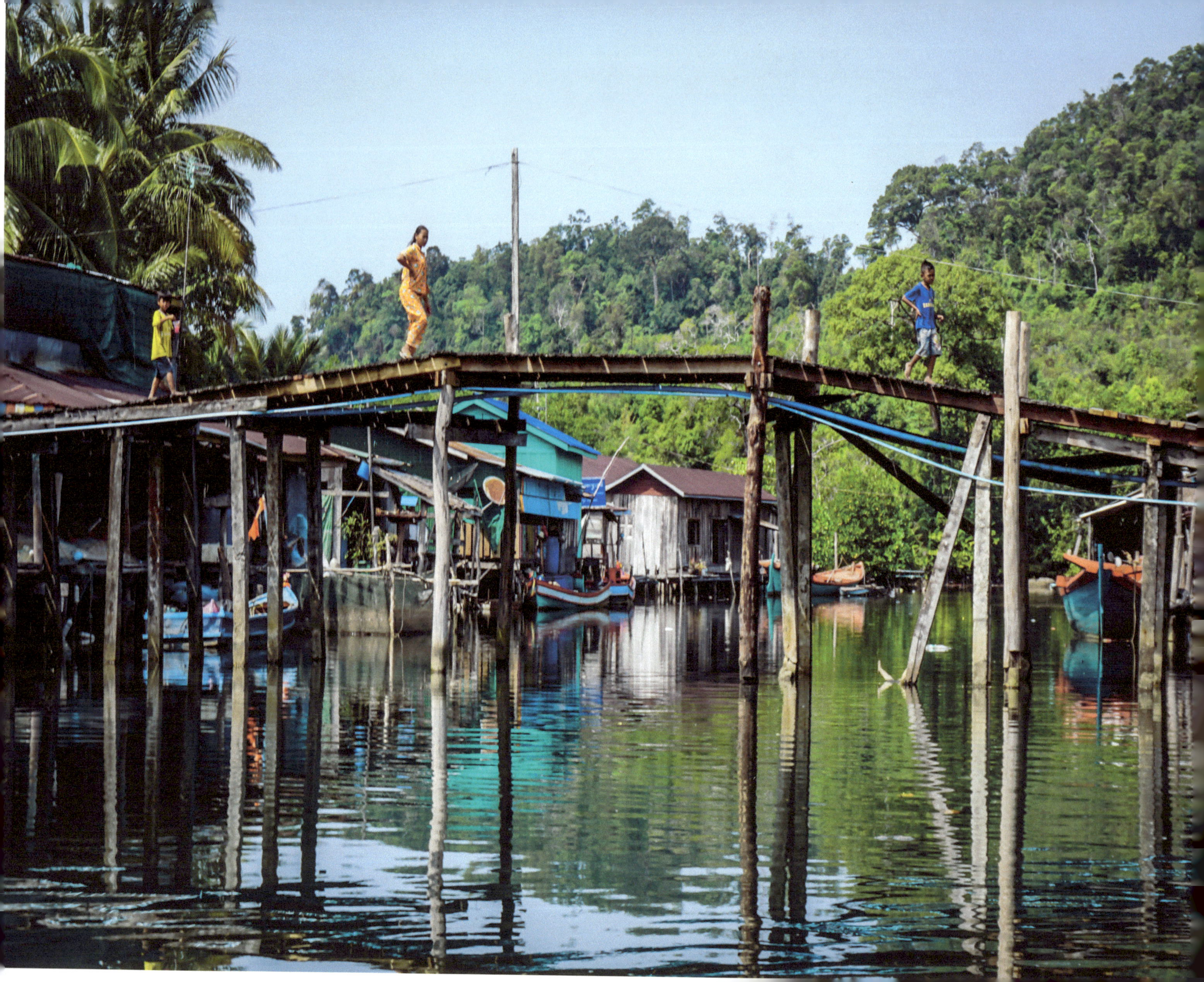

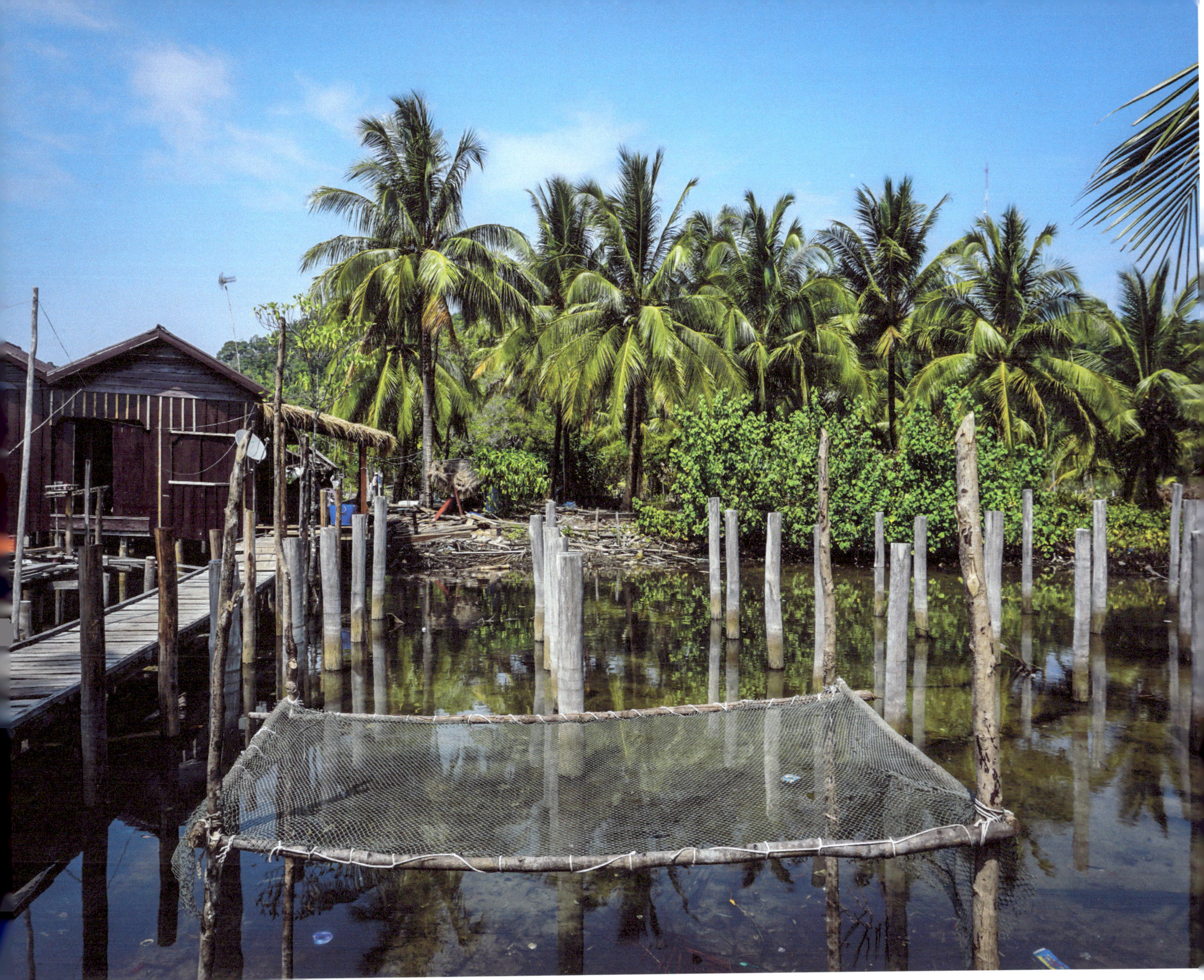

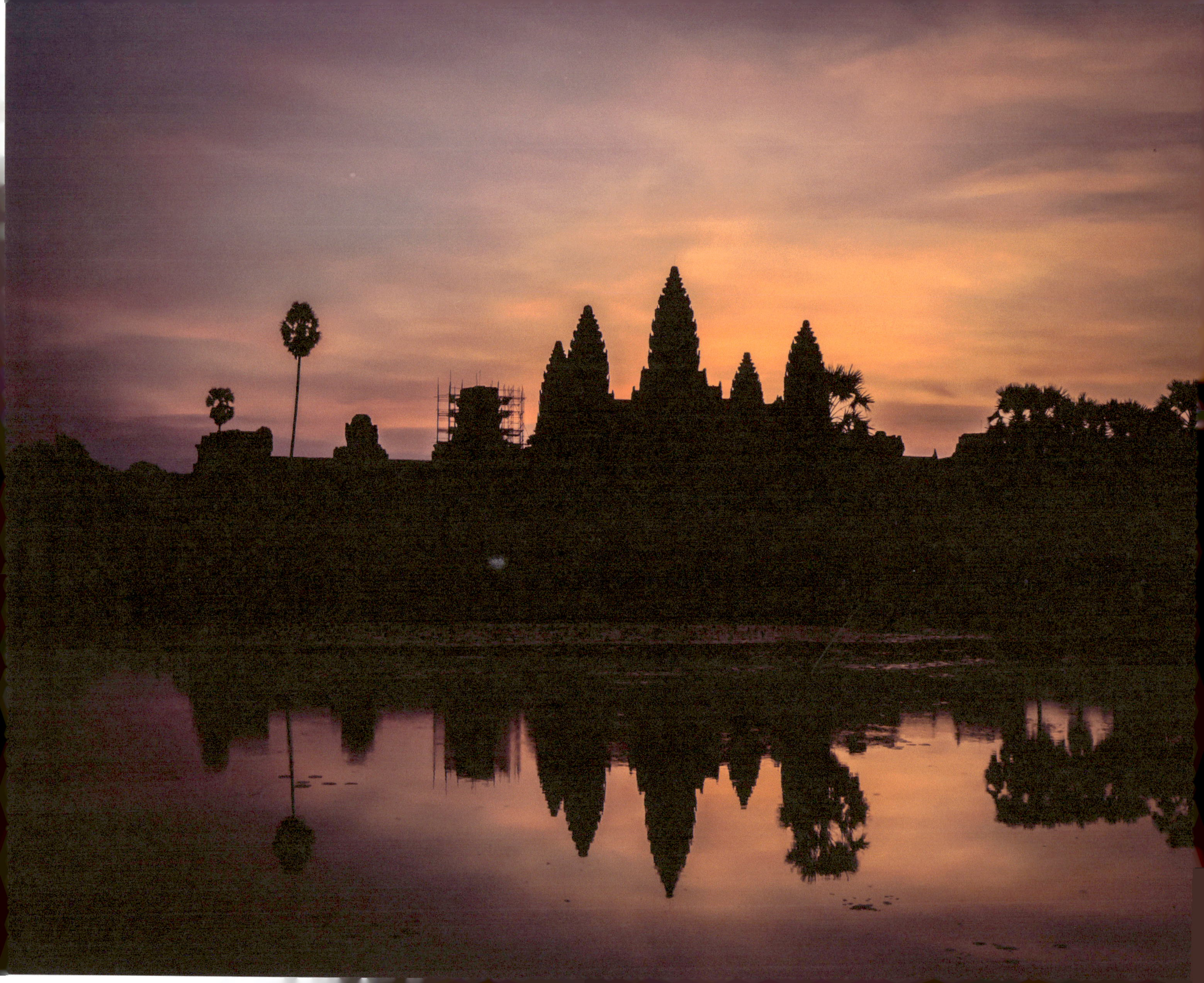

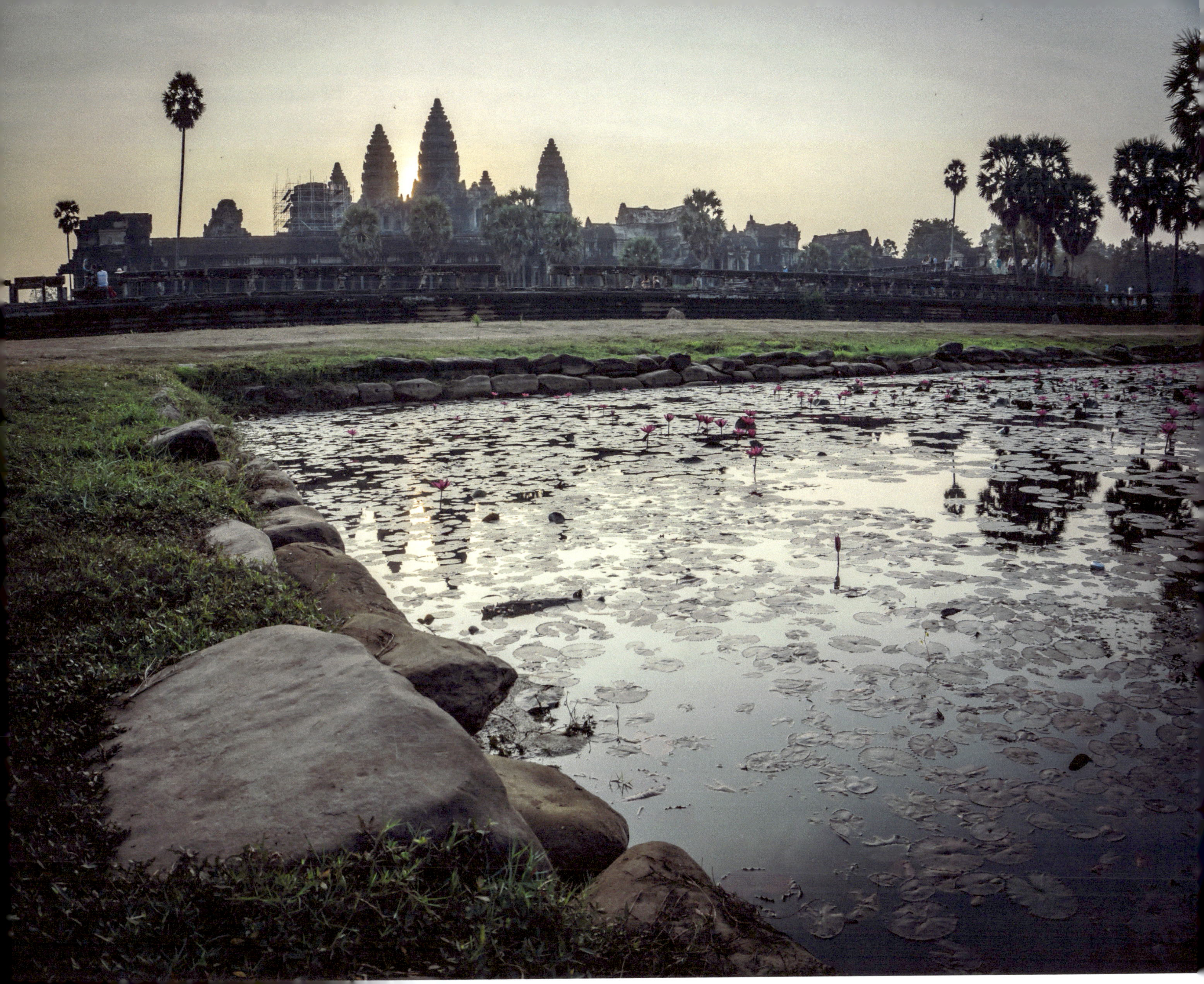

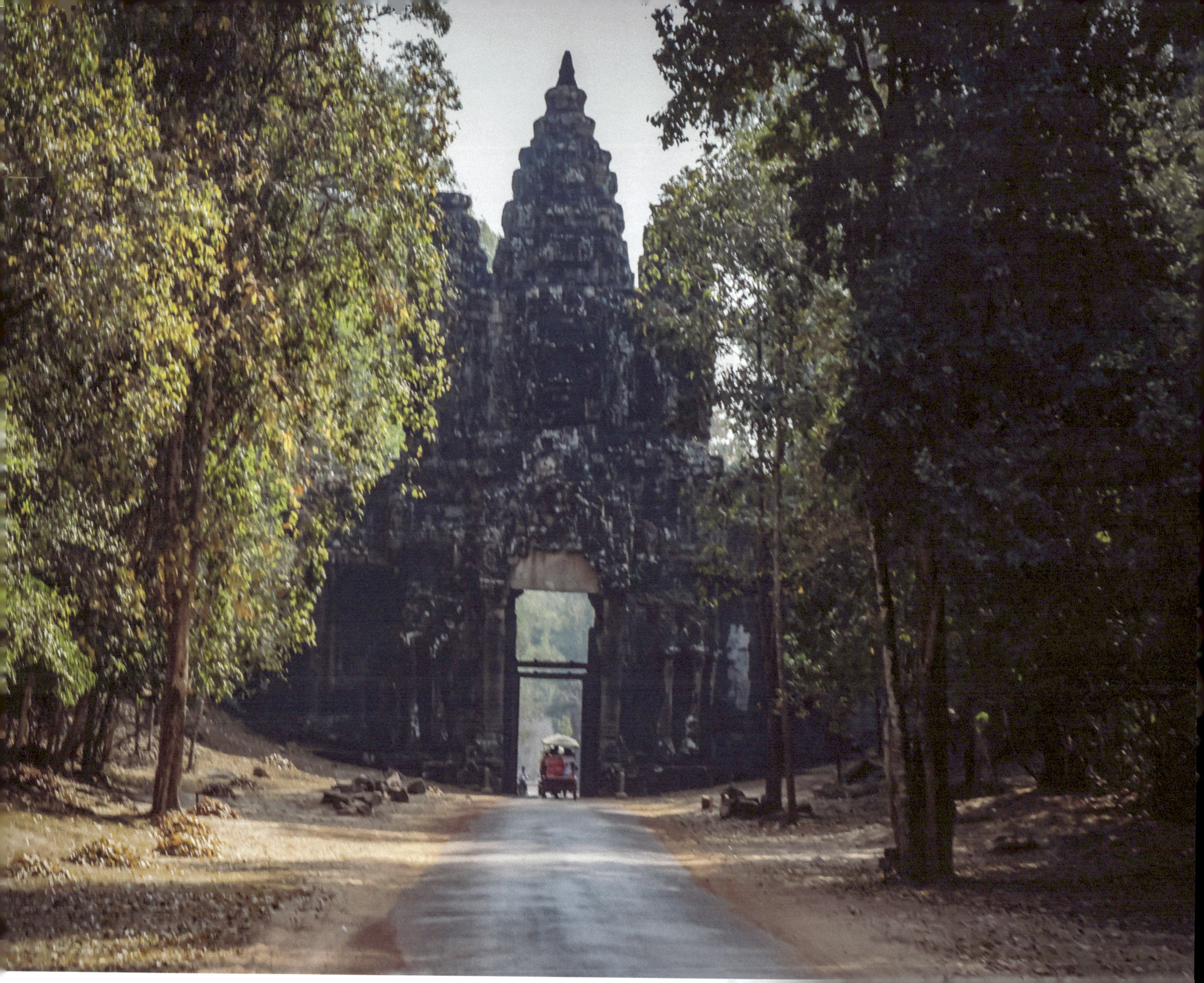

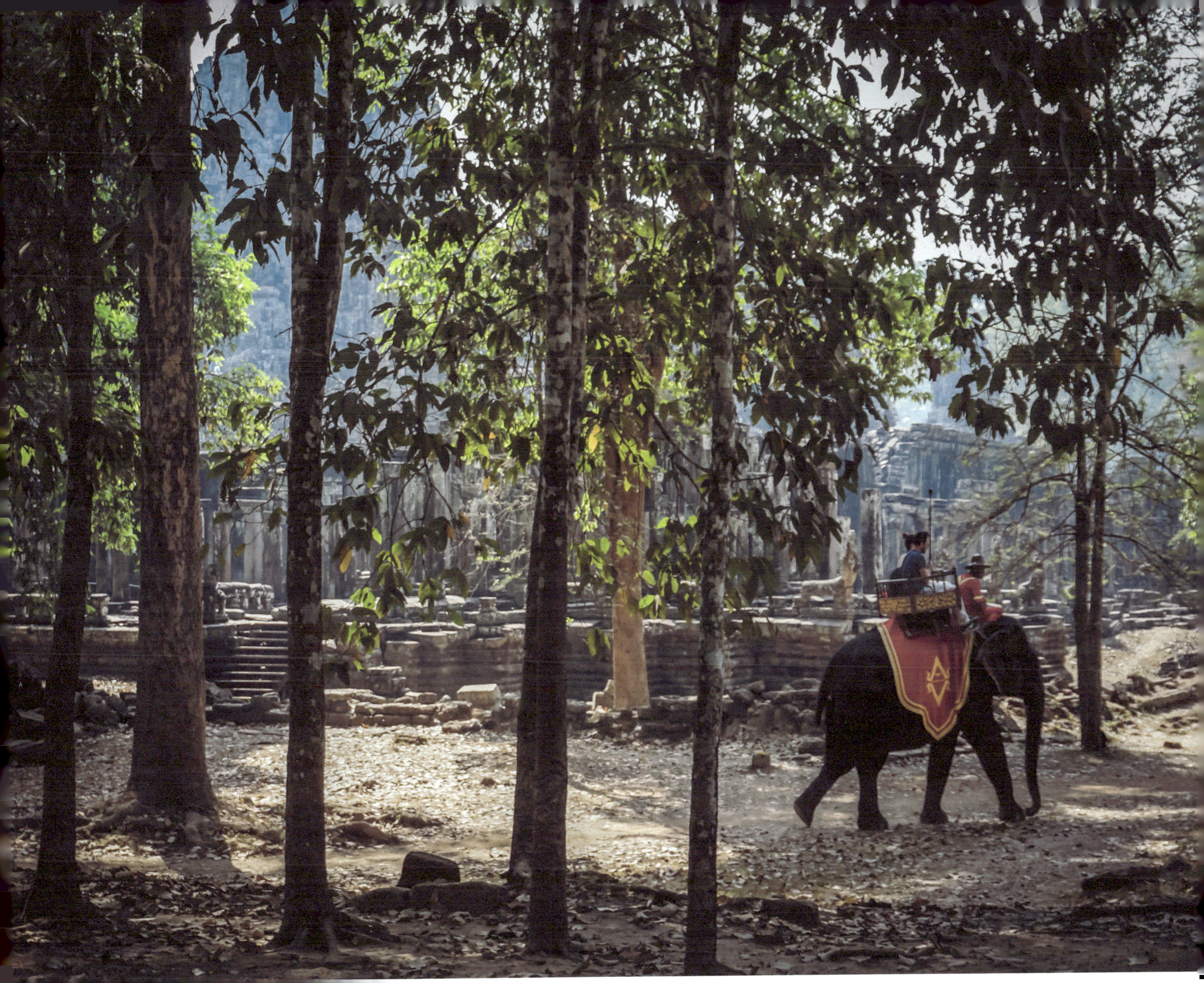

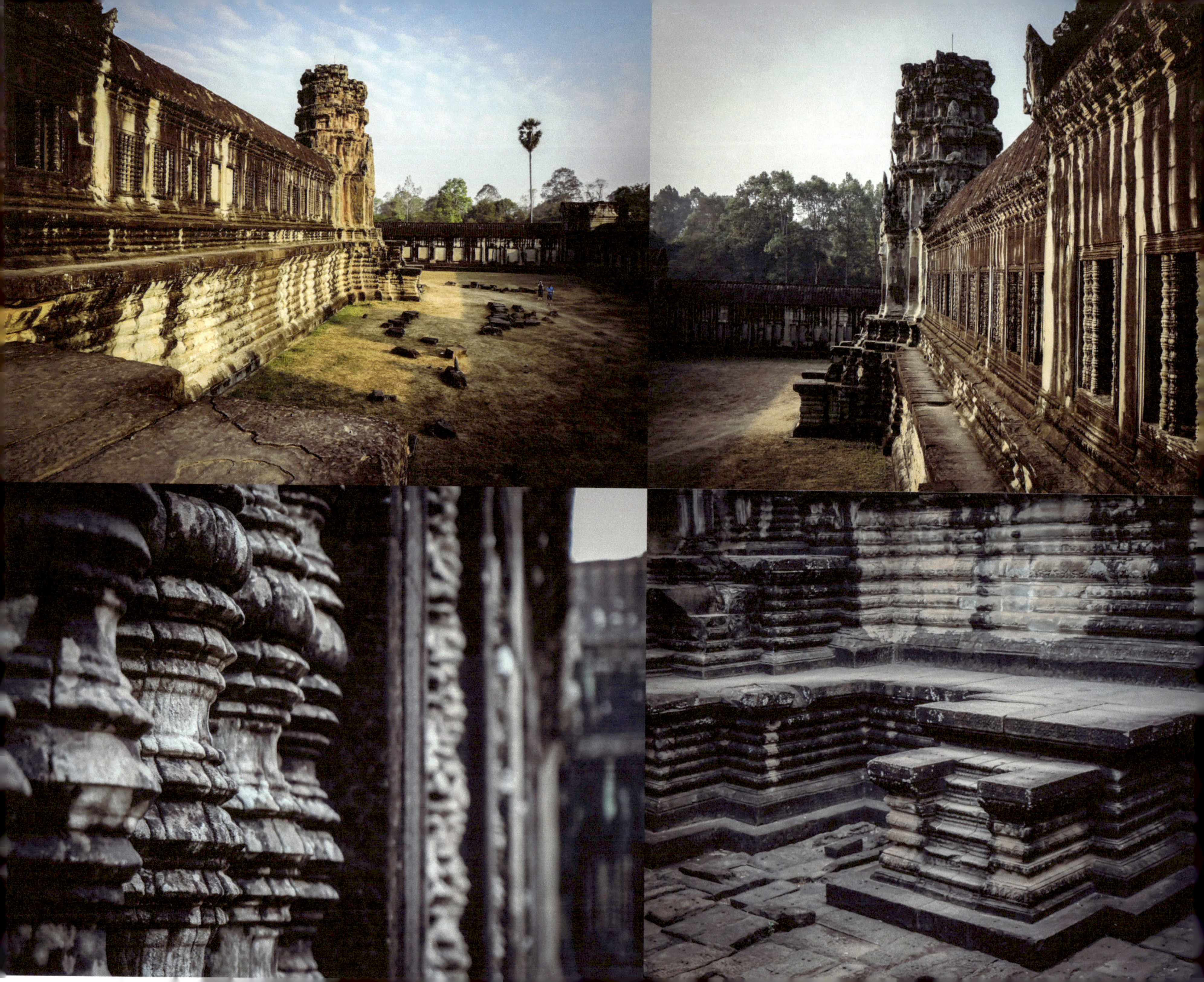

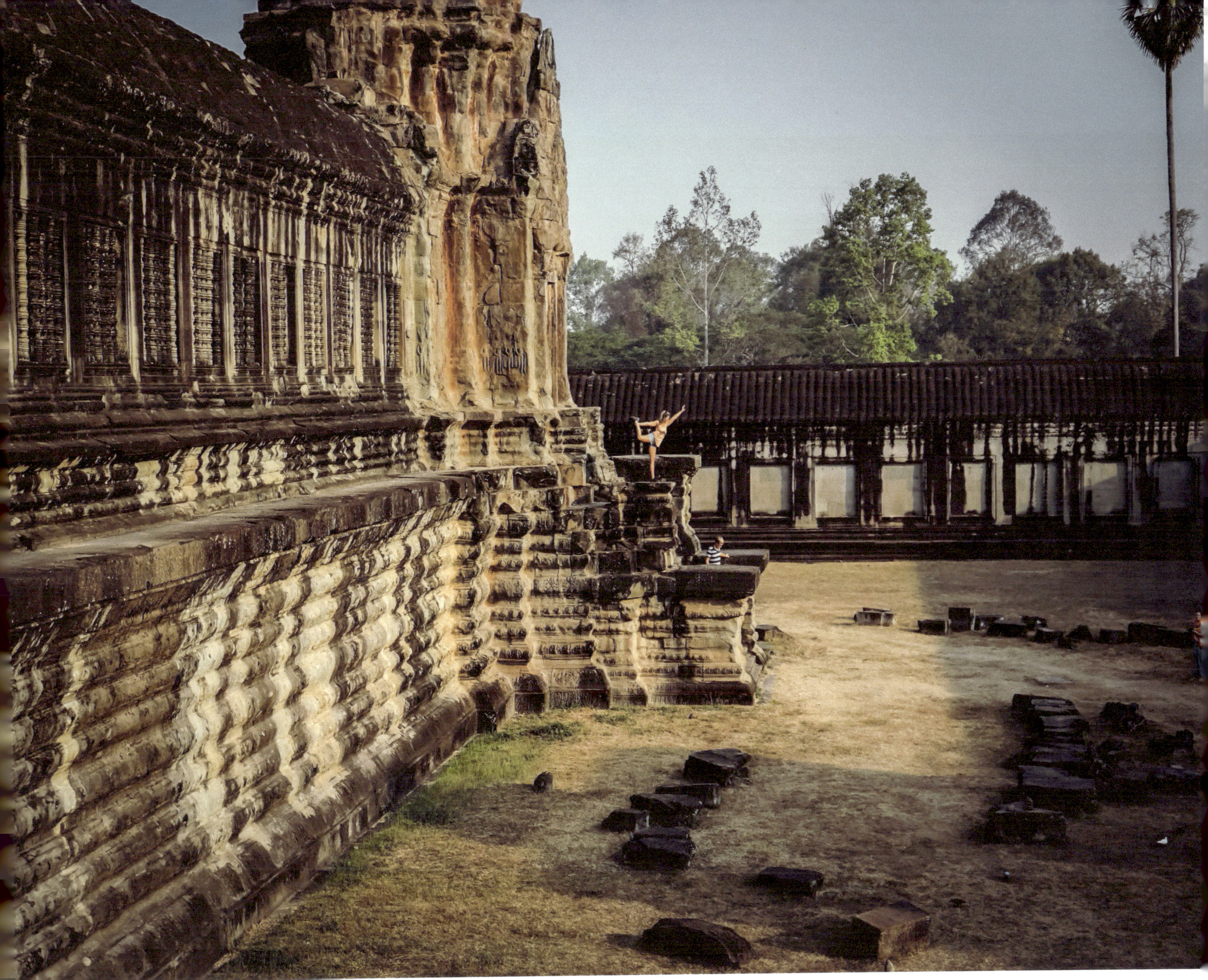

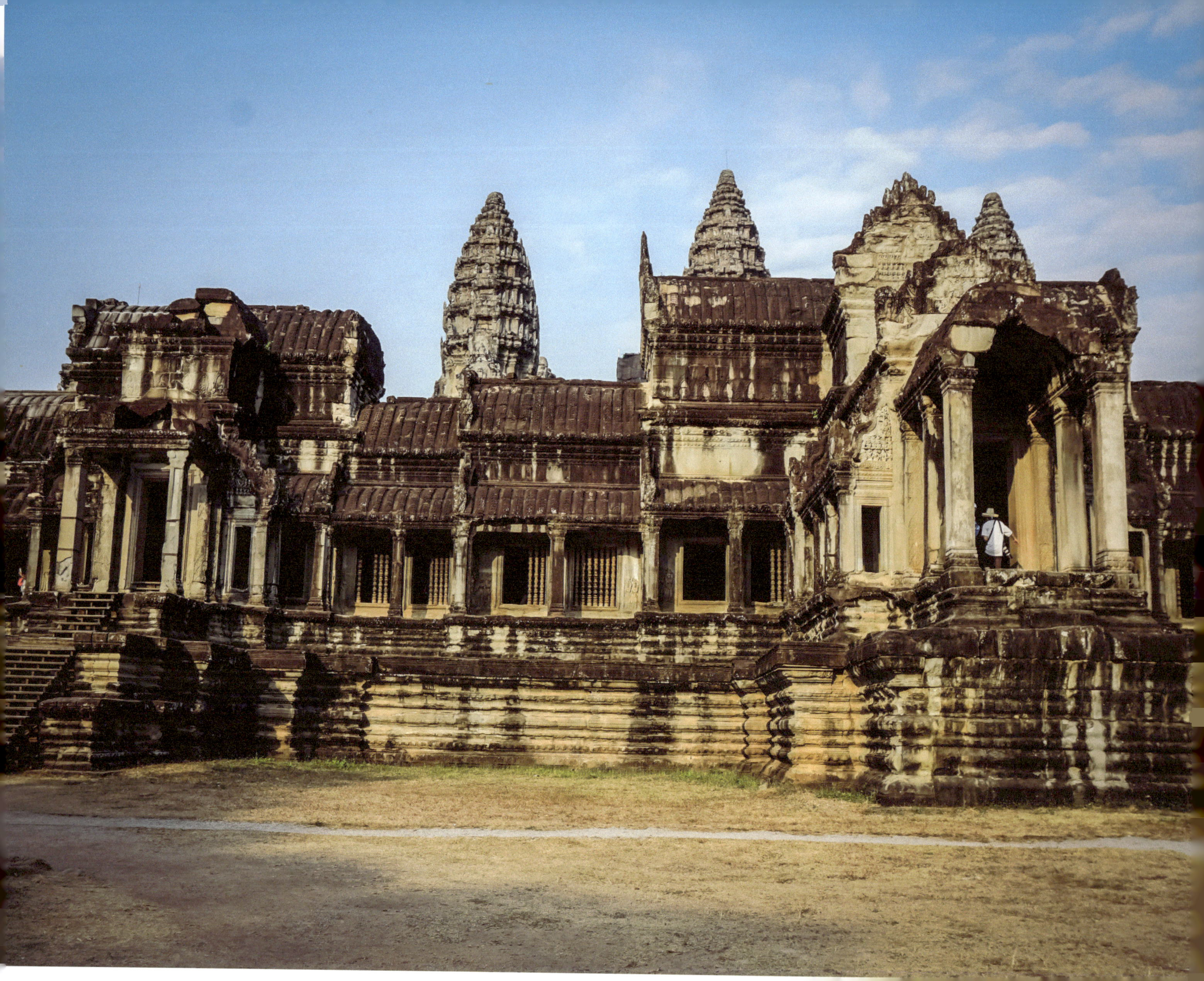

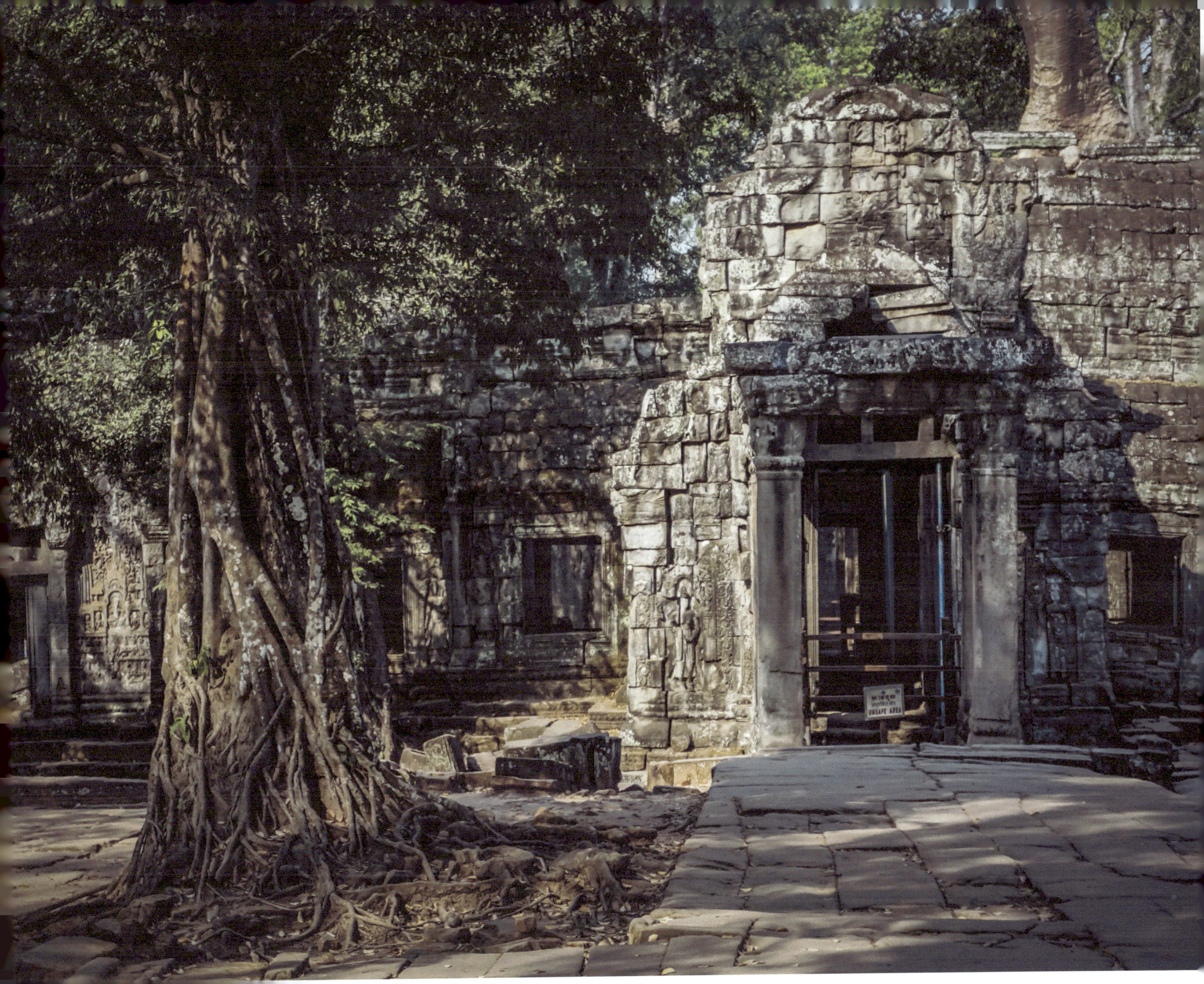
UNSAFE AREA

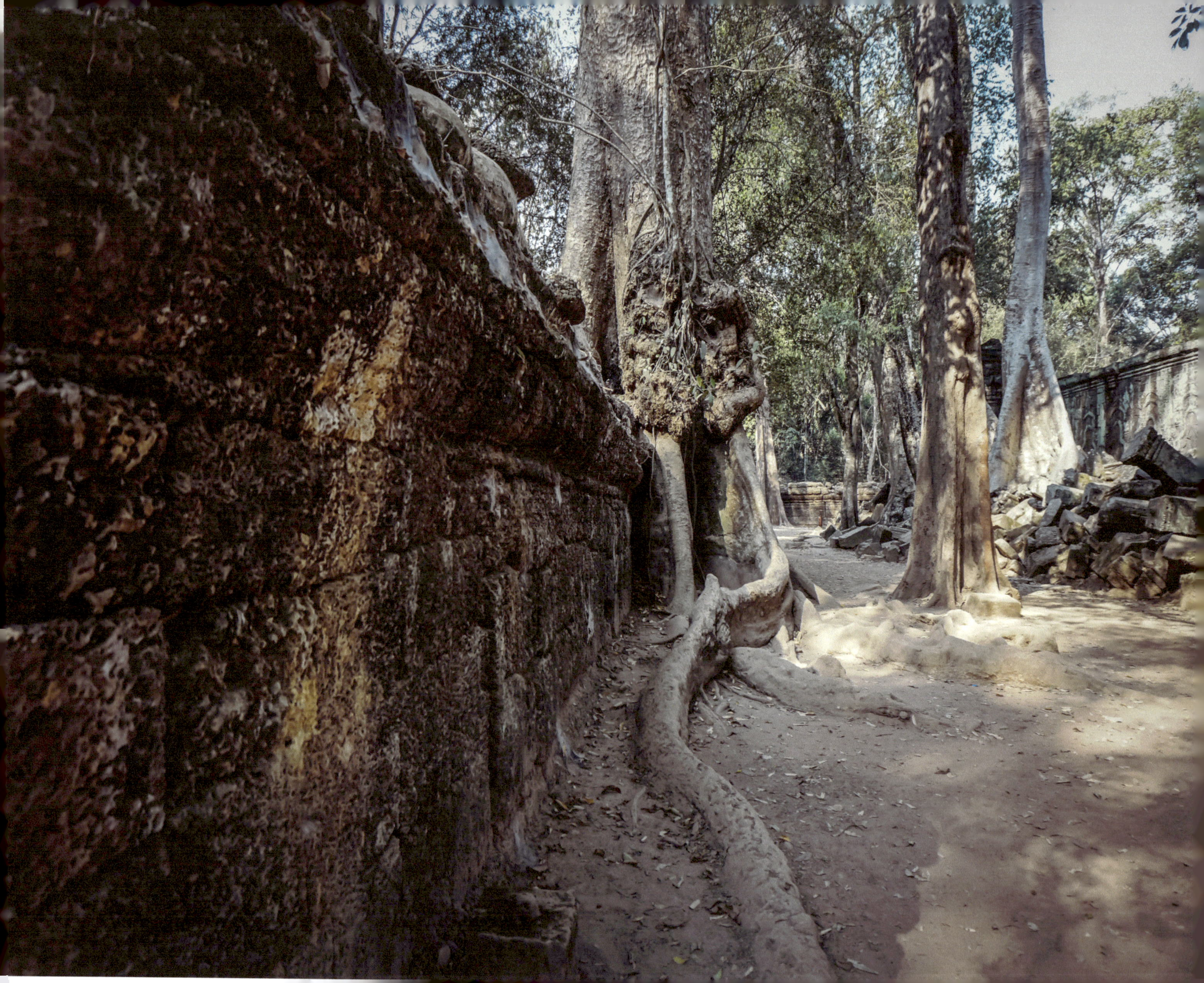

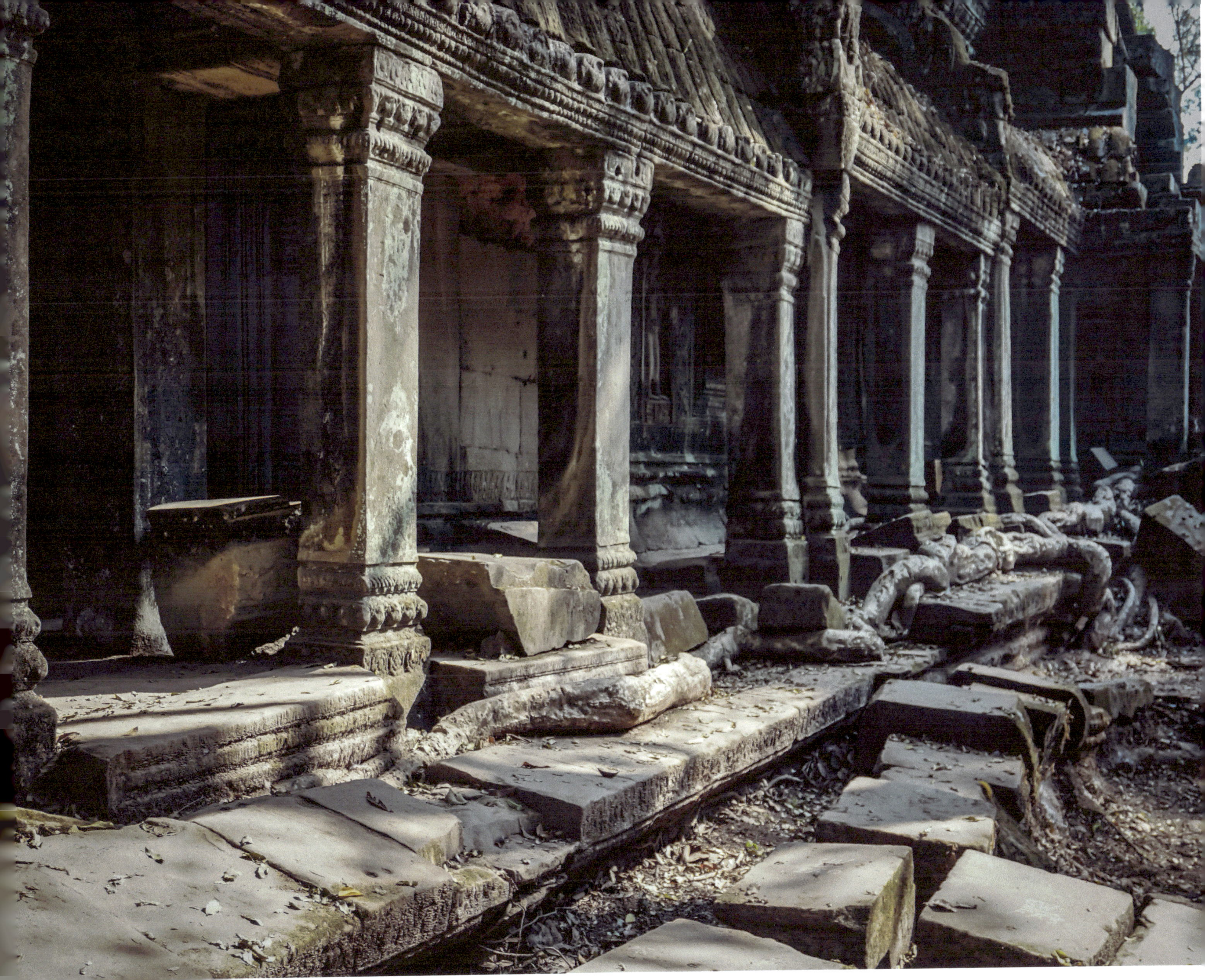

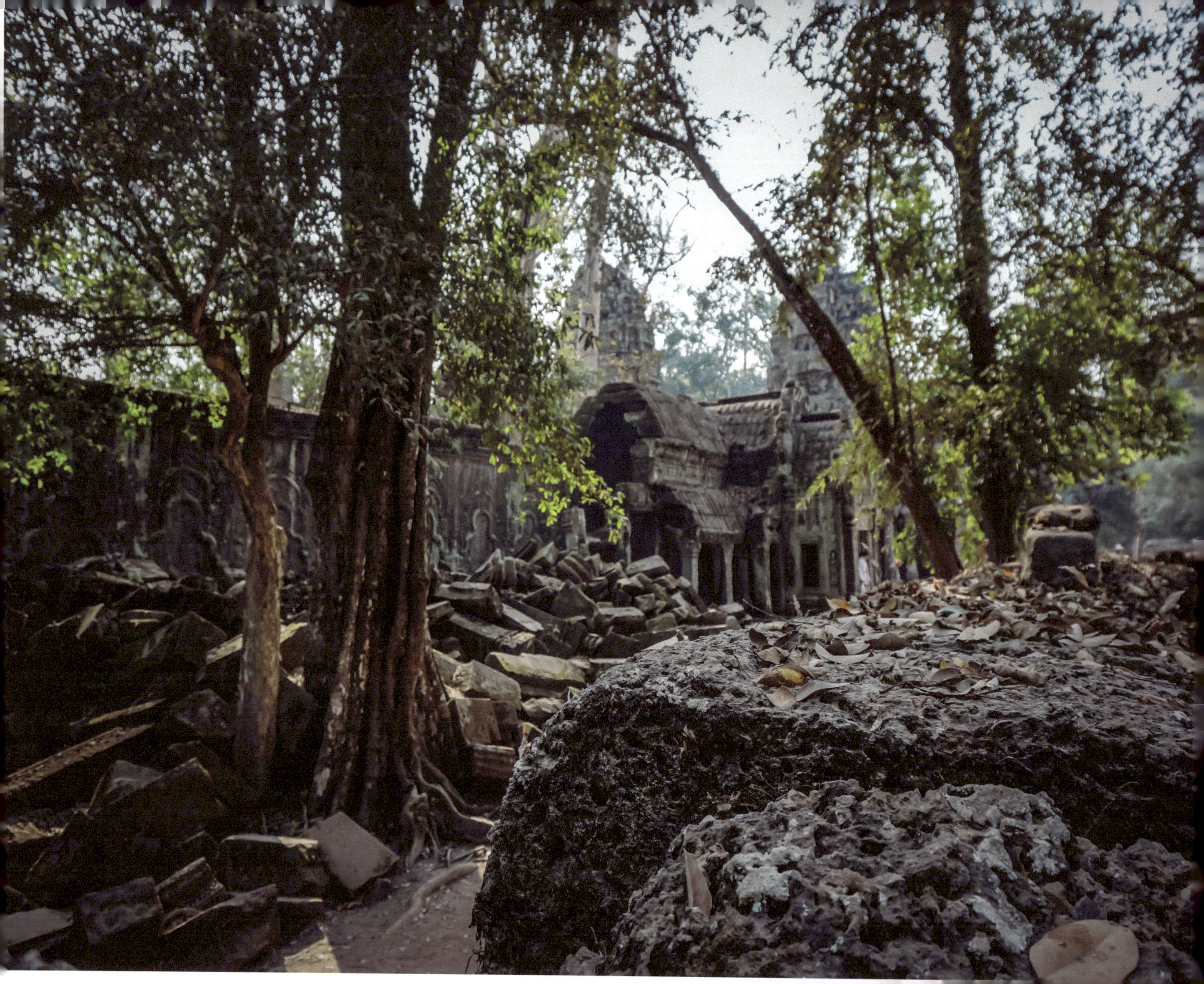

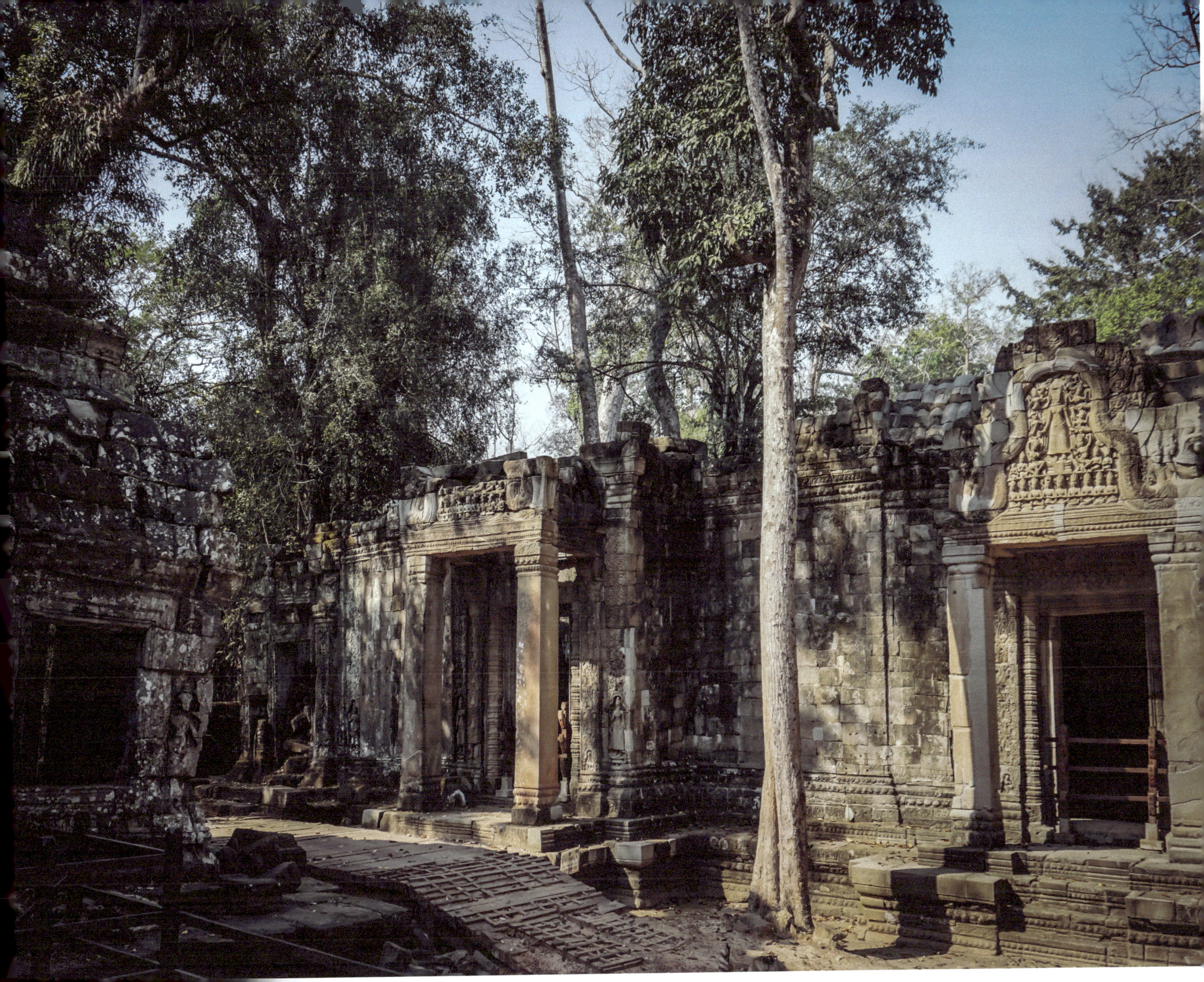

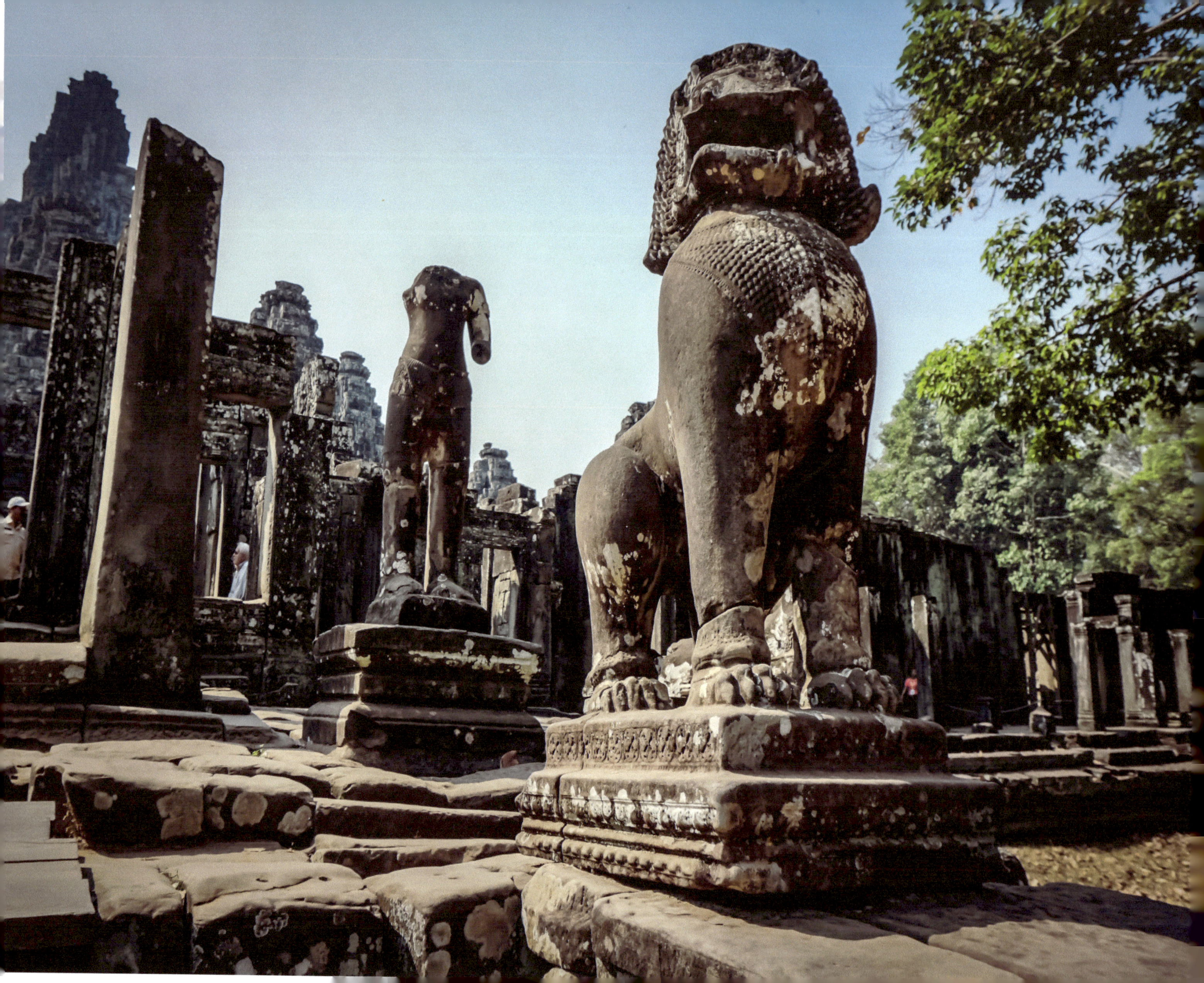

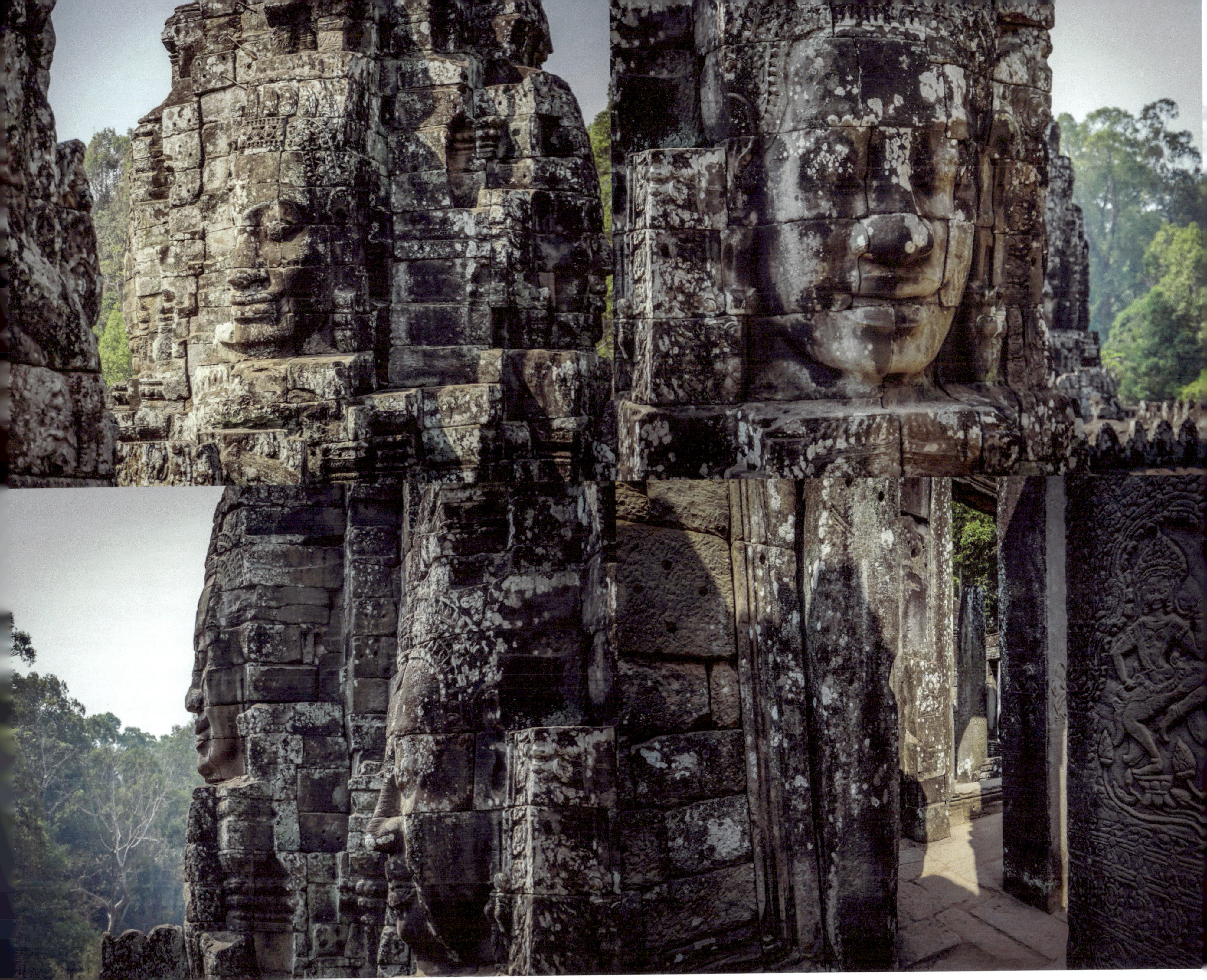

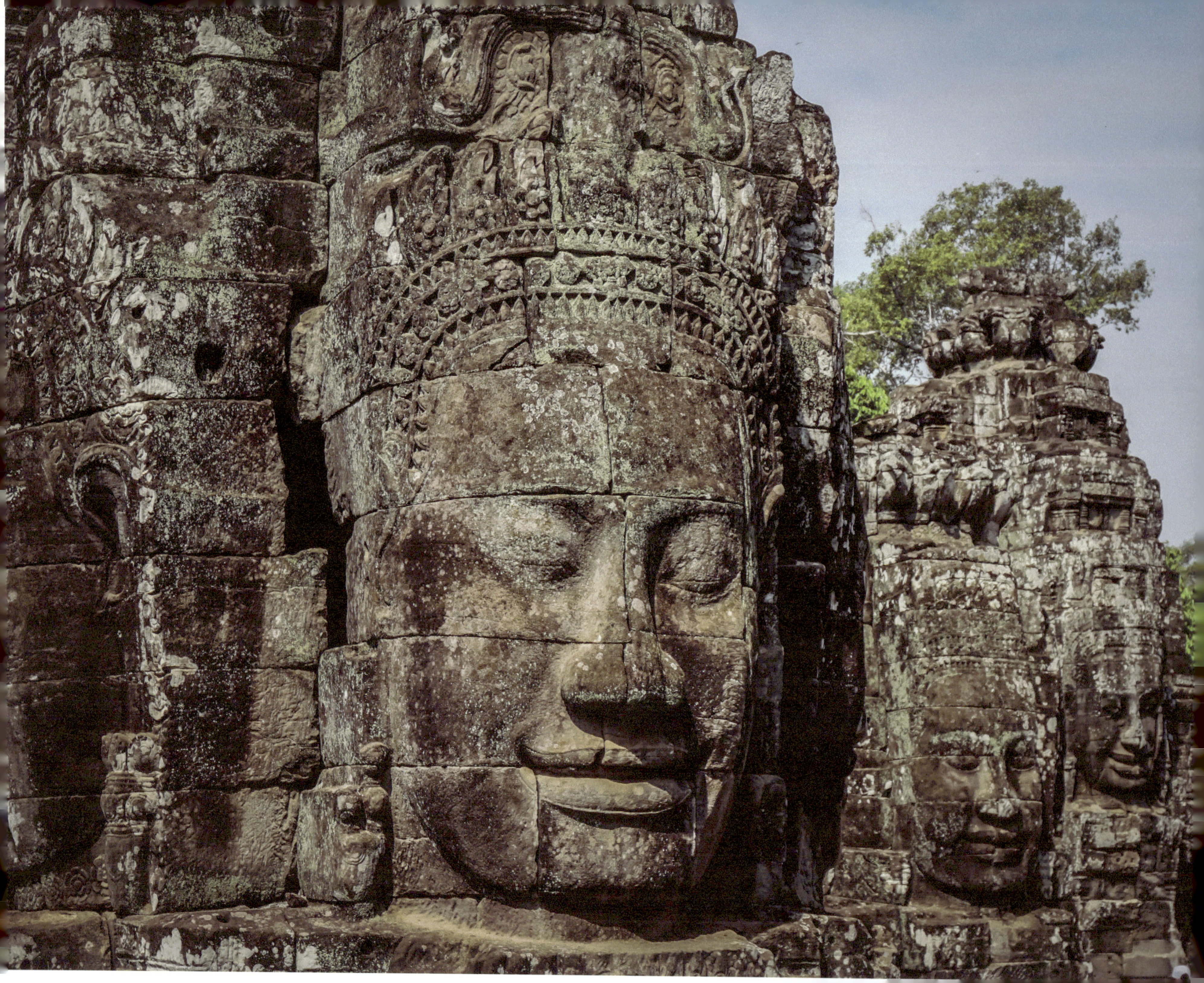

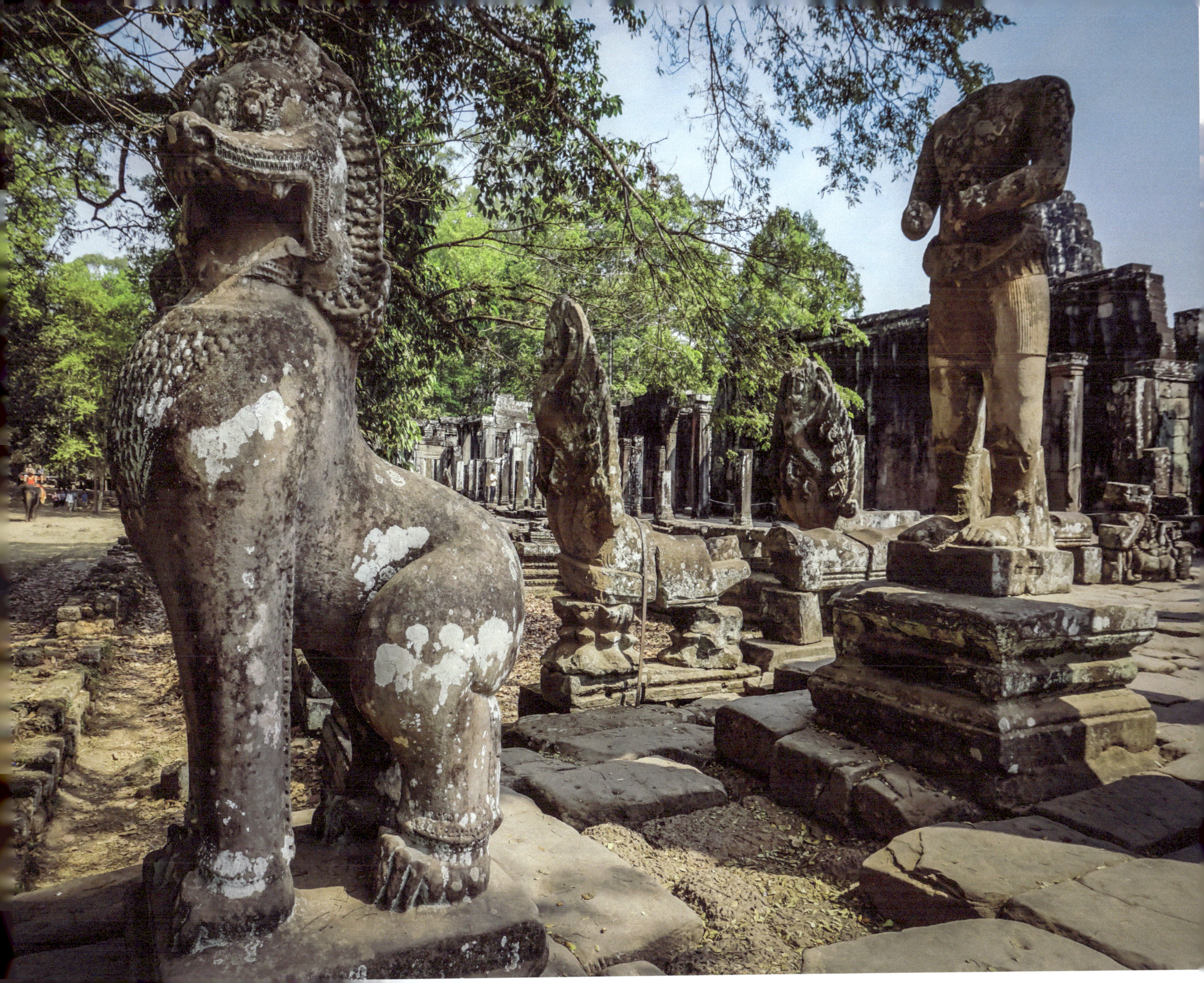

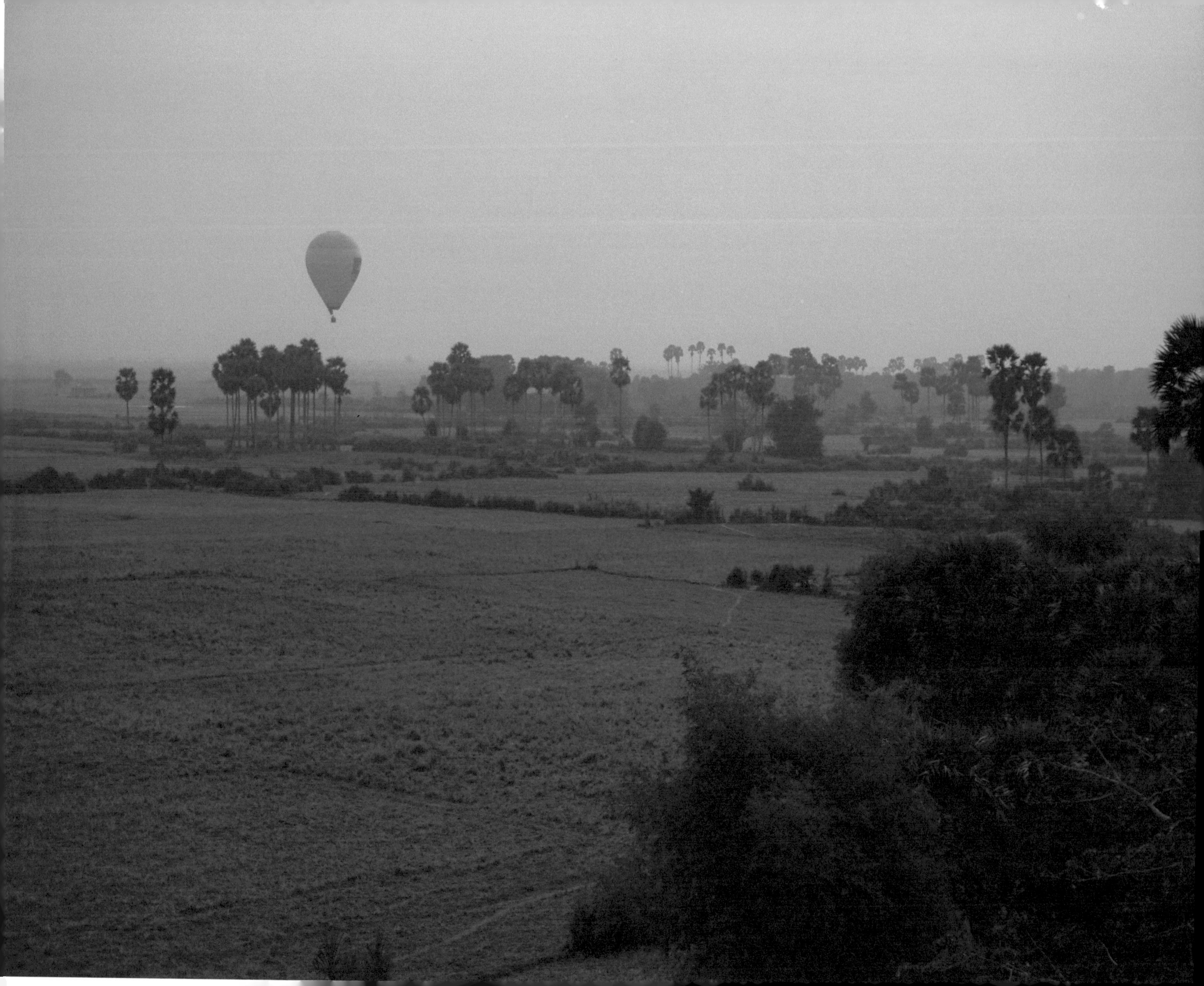

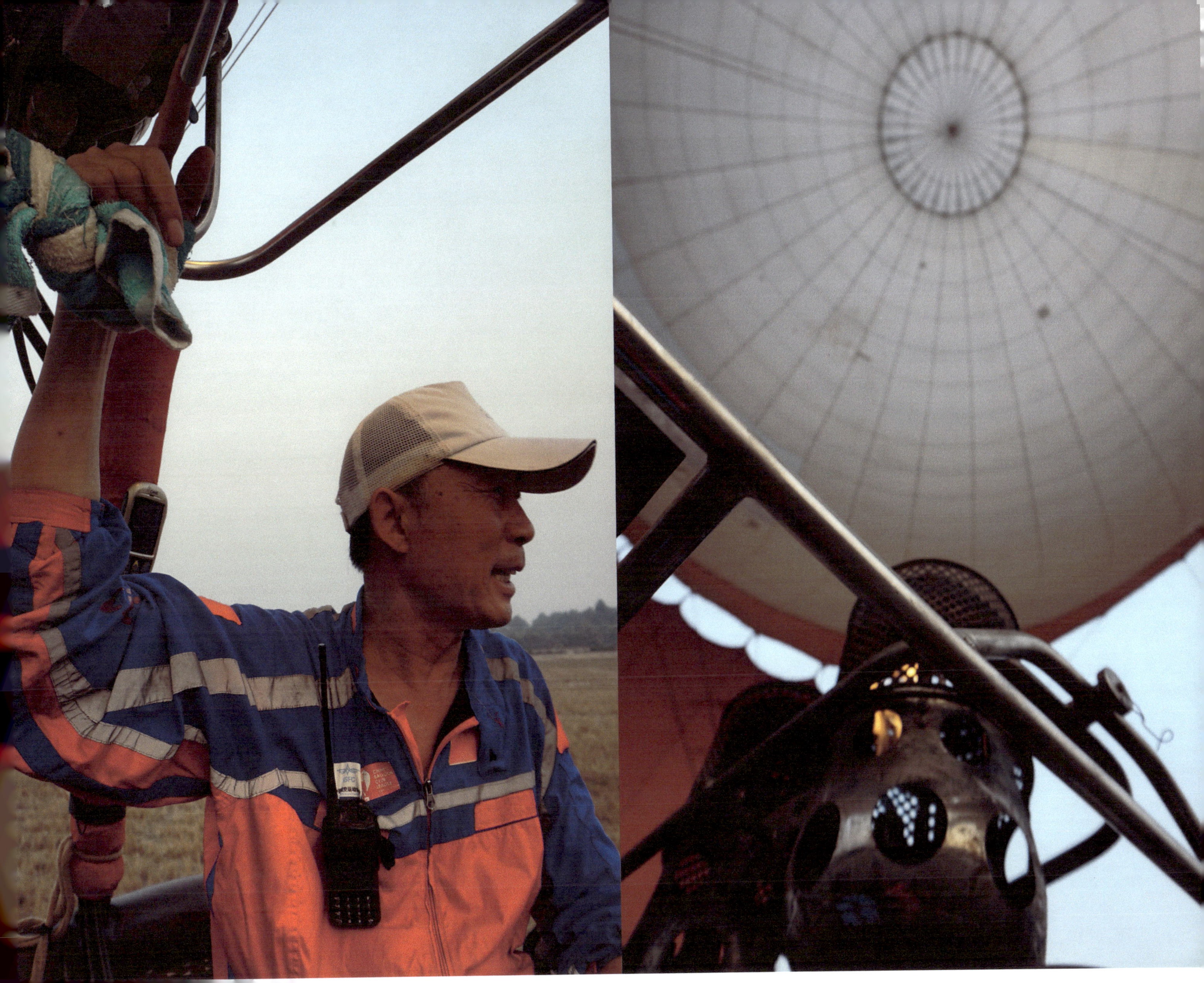

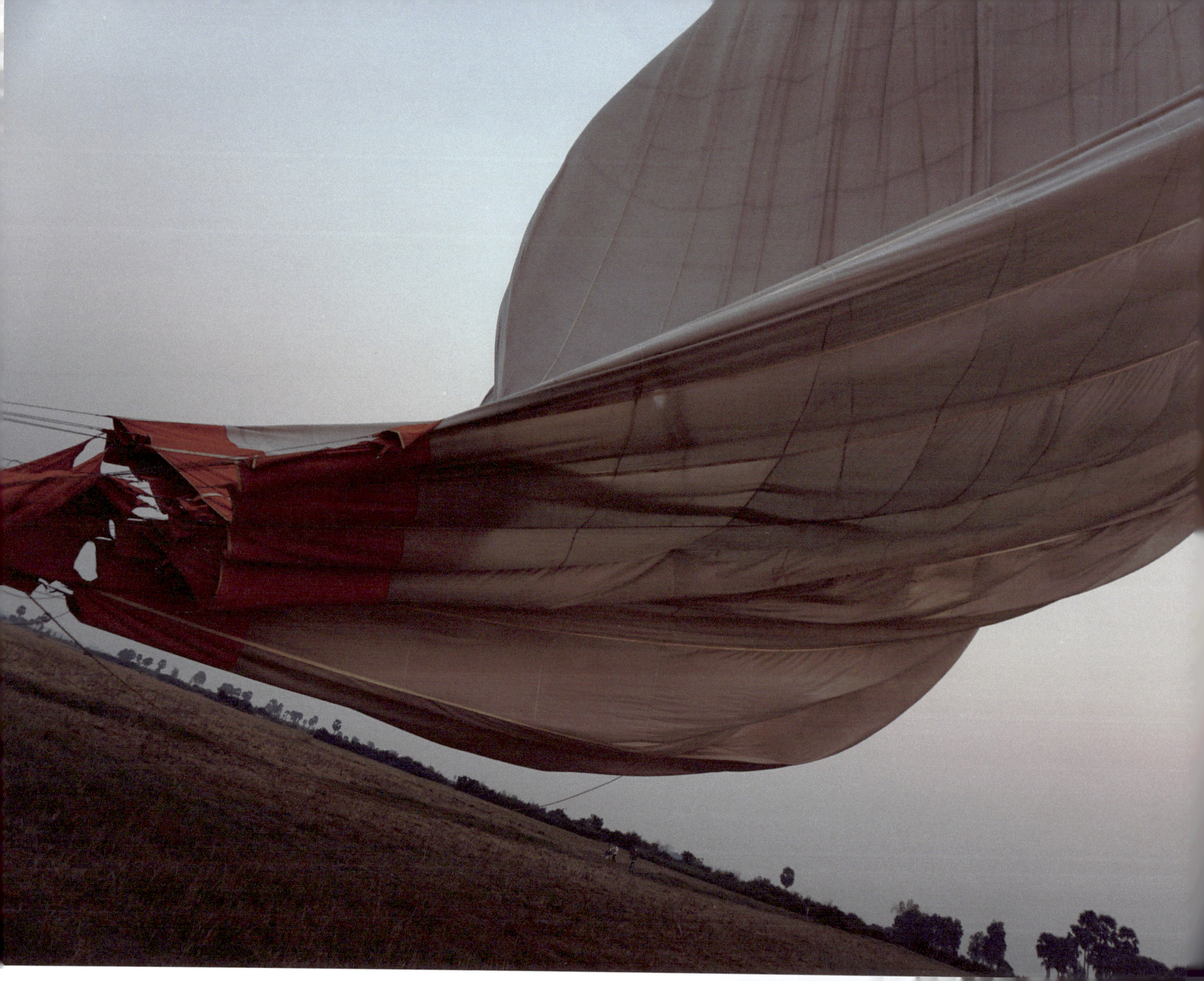

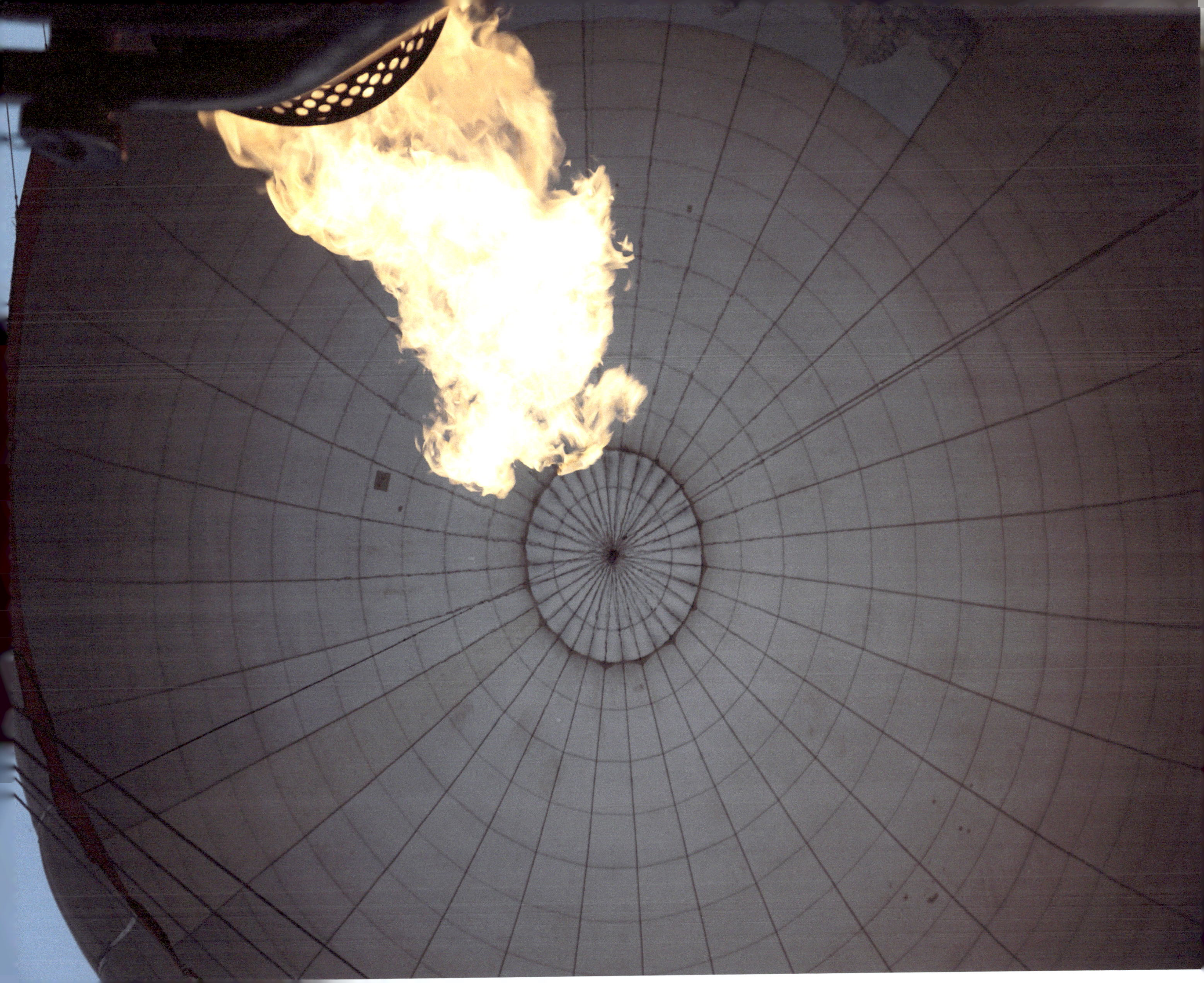

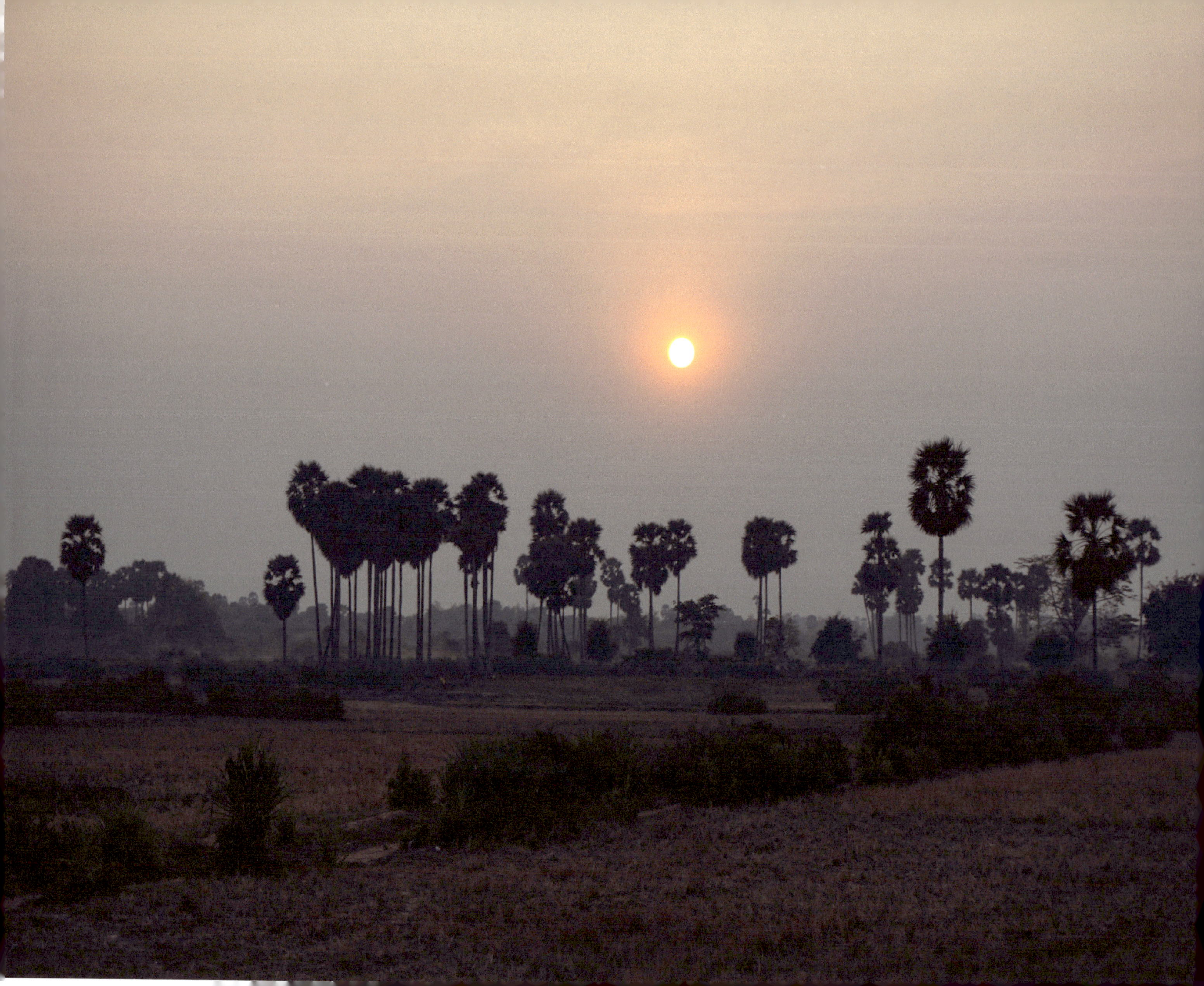

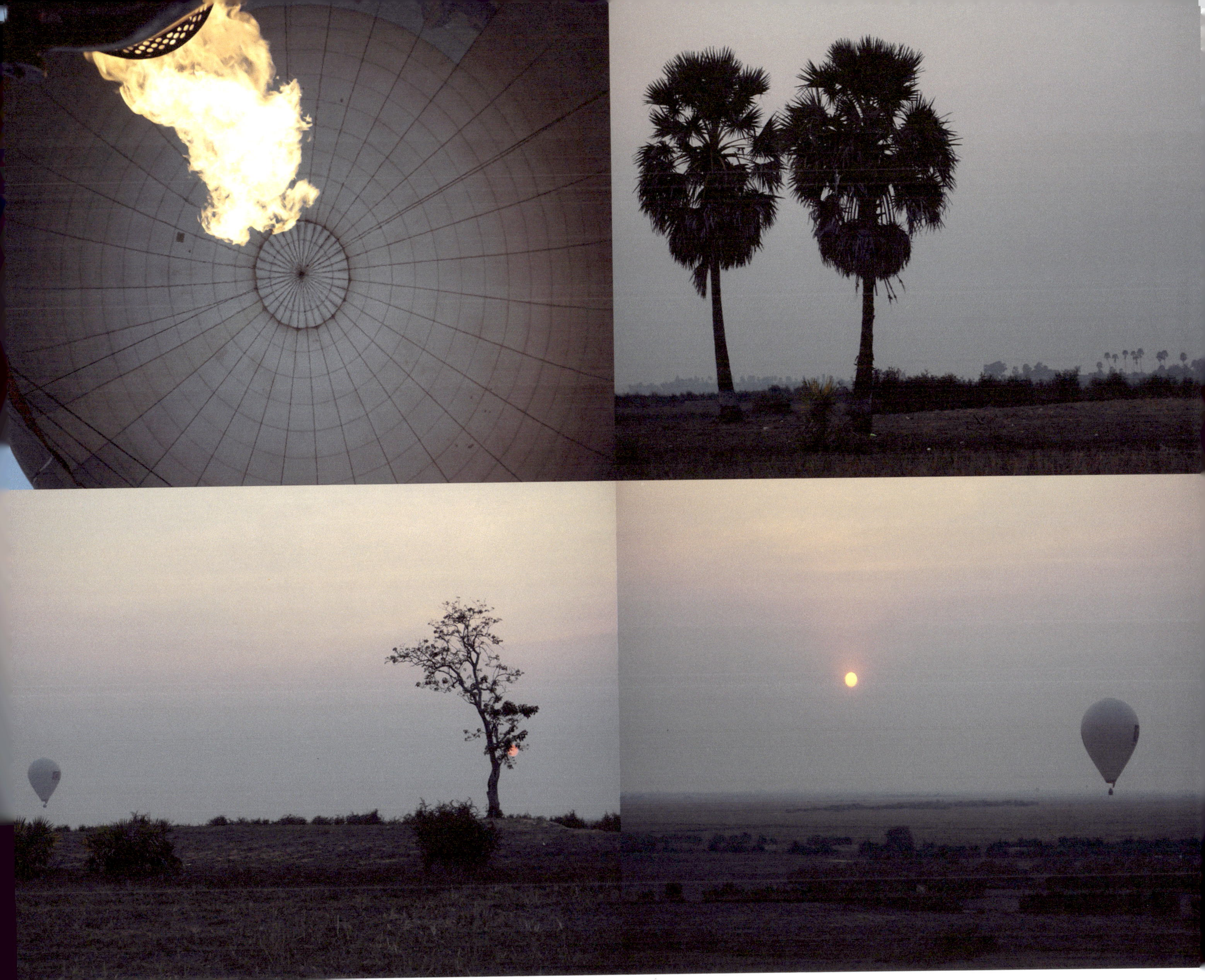

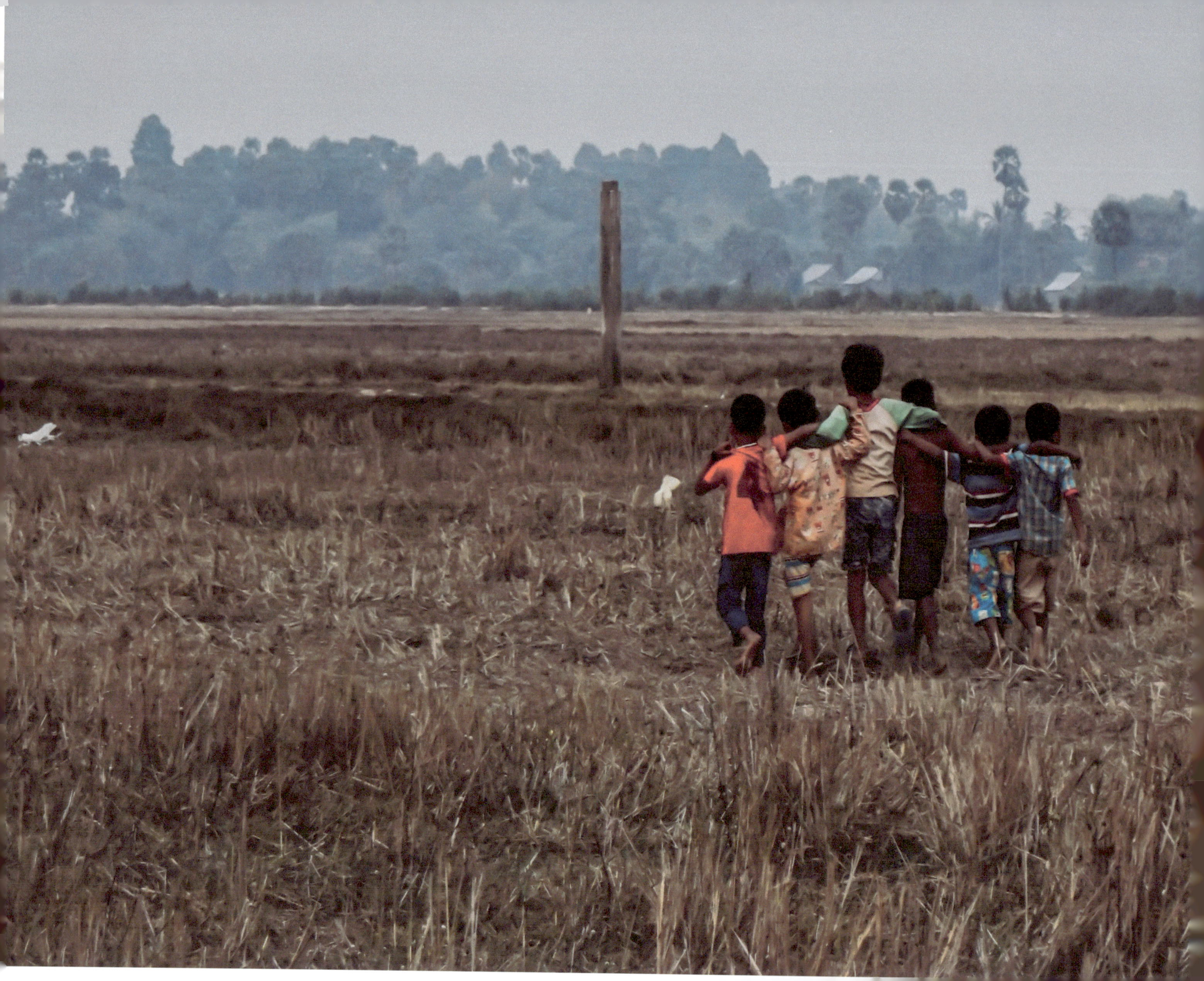

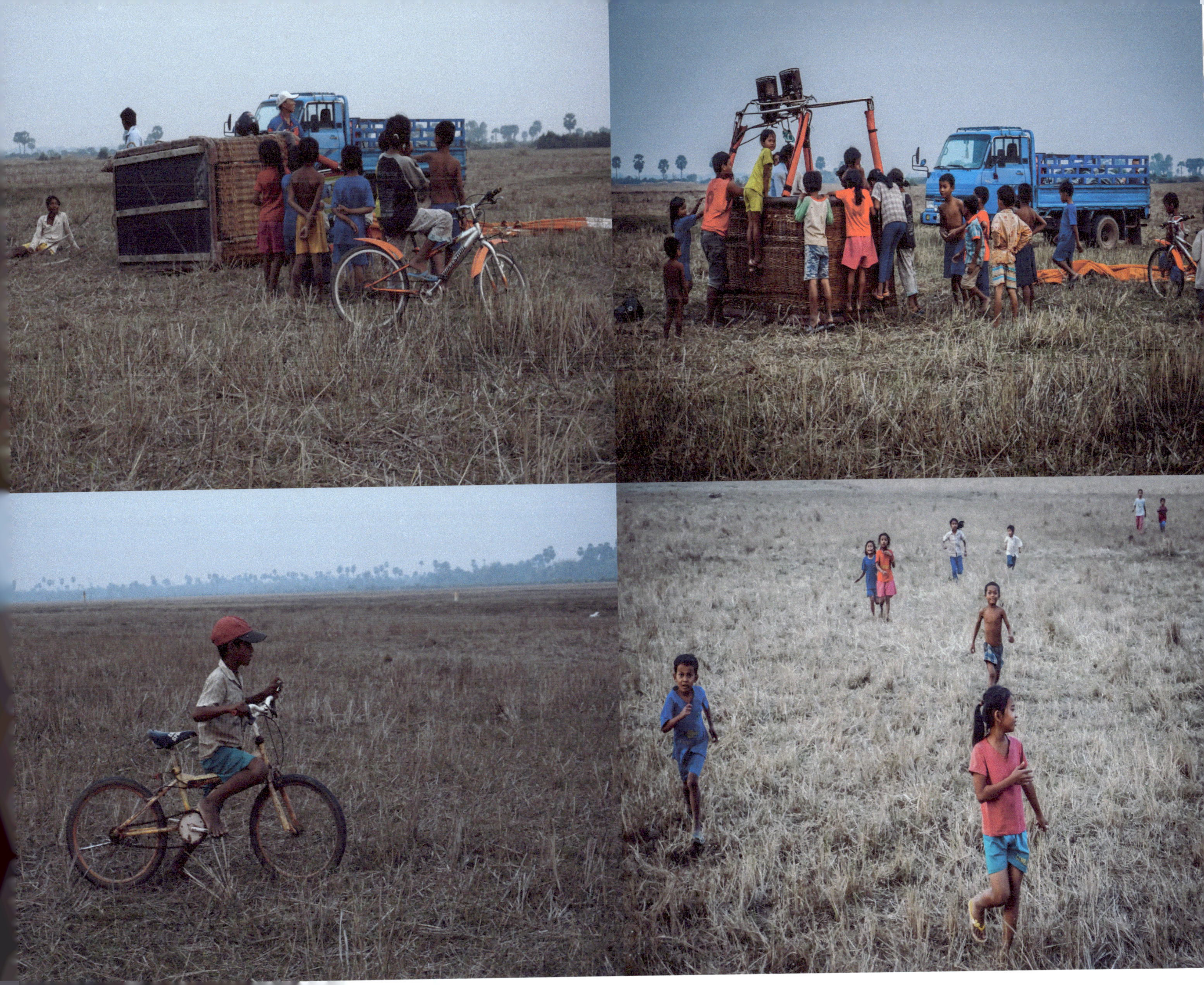

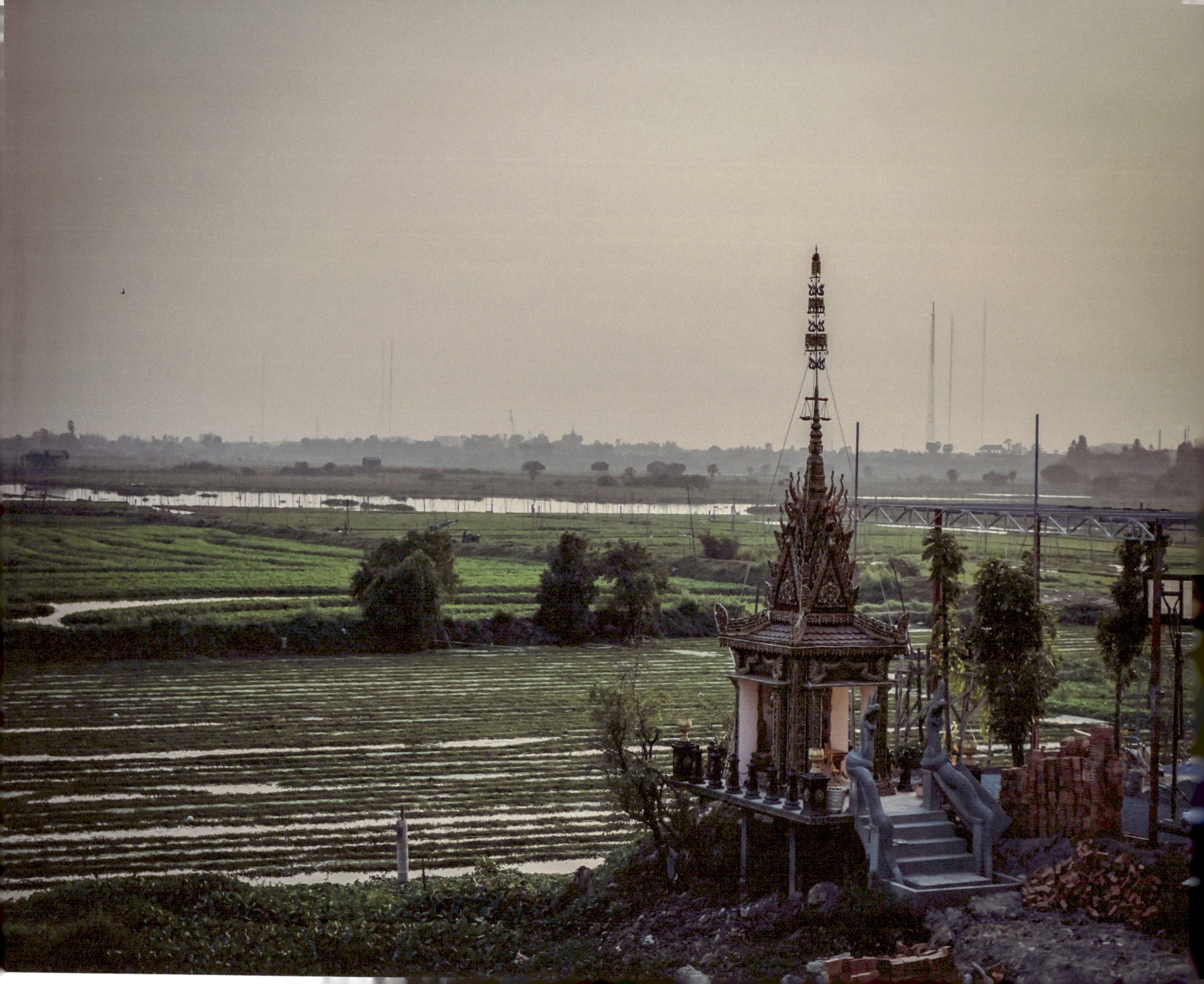

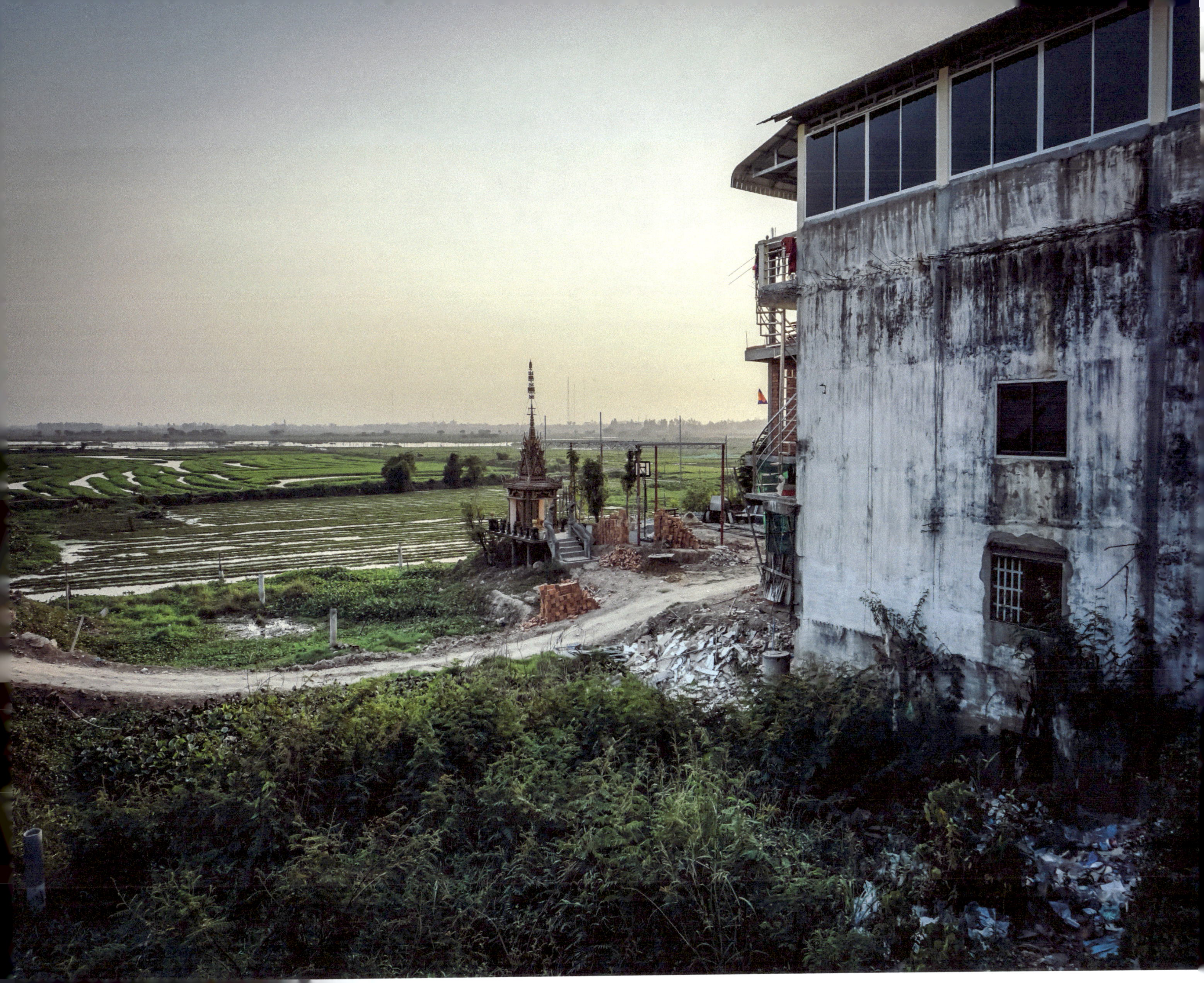

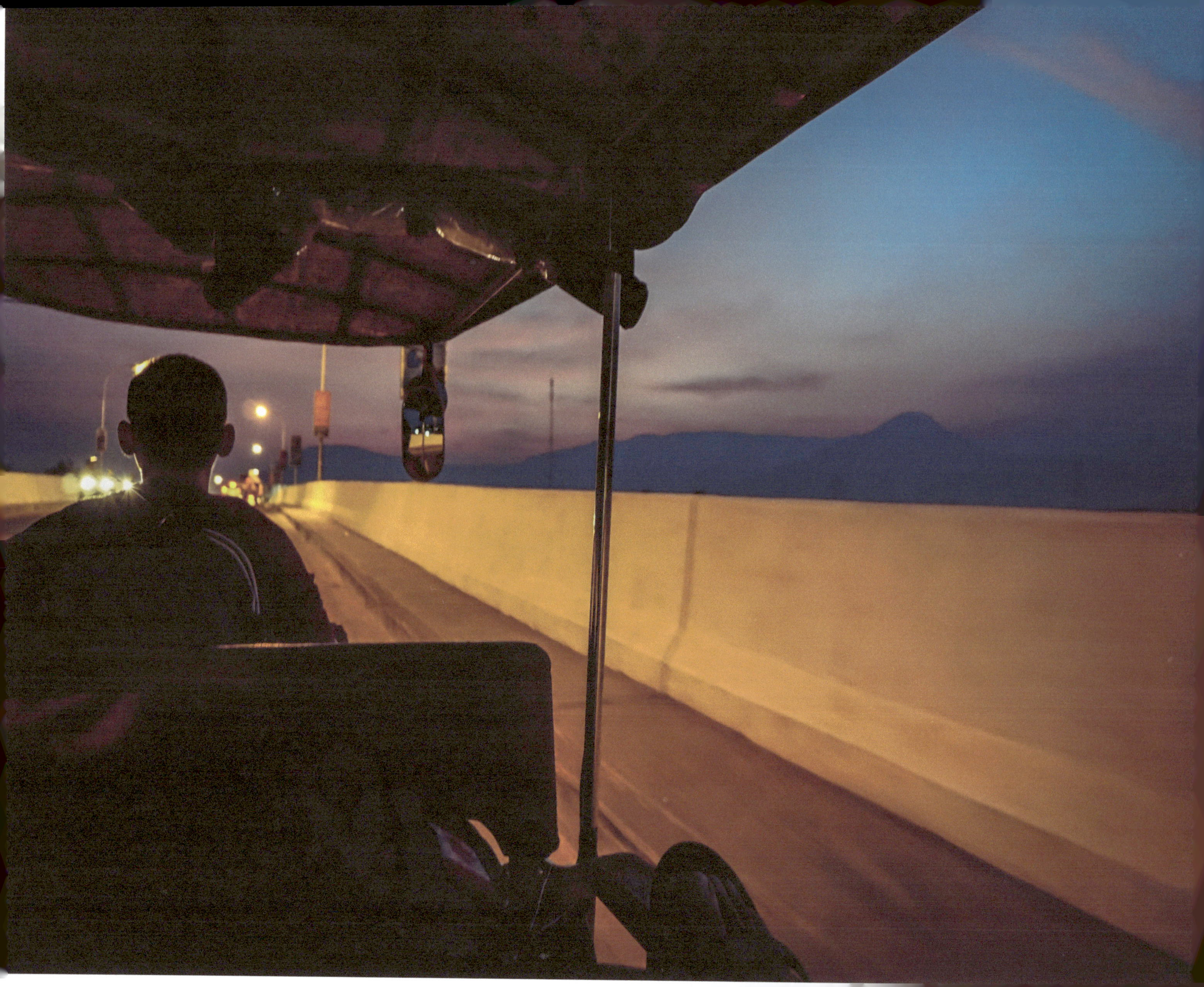

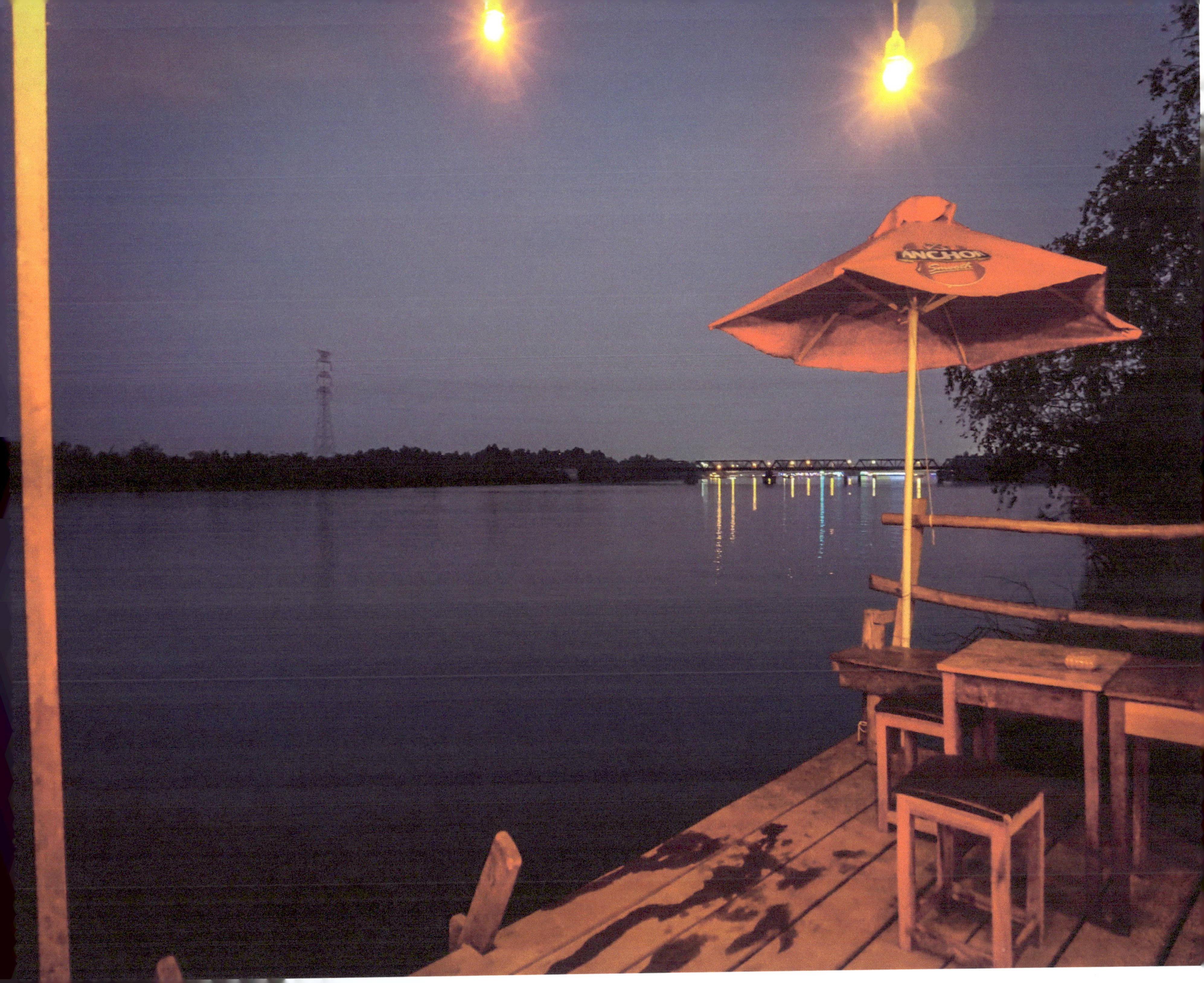

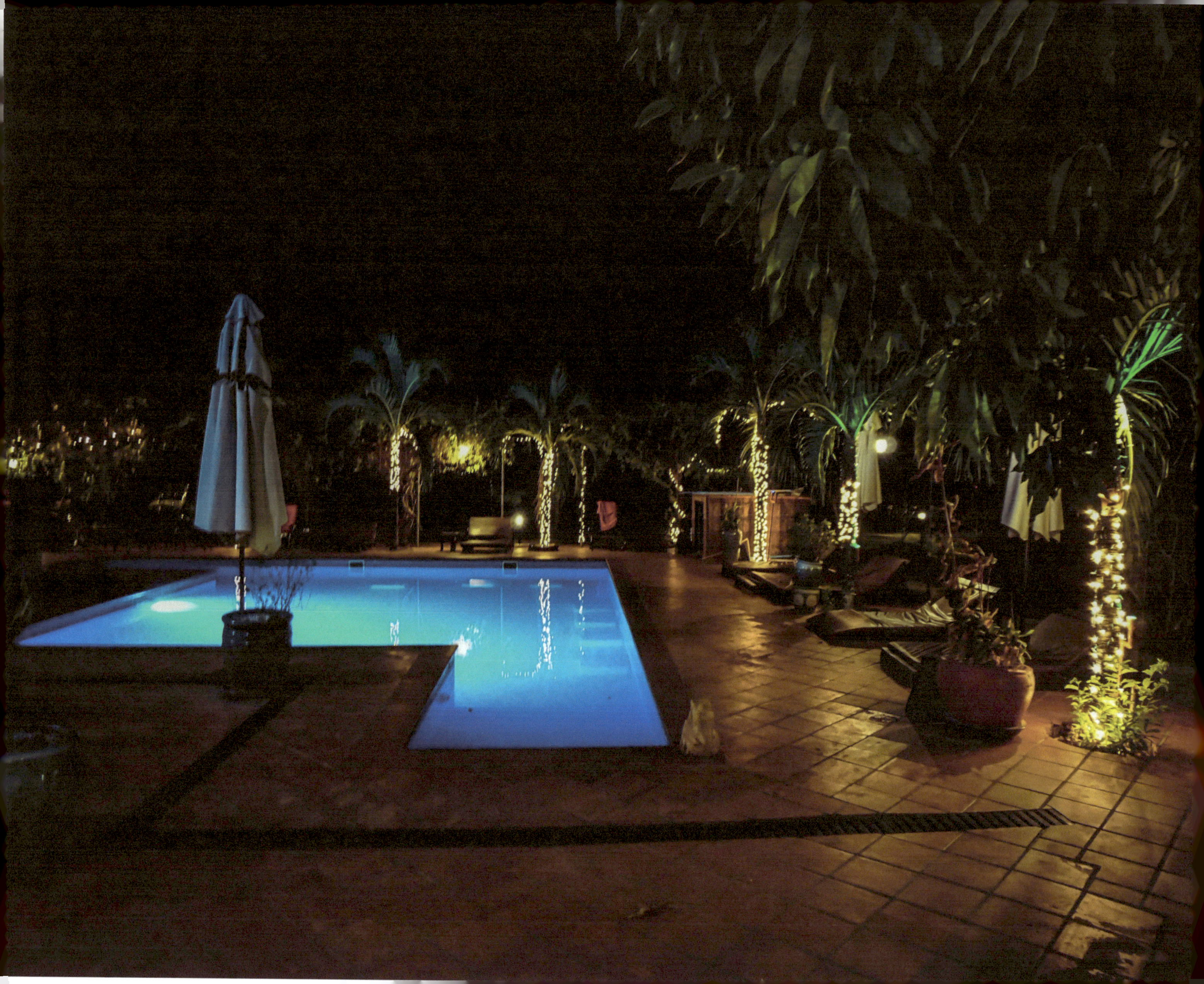

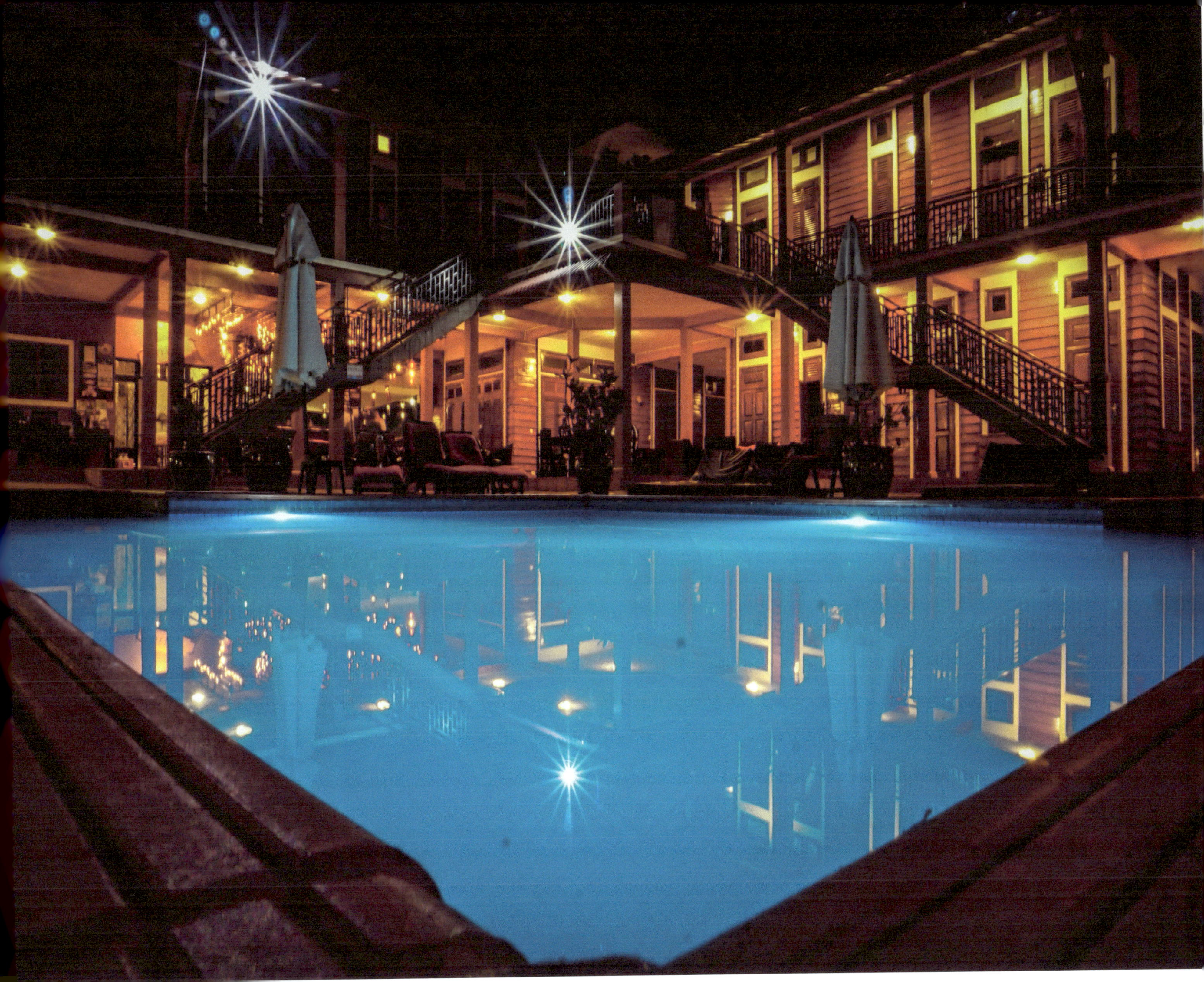

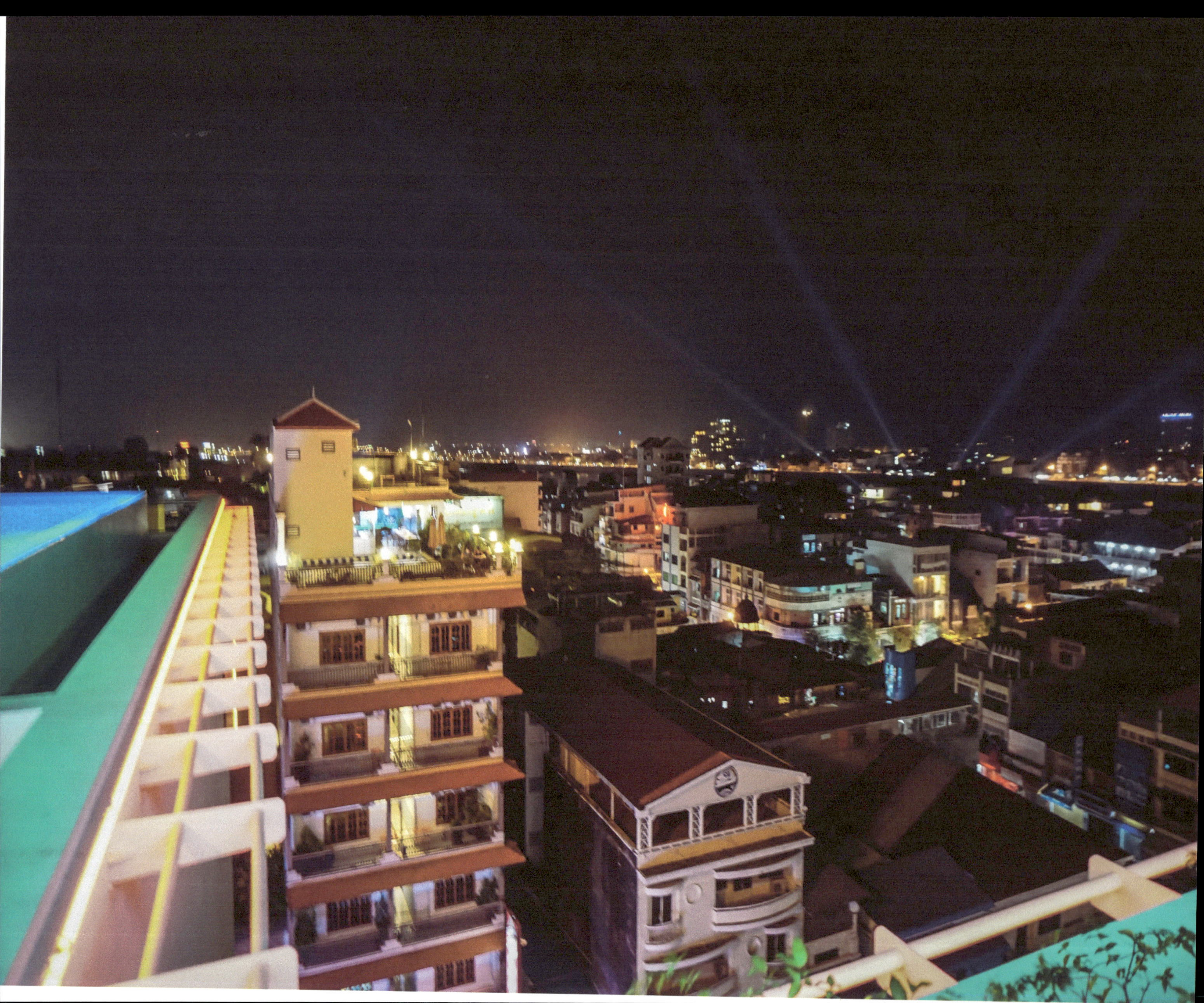

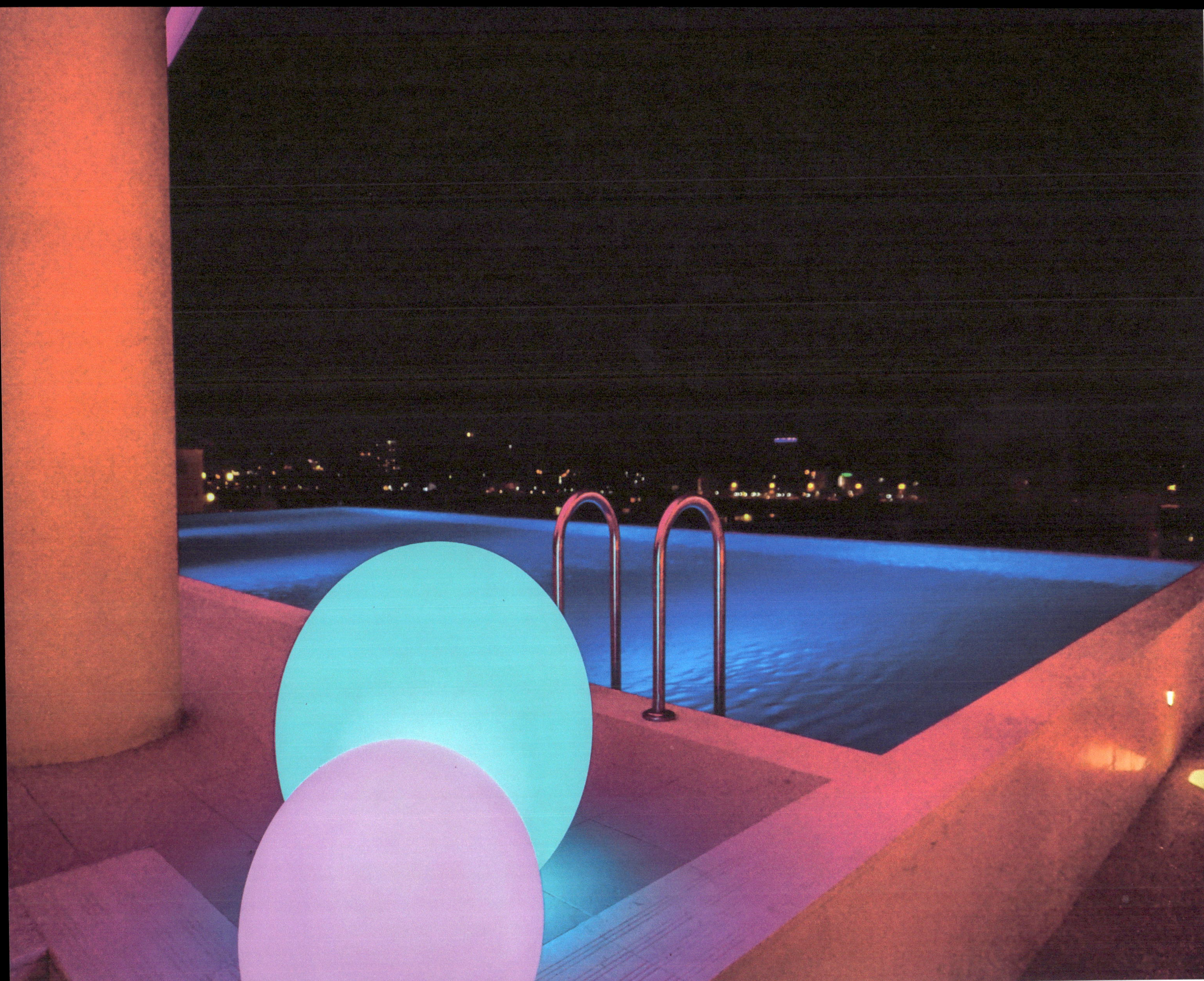

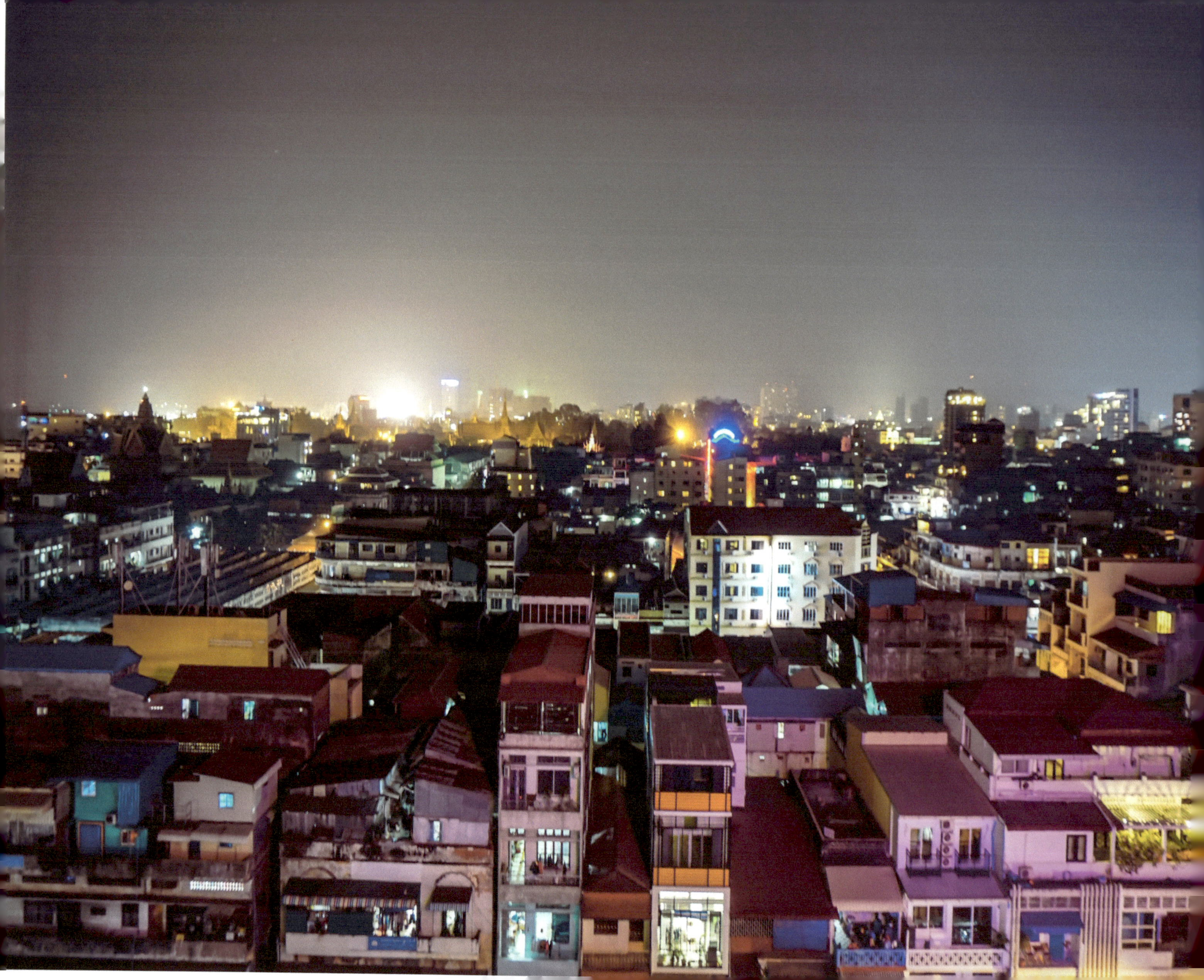

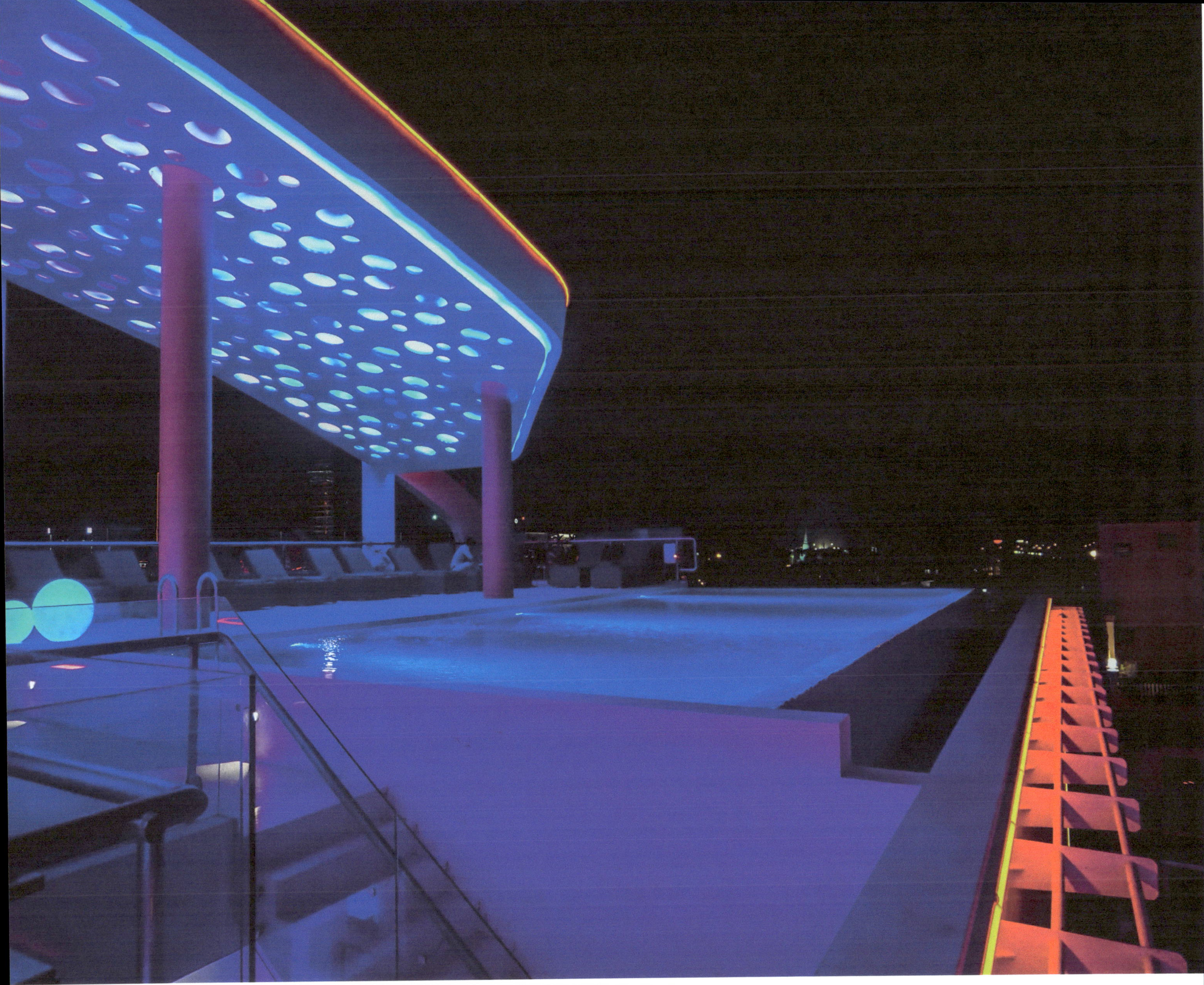

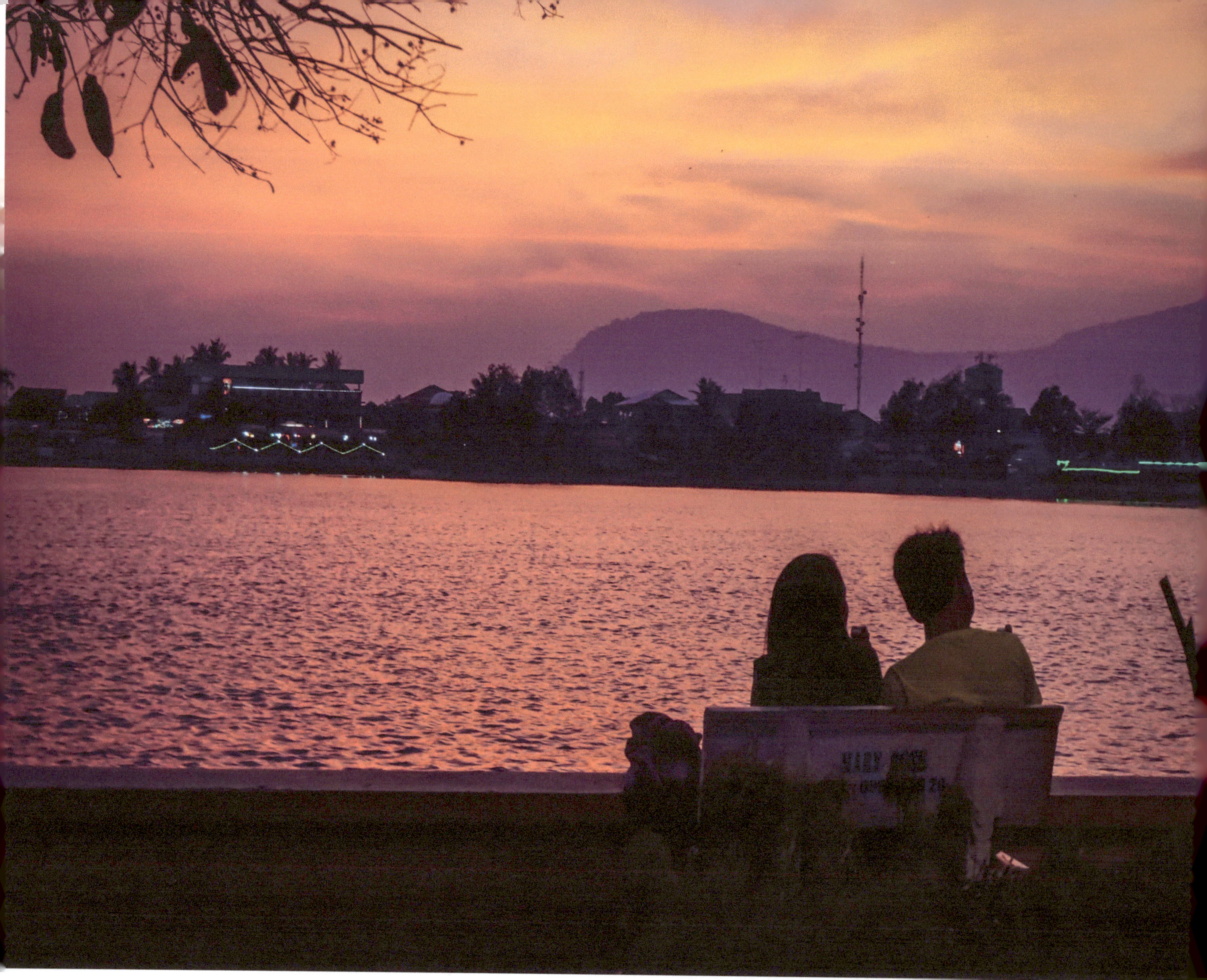

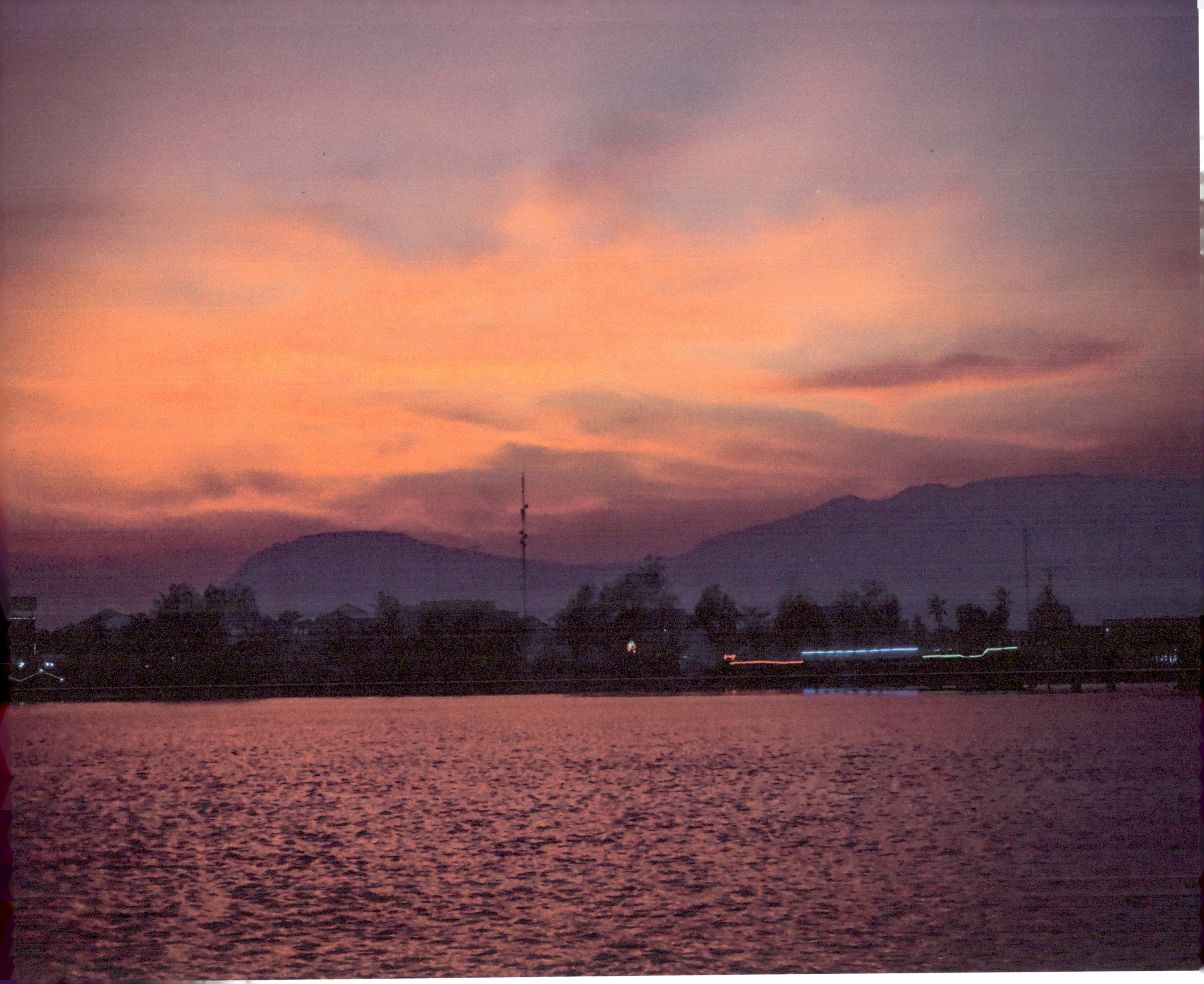

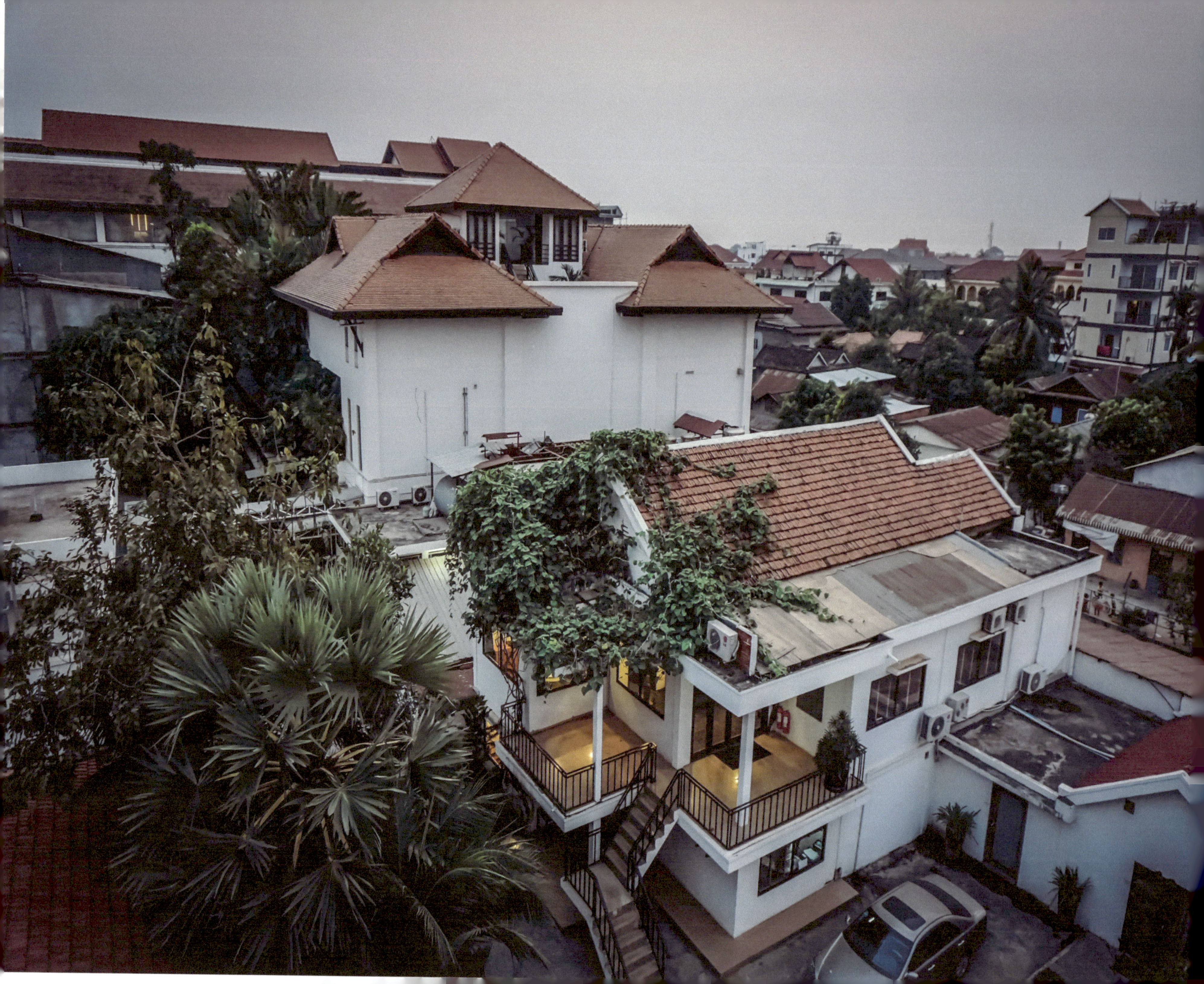

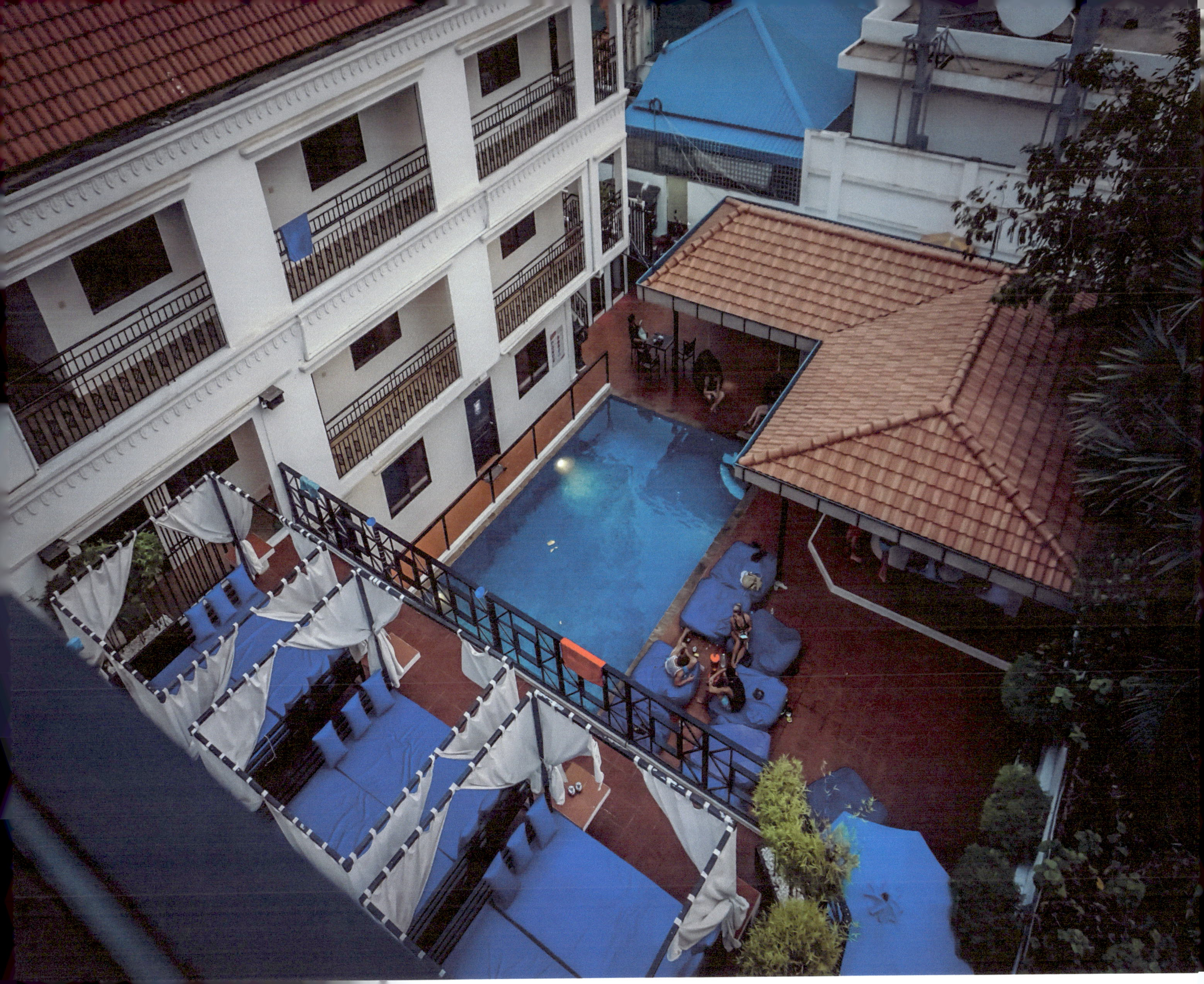

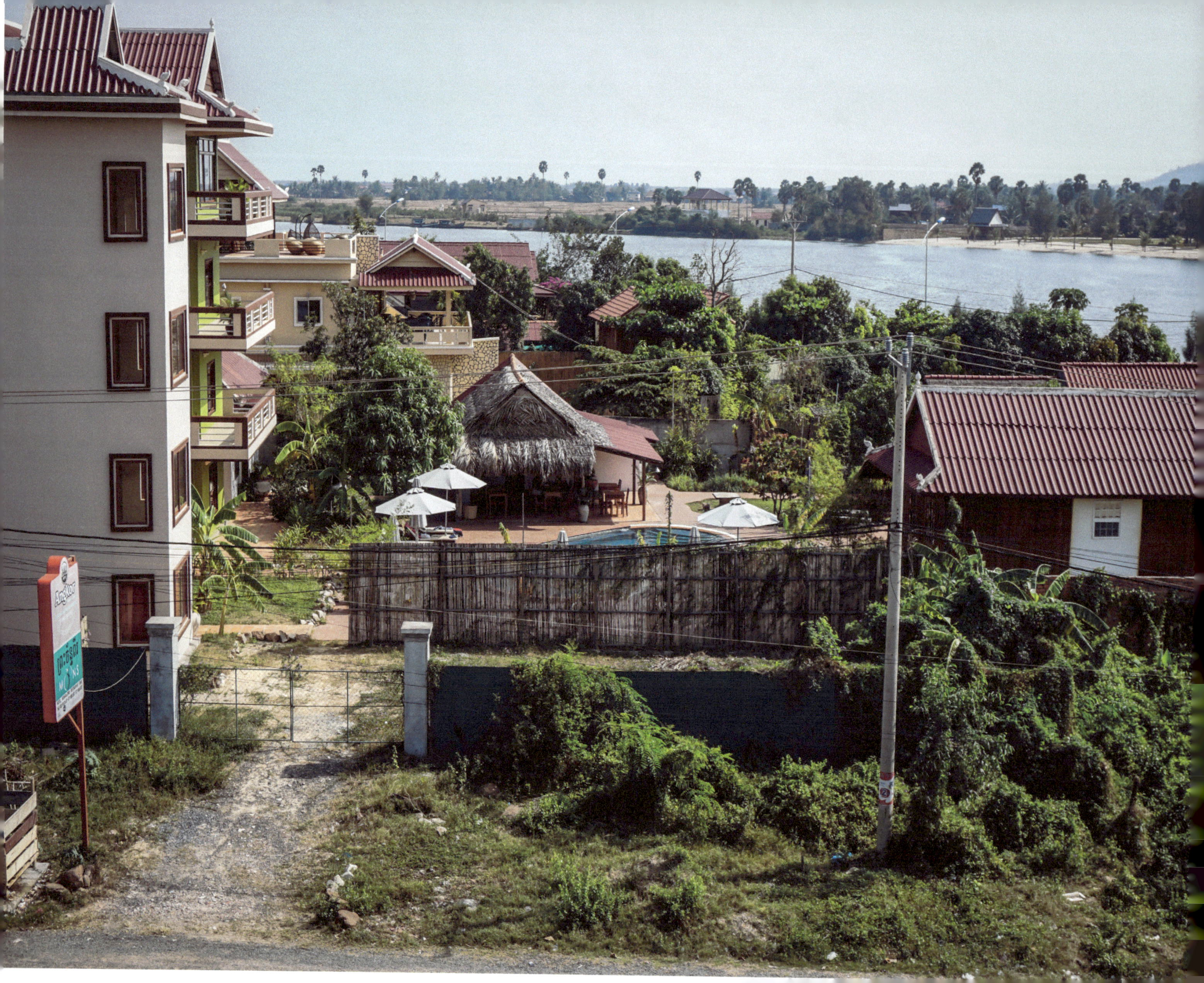

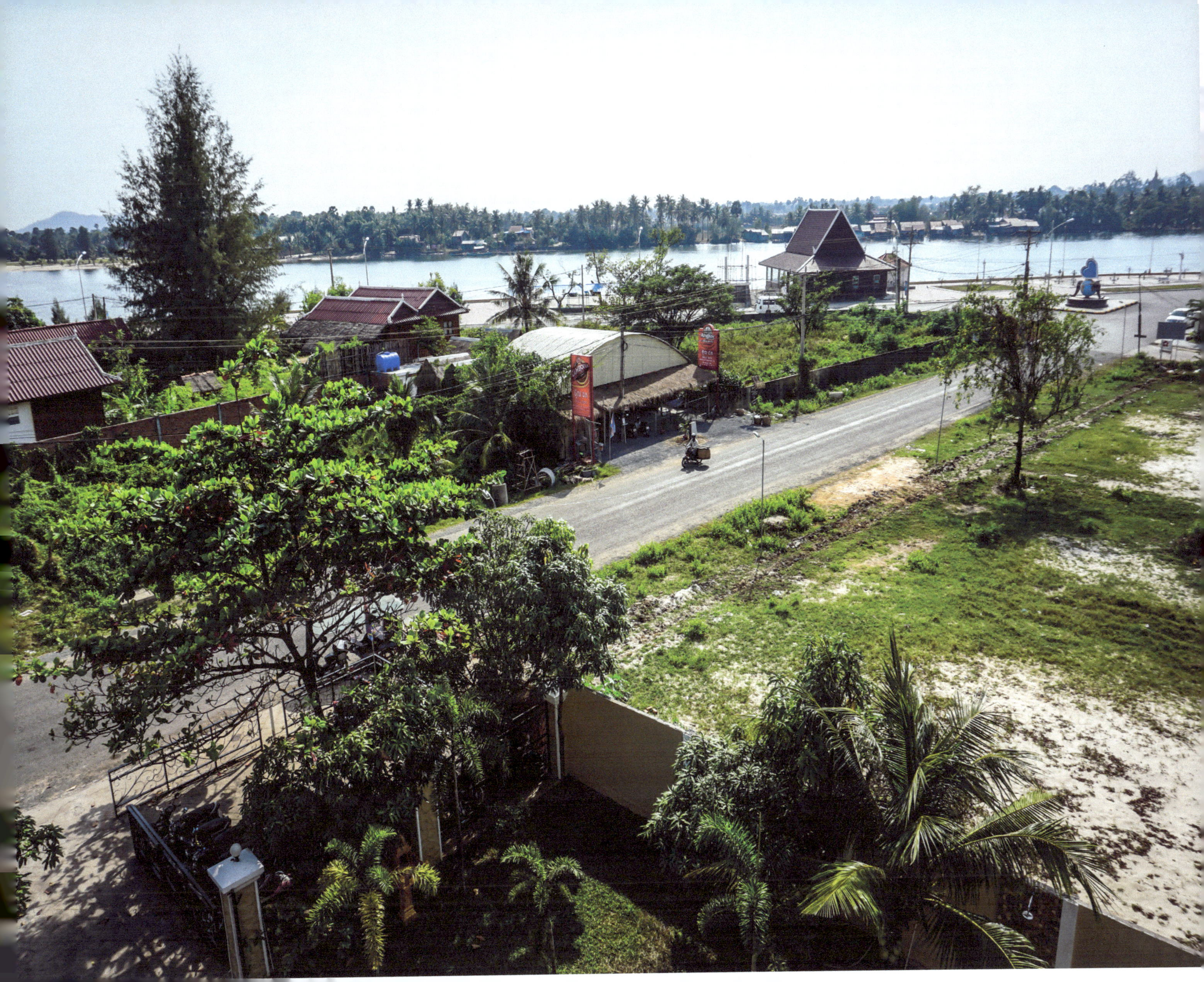

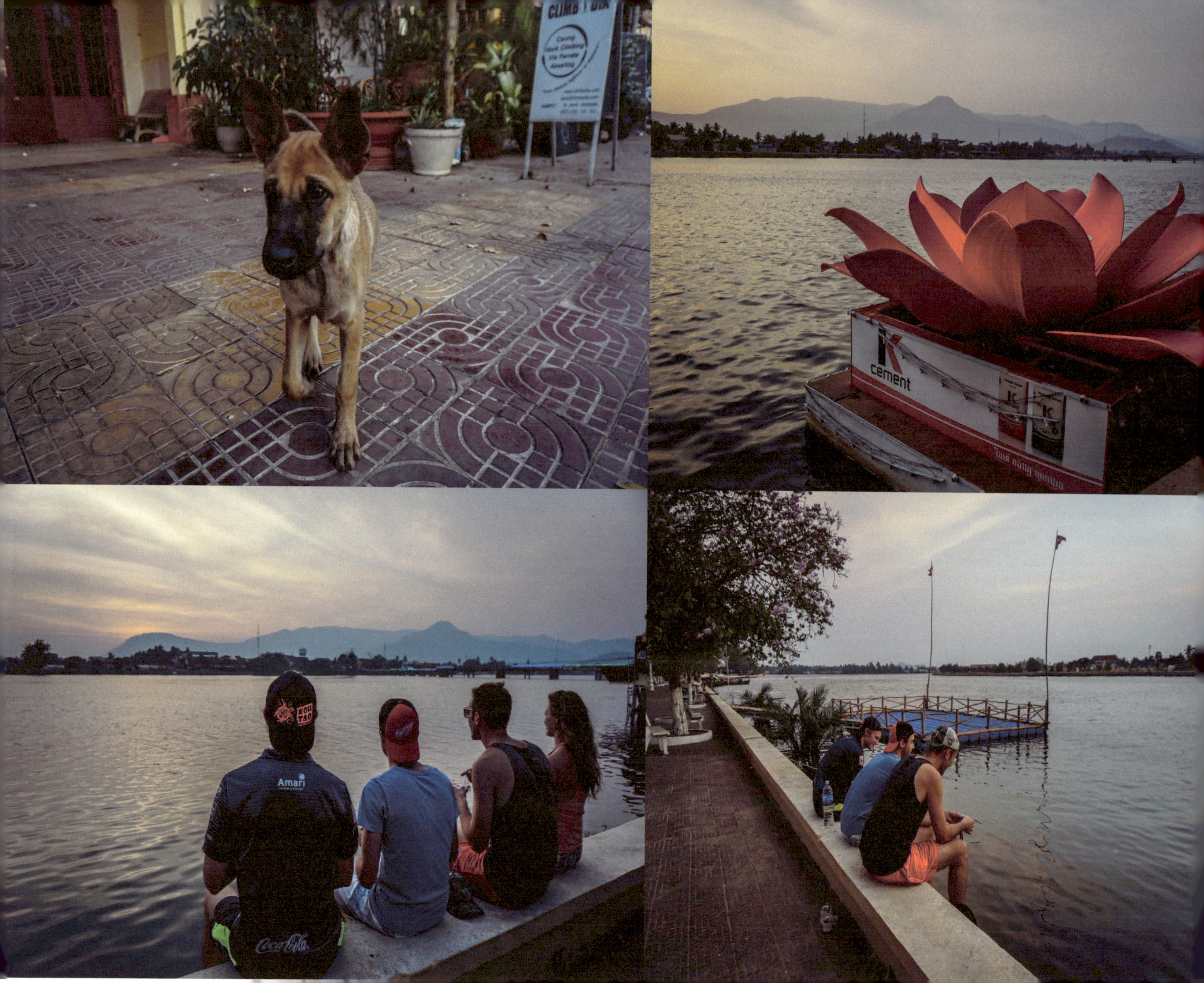

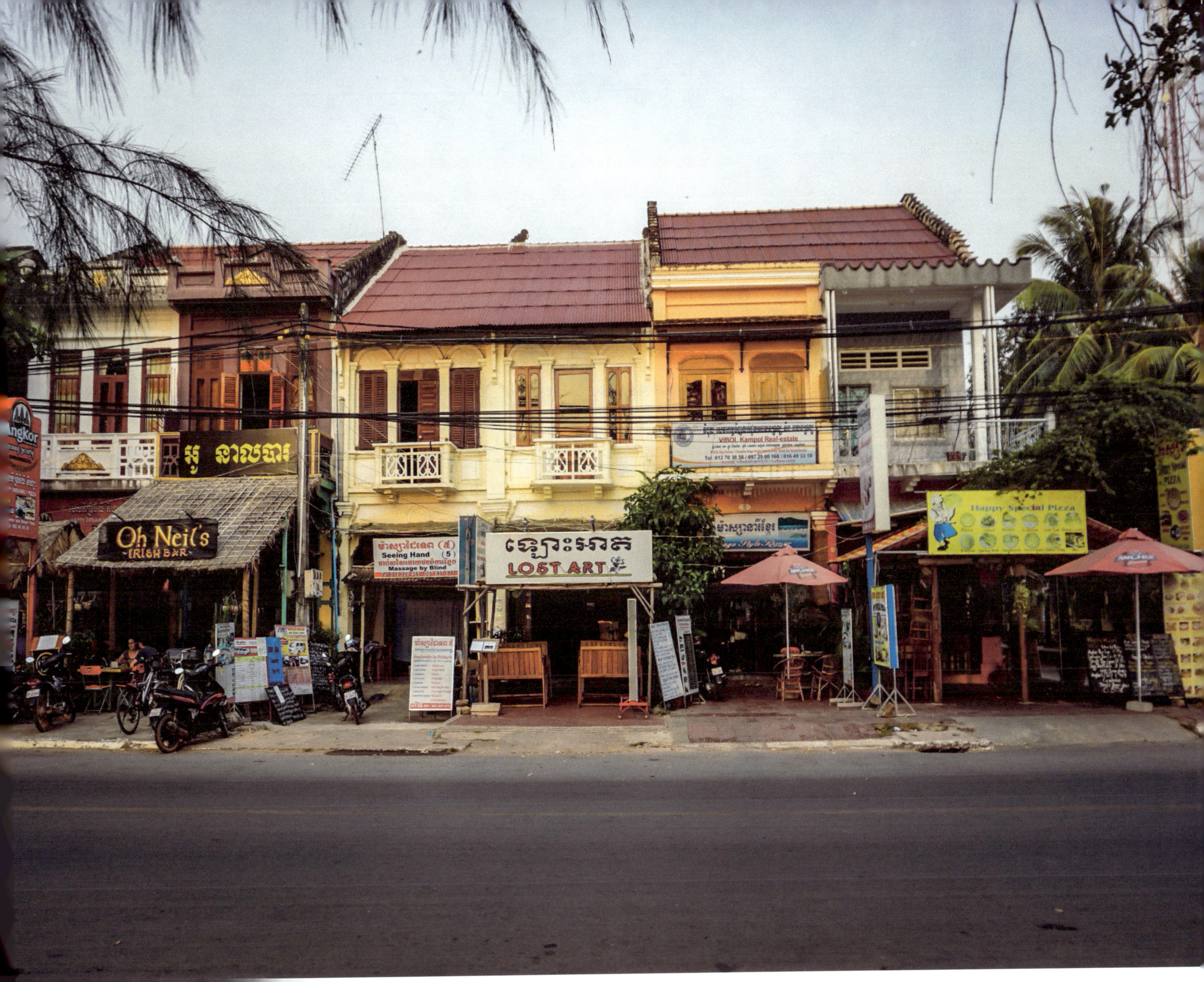
Oh Neil's
IRISH BAR
Seeing Hand (5)
Massage by Blind
VIBOL Kampot Real-estate
Tel. 012 70 30 58 / 097 25 60 168 / 016 49 33 19
LOST ART
Happy Special Pizza
Angkor

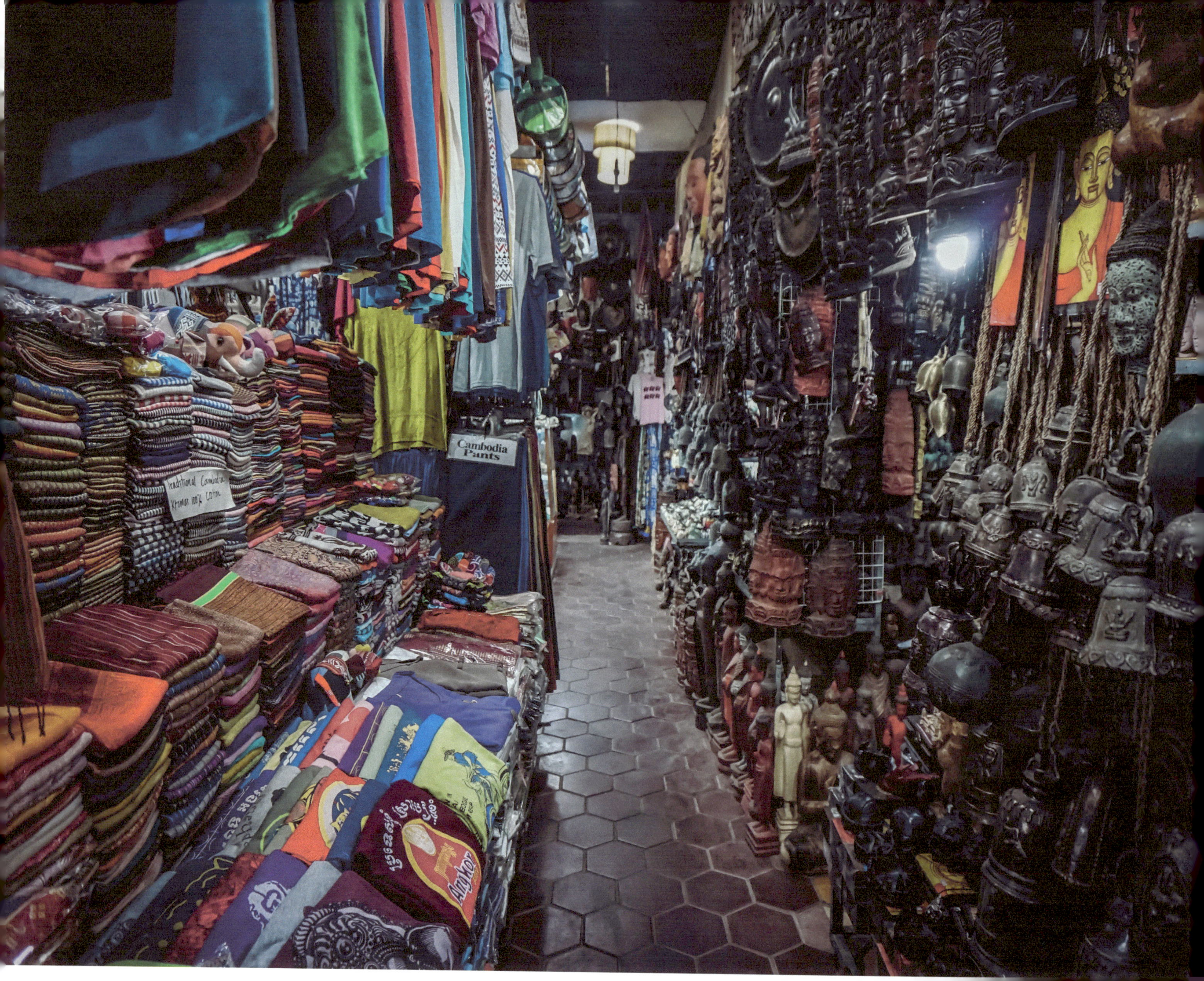

Traditional Cambodia
Kroman 100% Cotton
Cambodia
Pants

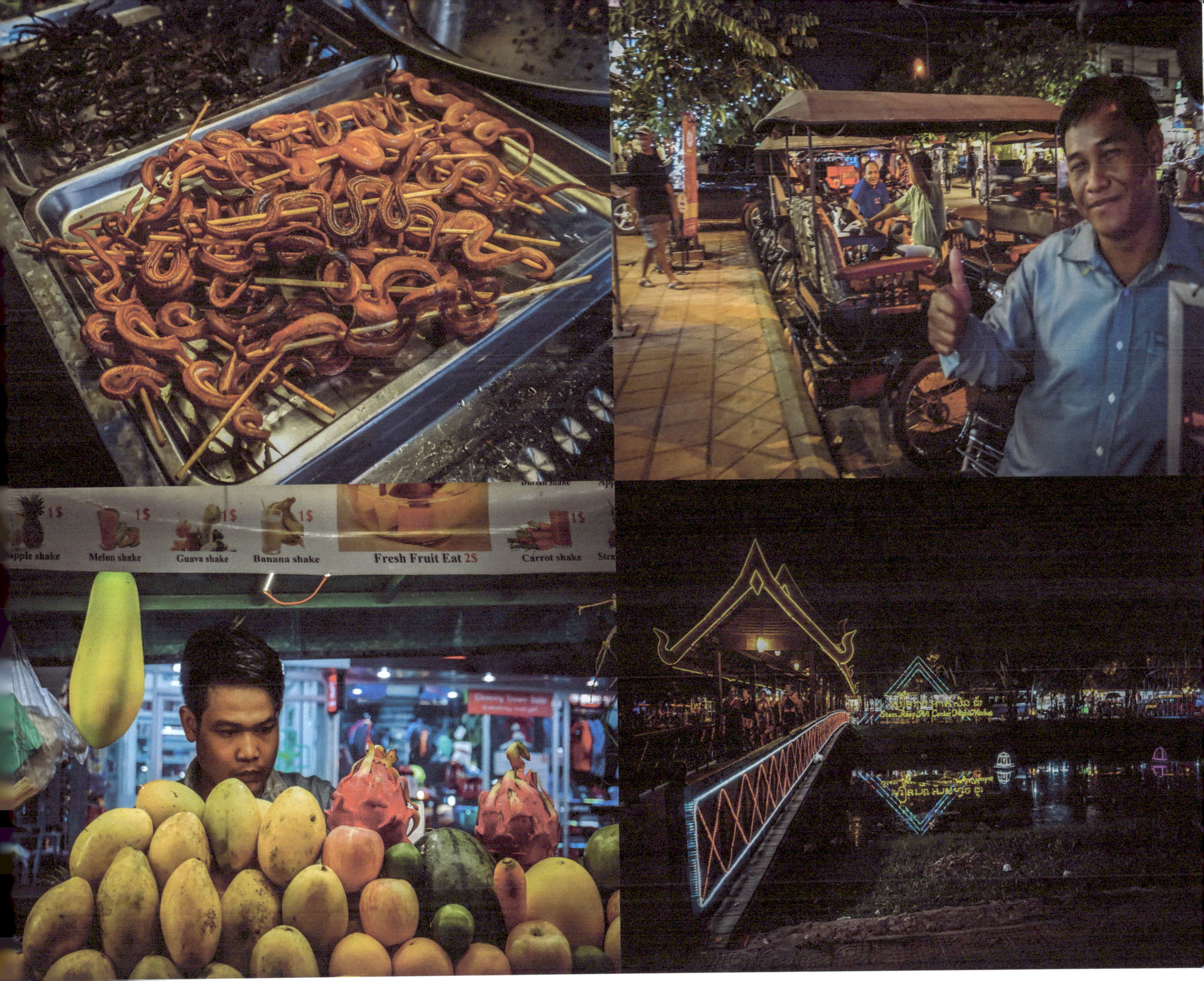
Durian shake    Apple
Pineapple shake 1$    Melon shake 1$    Guava shake 1$    Banana shake 1$    Fresh Fruit Eat 2$    Carrot shake 1$    Straw
apple shake    Melon shake    Guava shake    Banana shake    Fresh Fruit Eat 2$    Carrot shake
Siem Reap Art Center Night Market

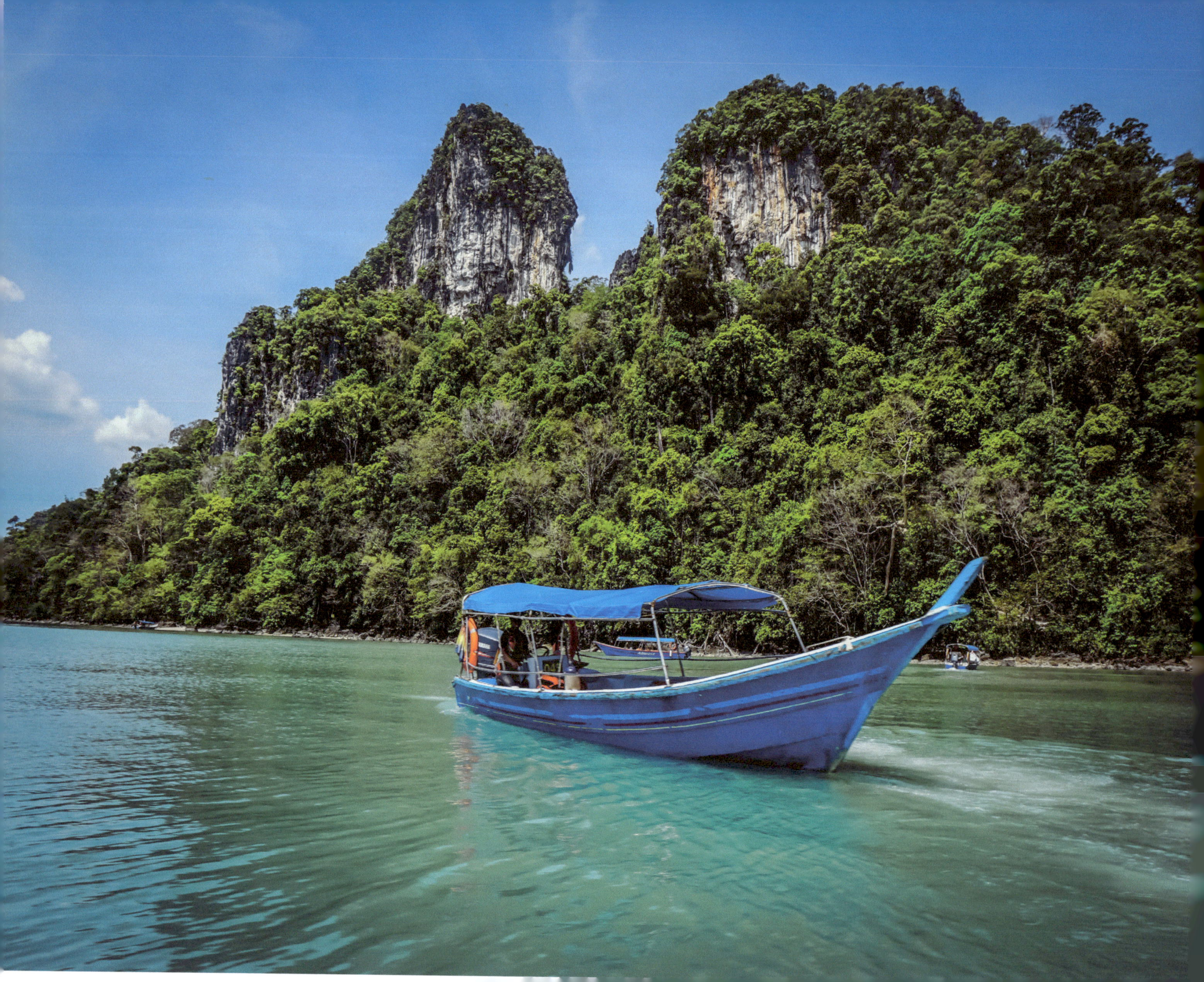

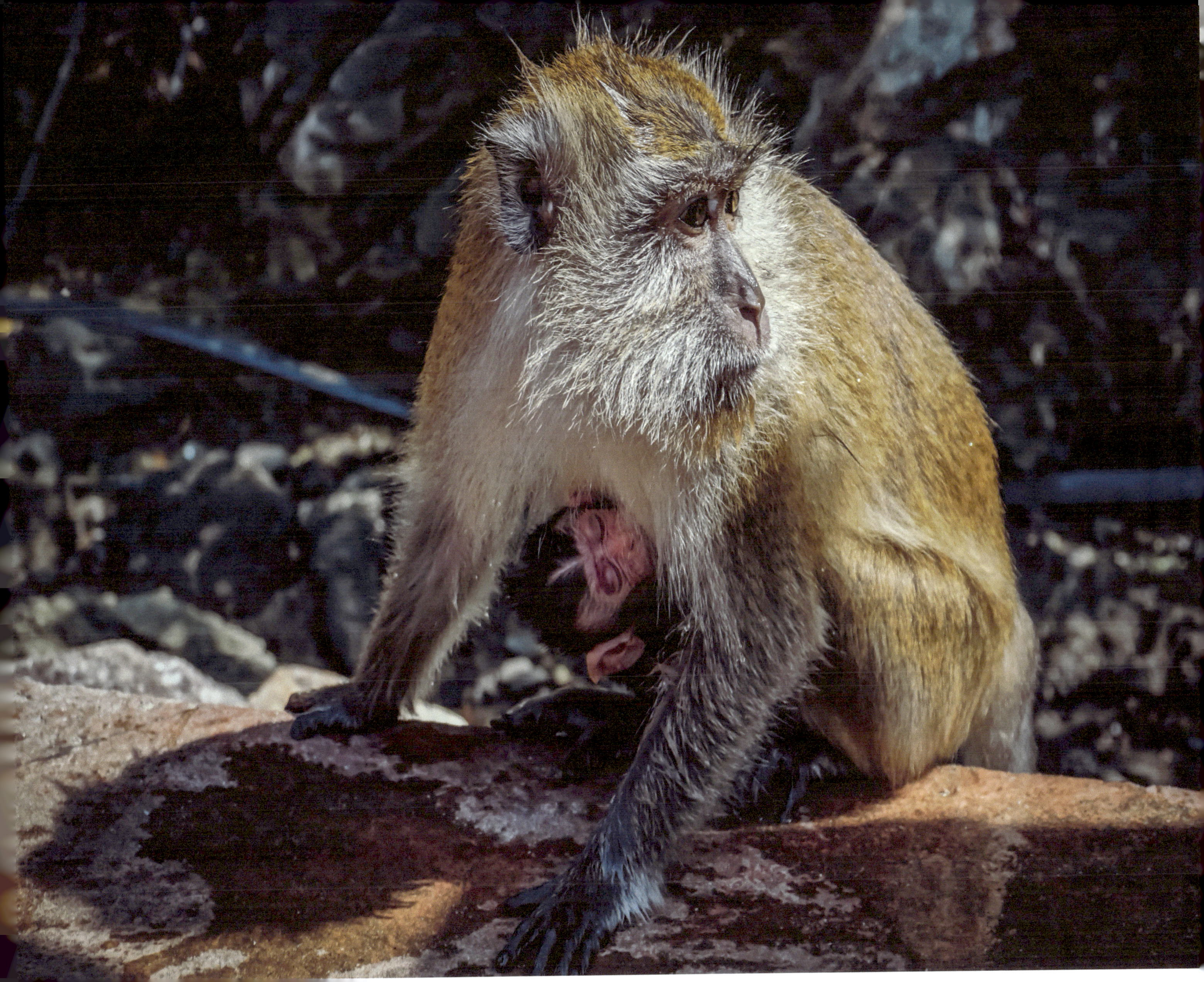

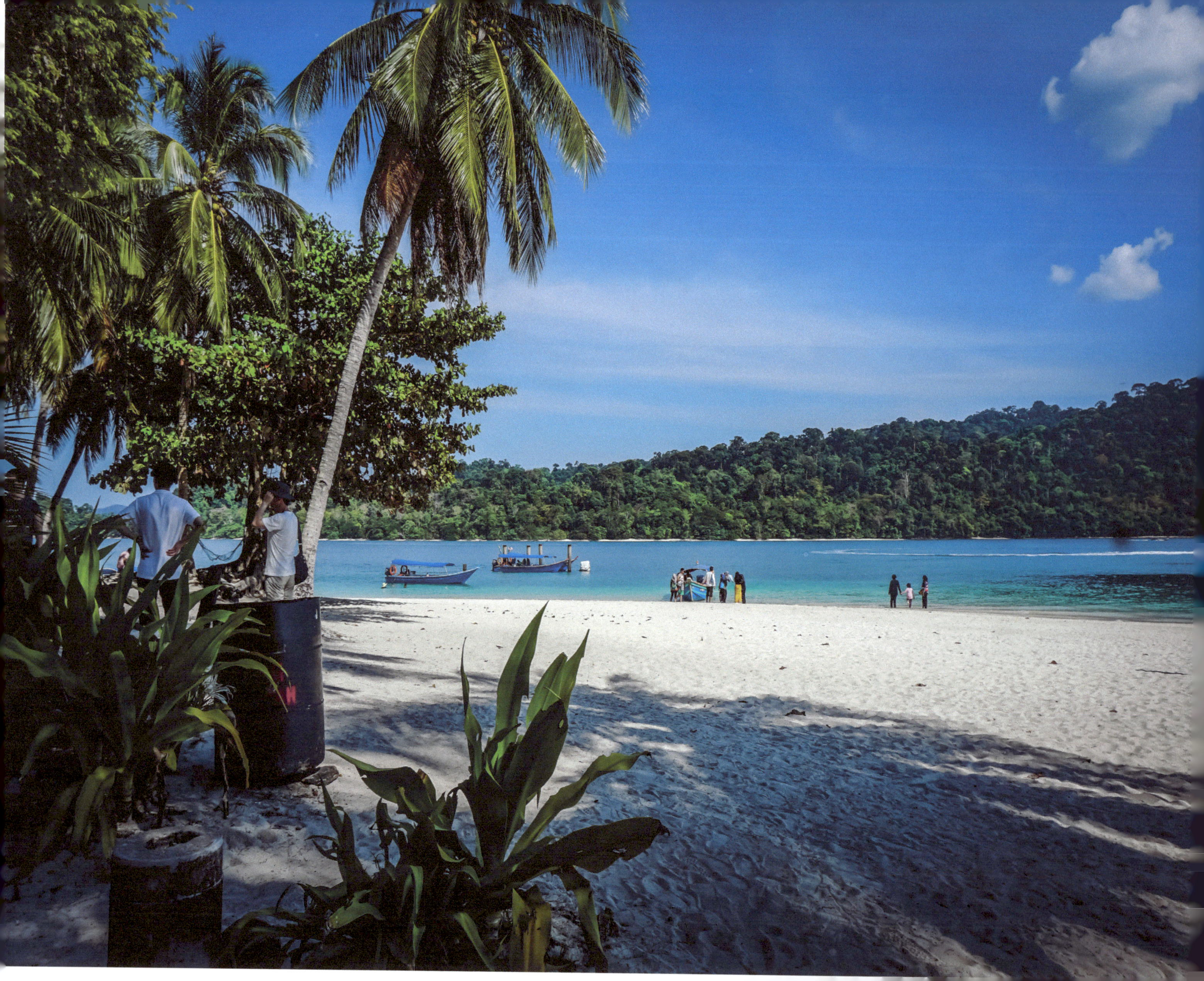

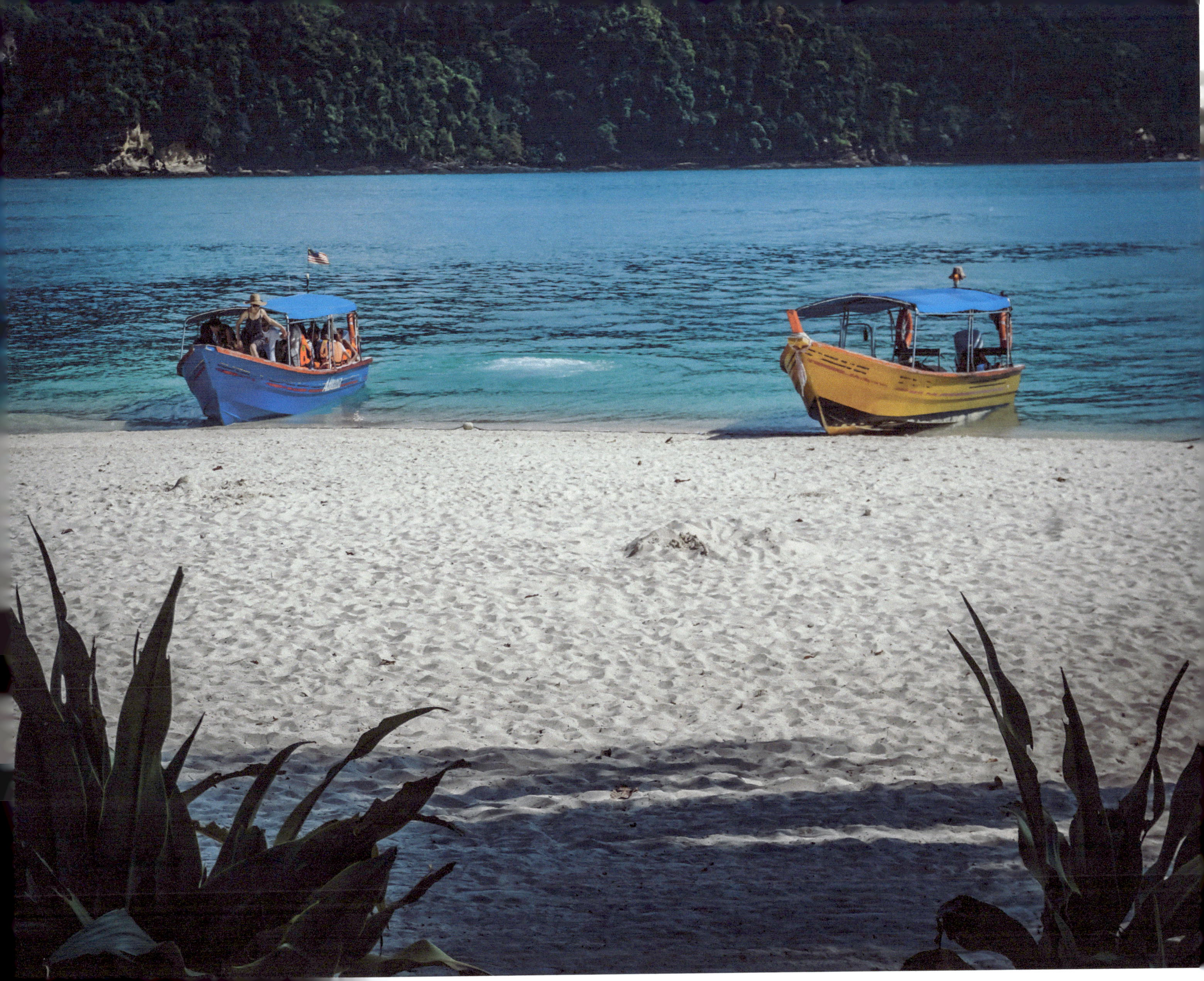

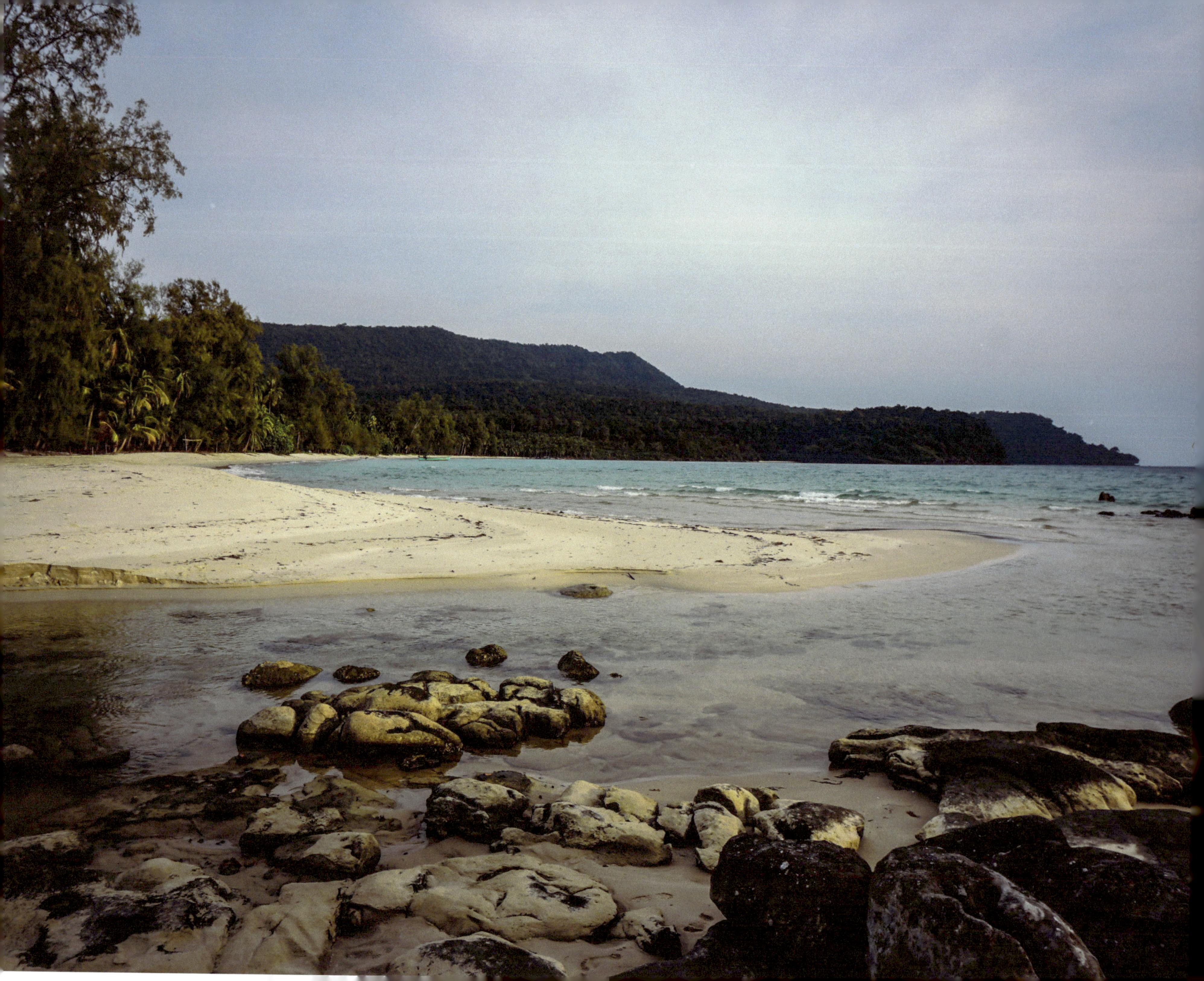

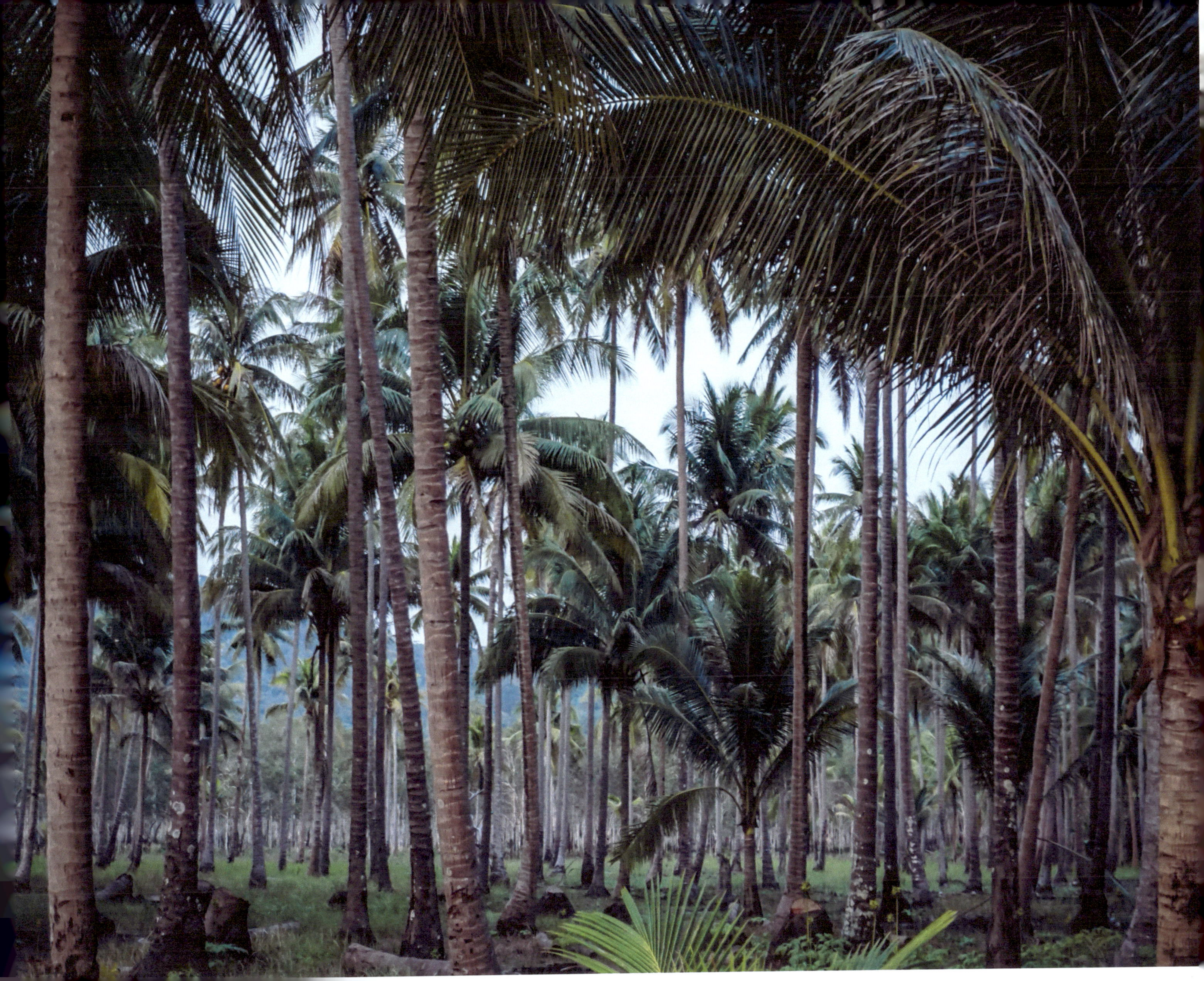

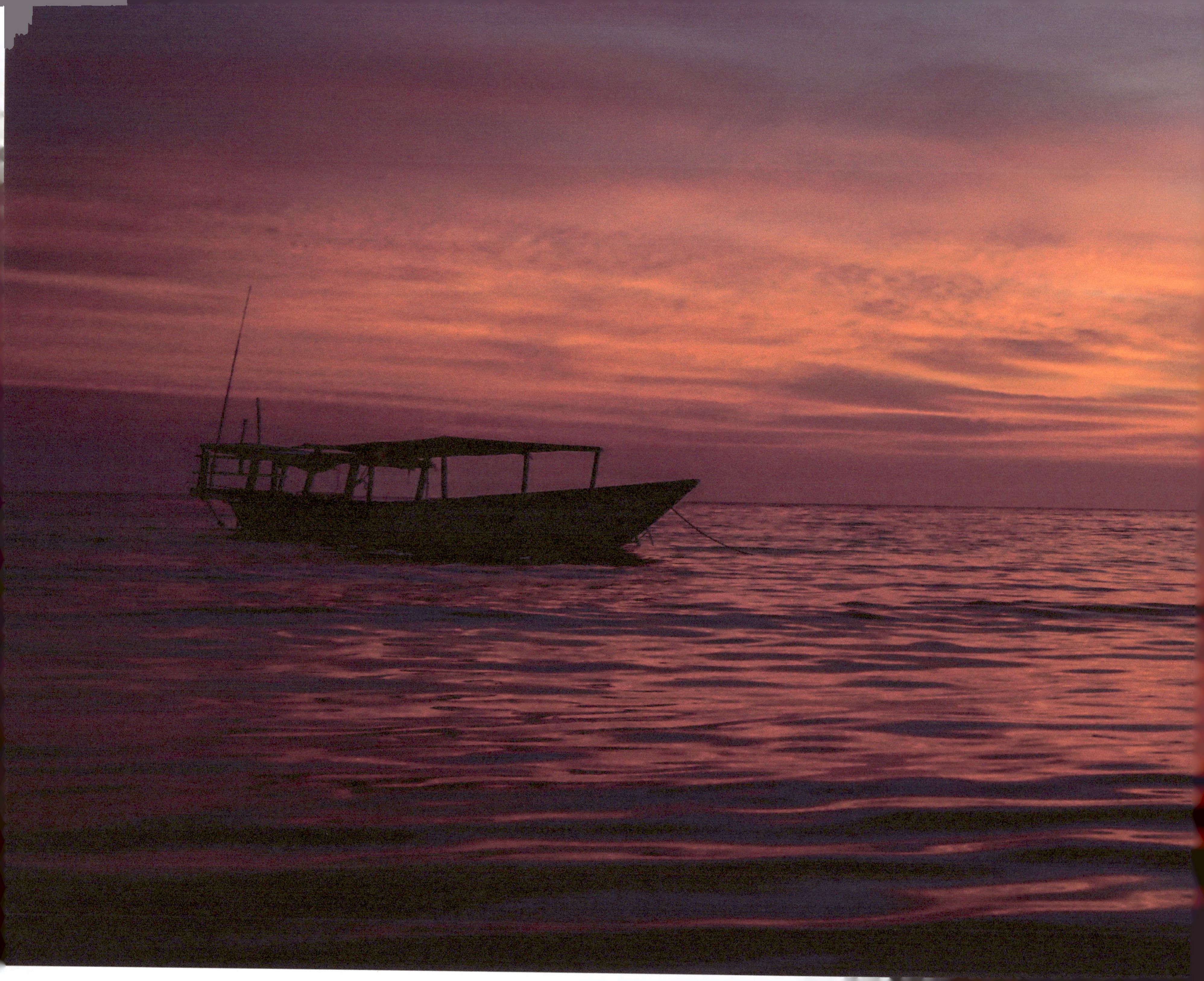

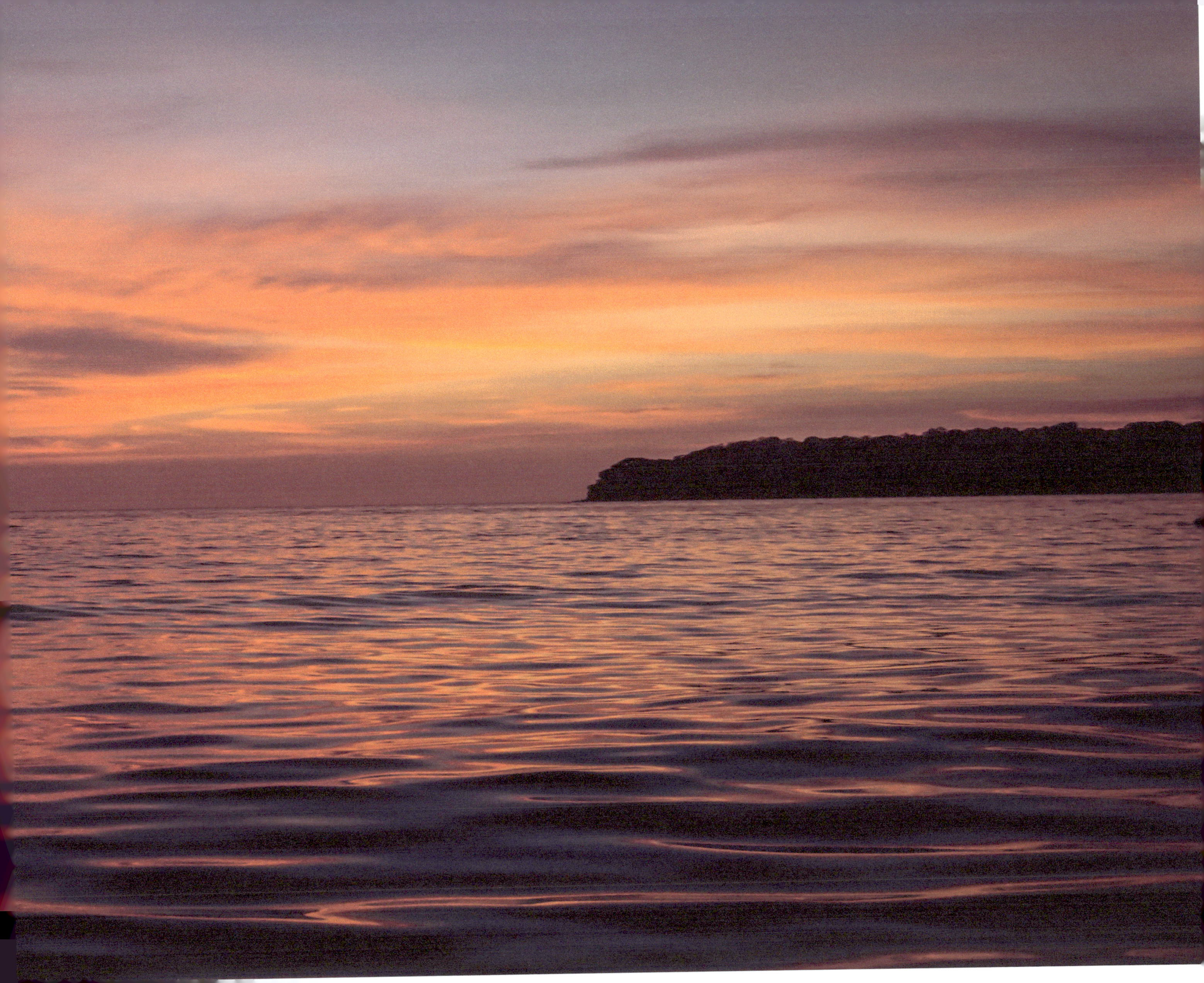

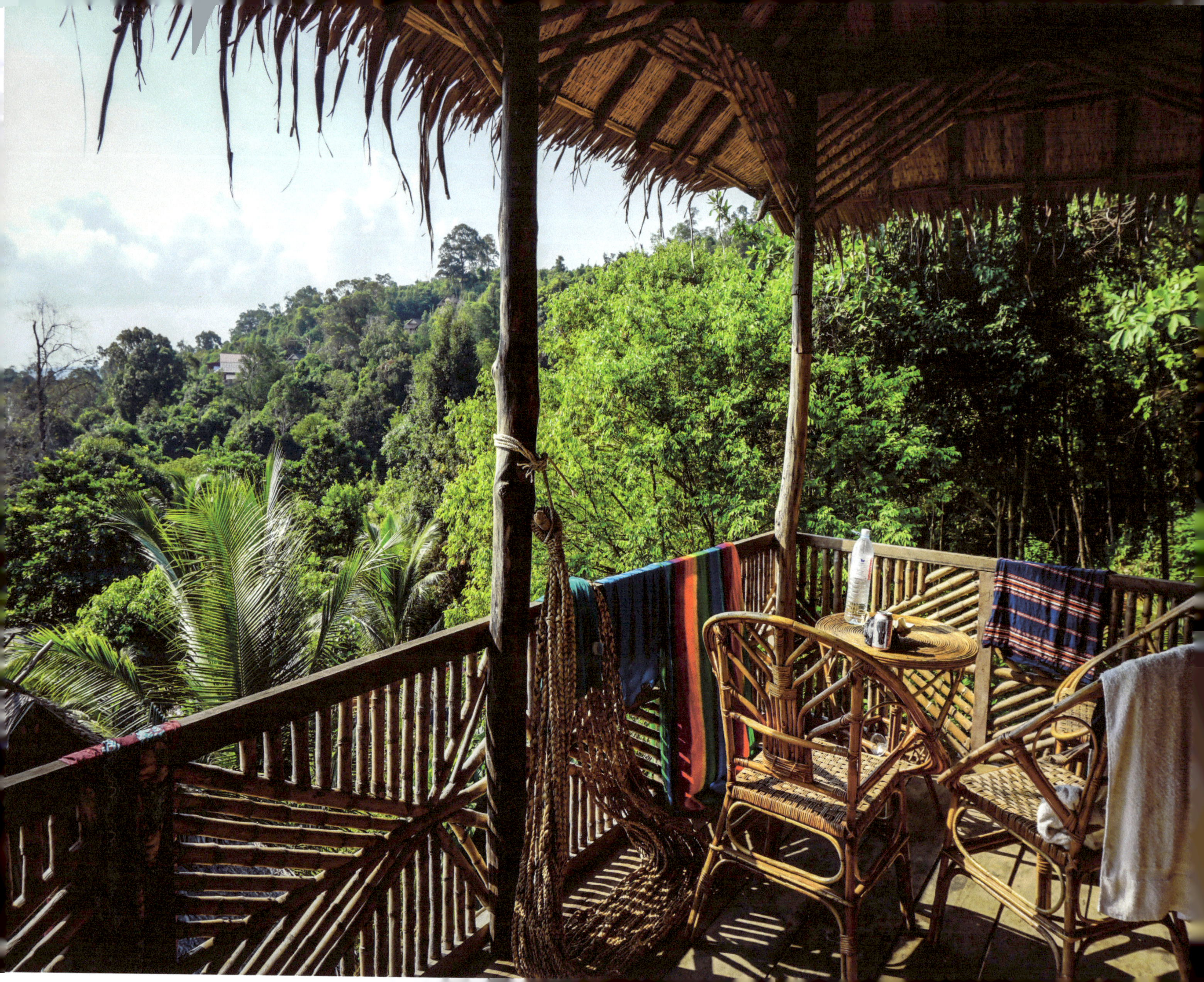

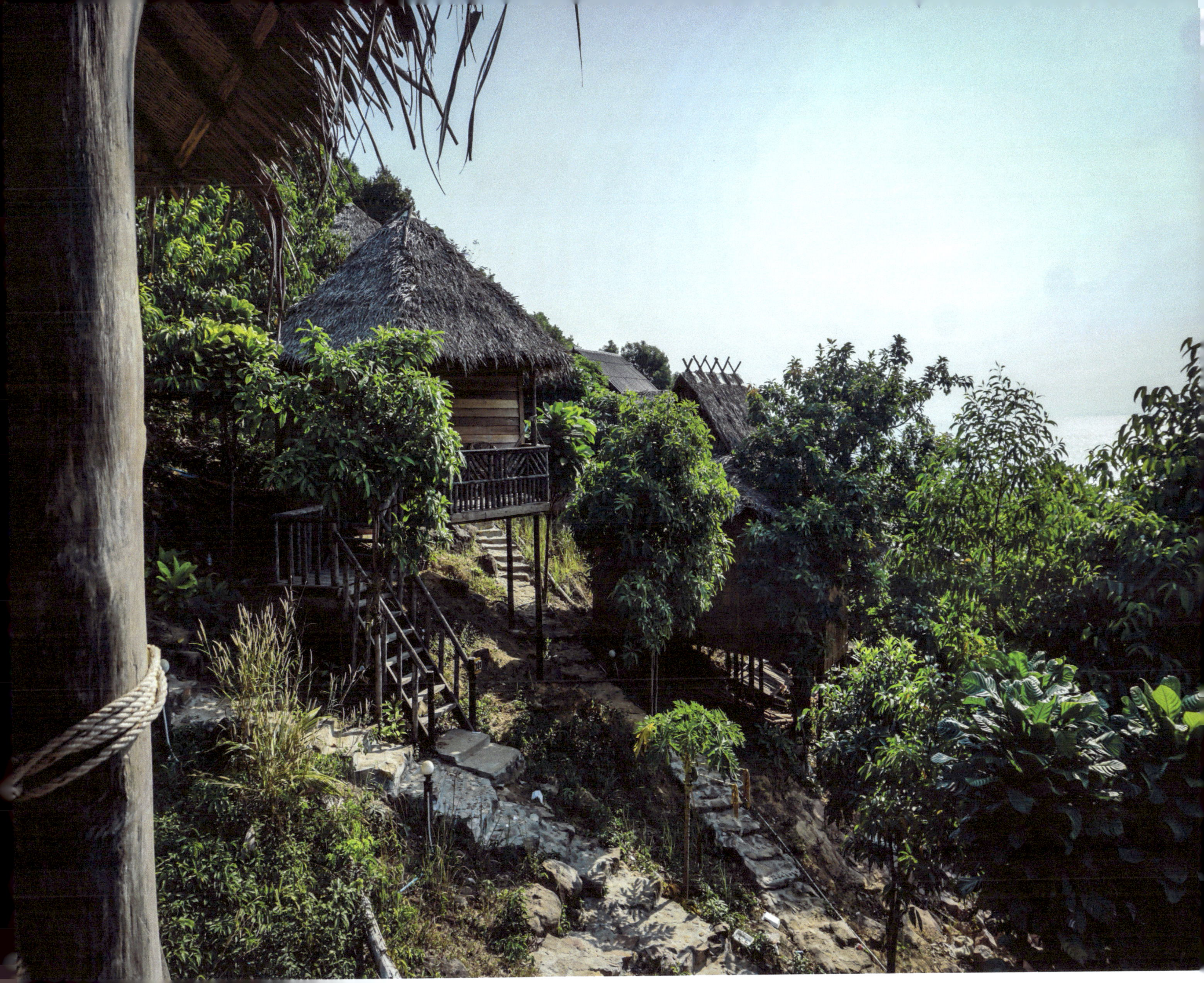

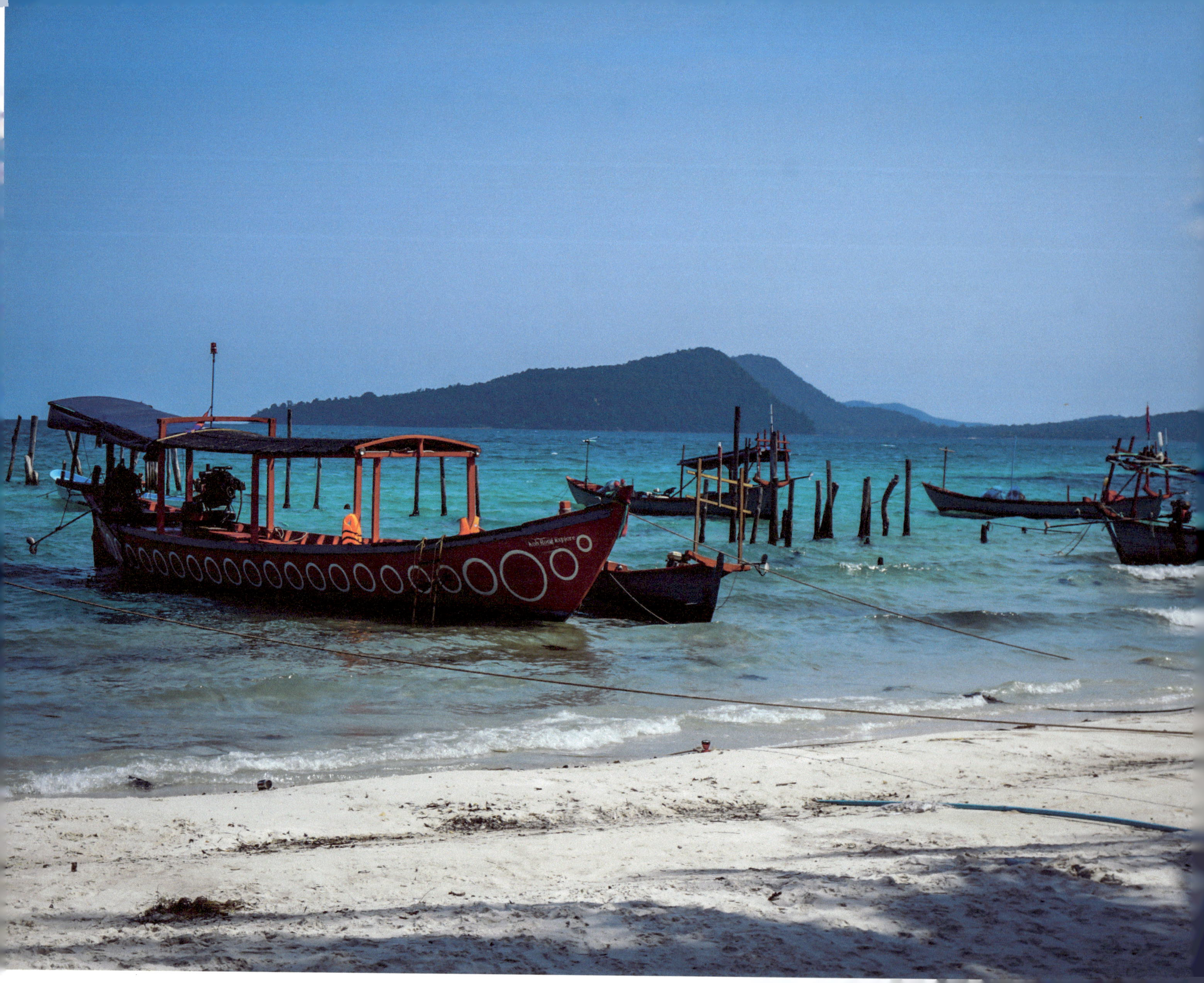

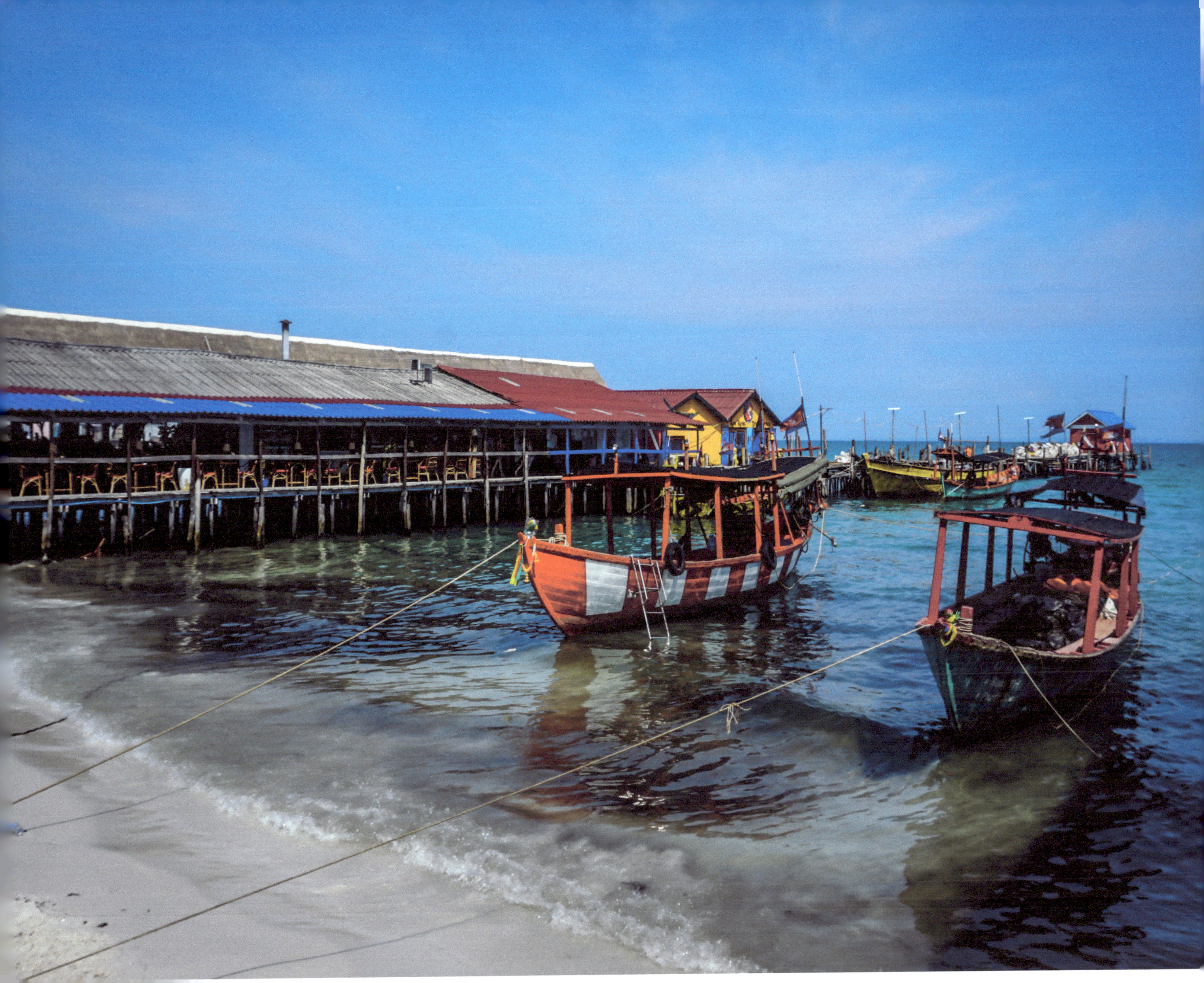

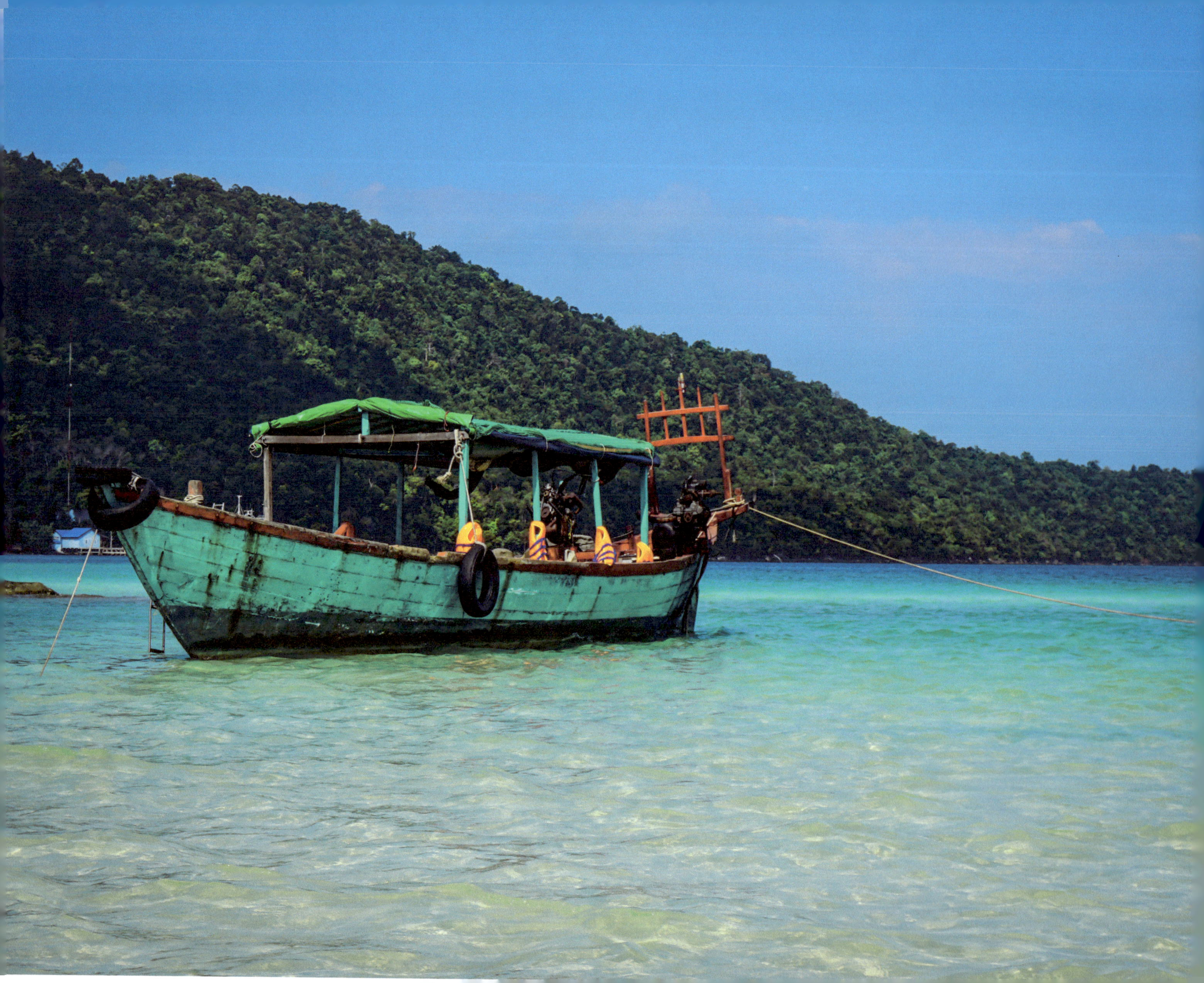

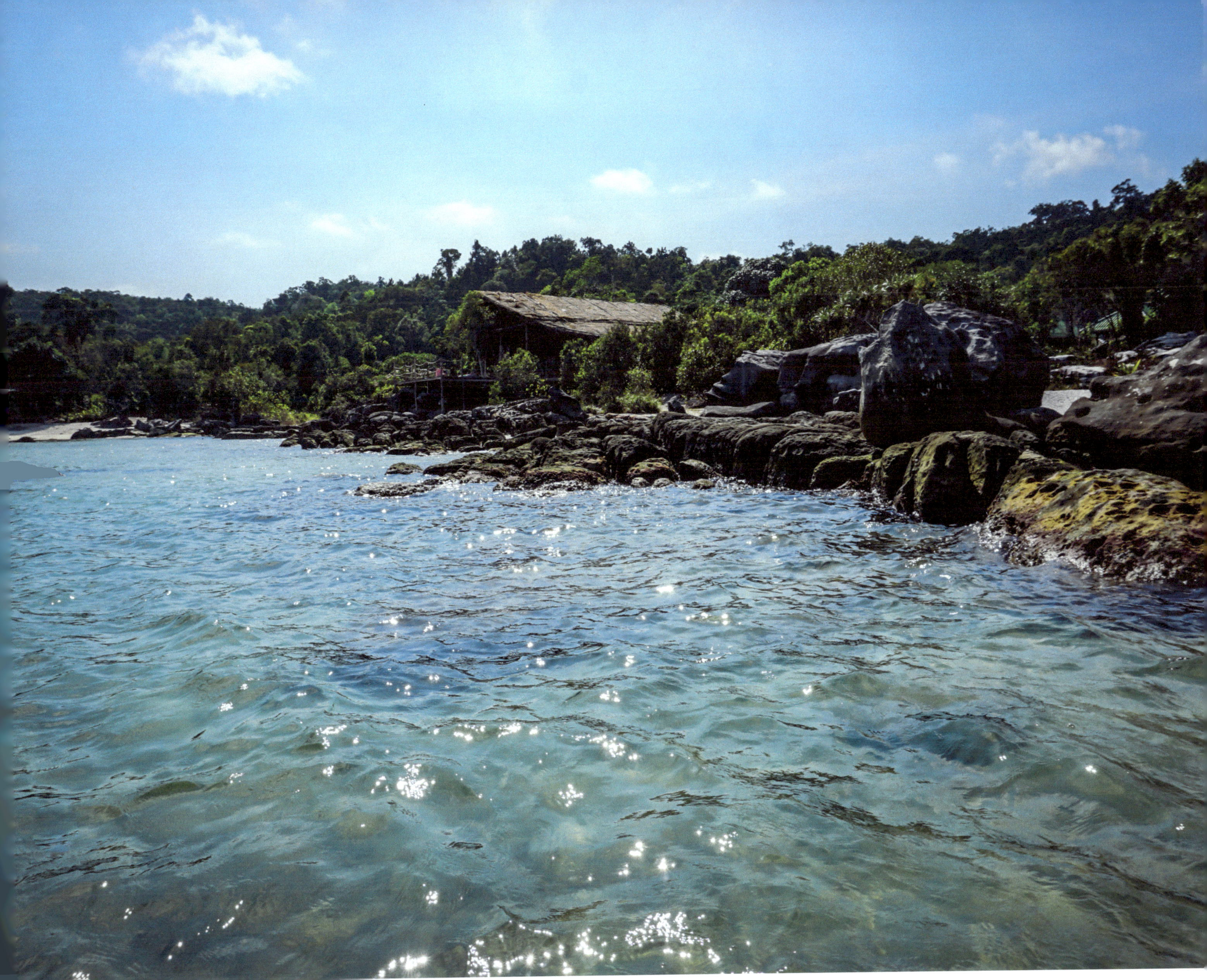

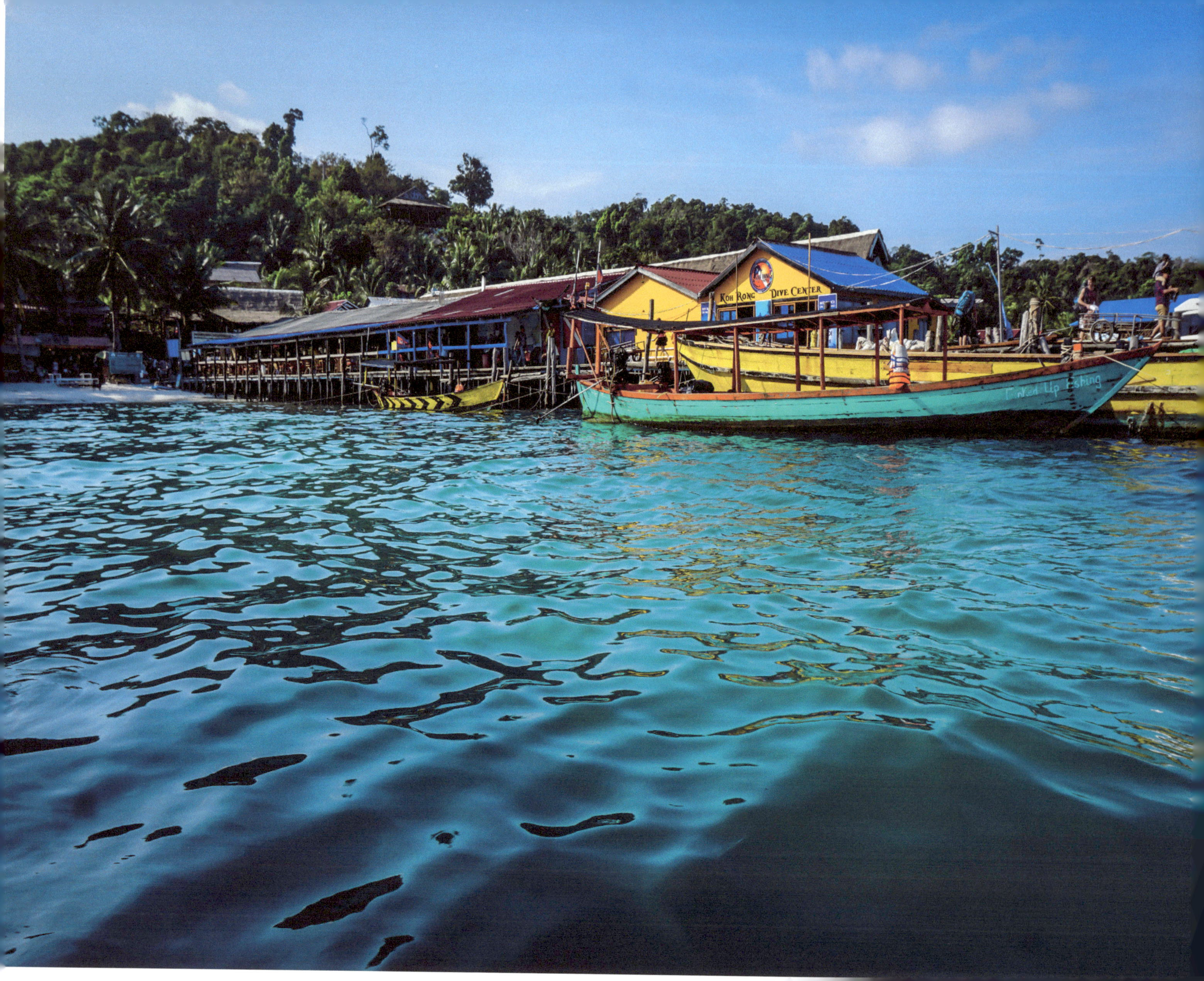

KOH RONG DIVE CENTER

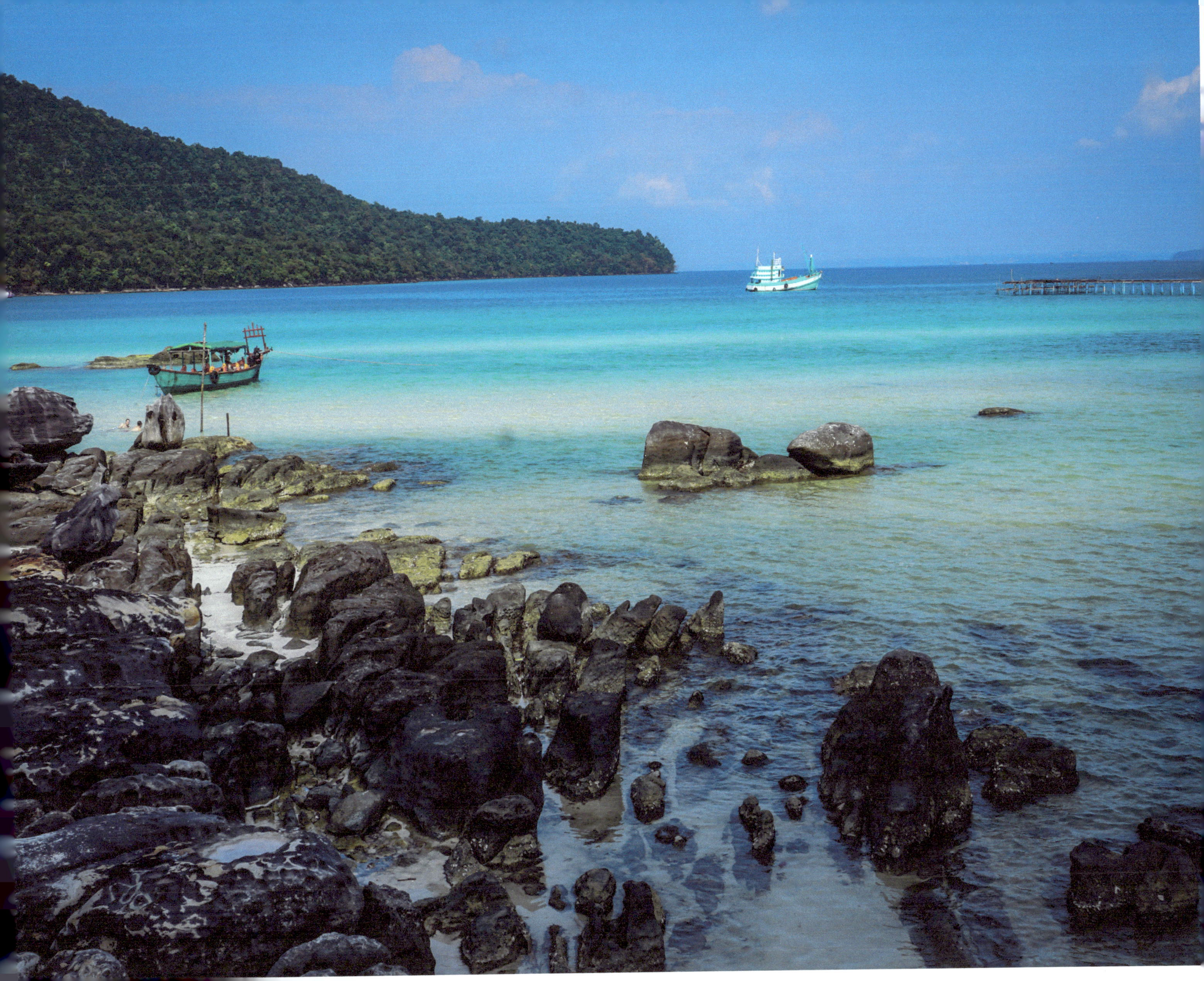

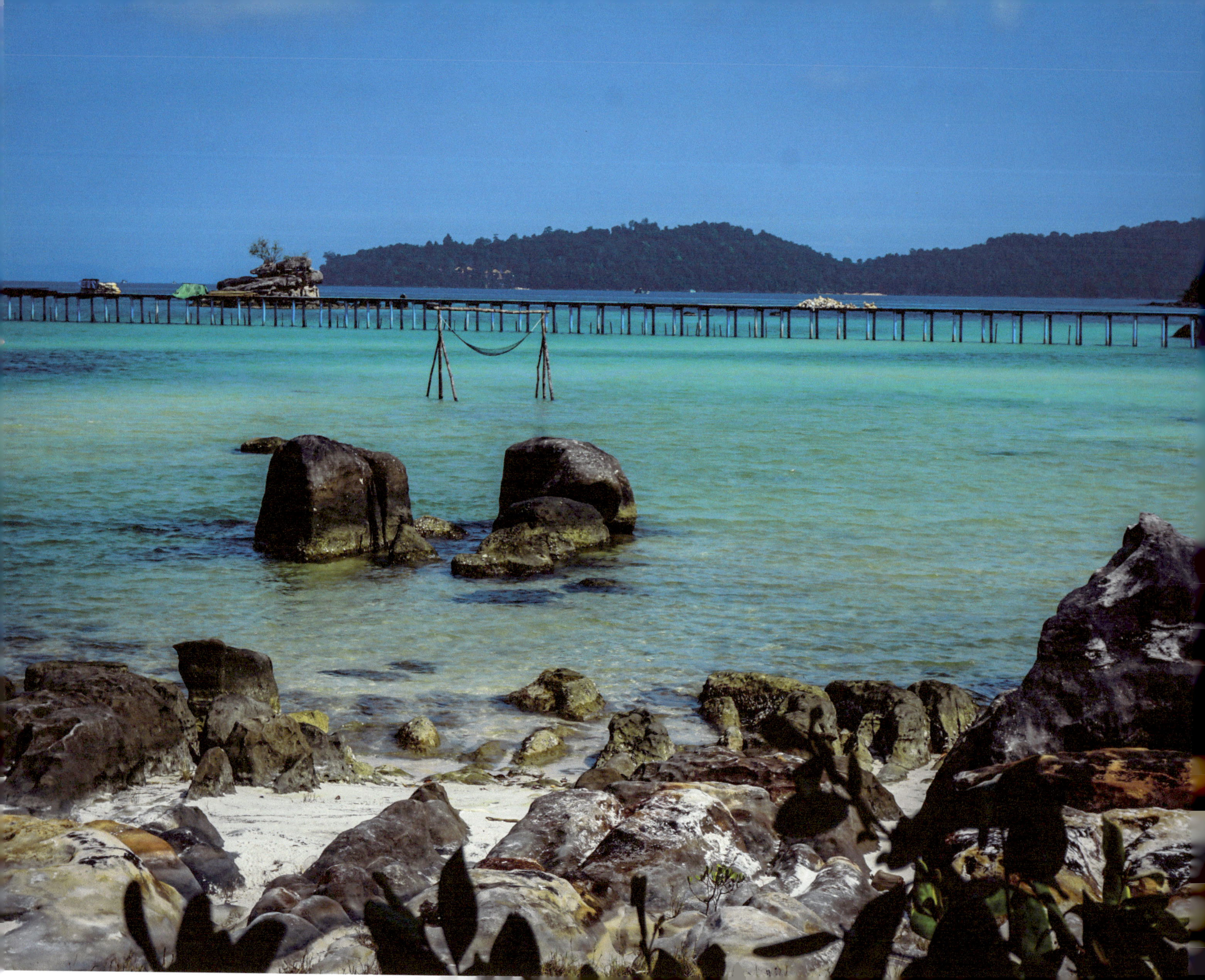

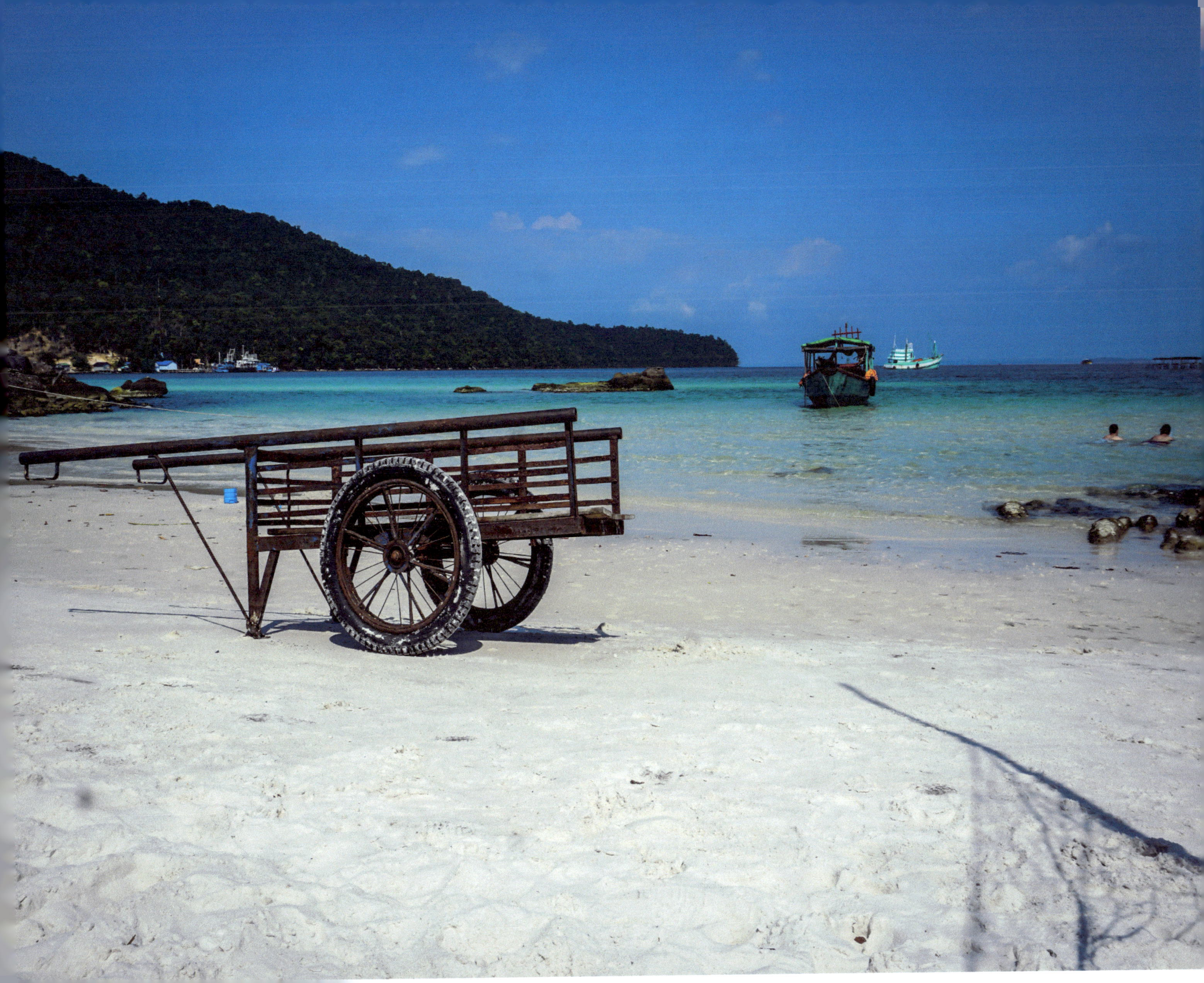

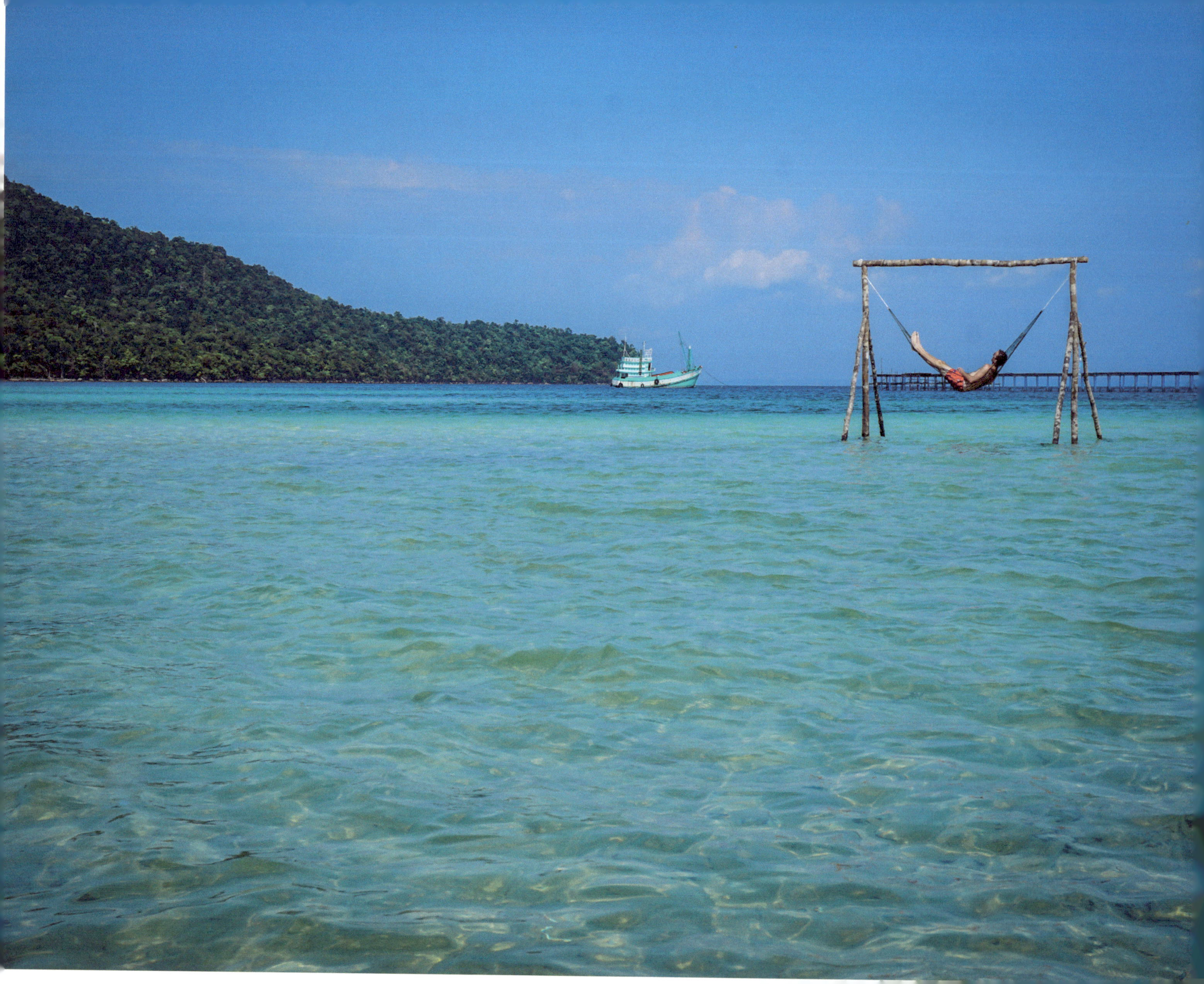

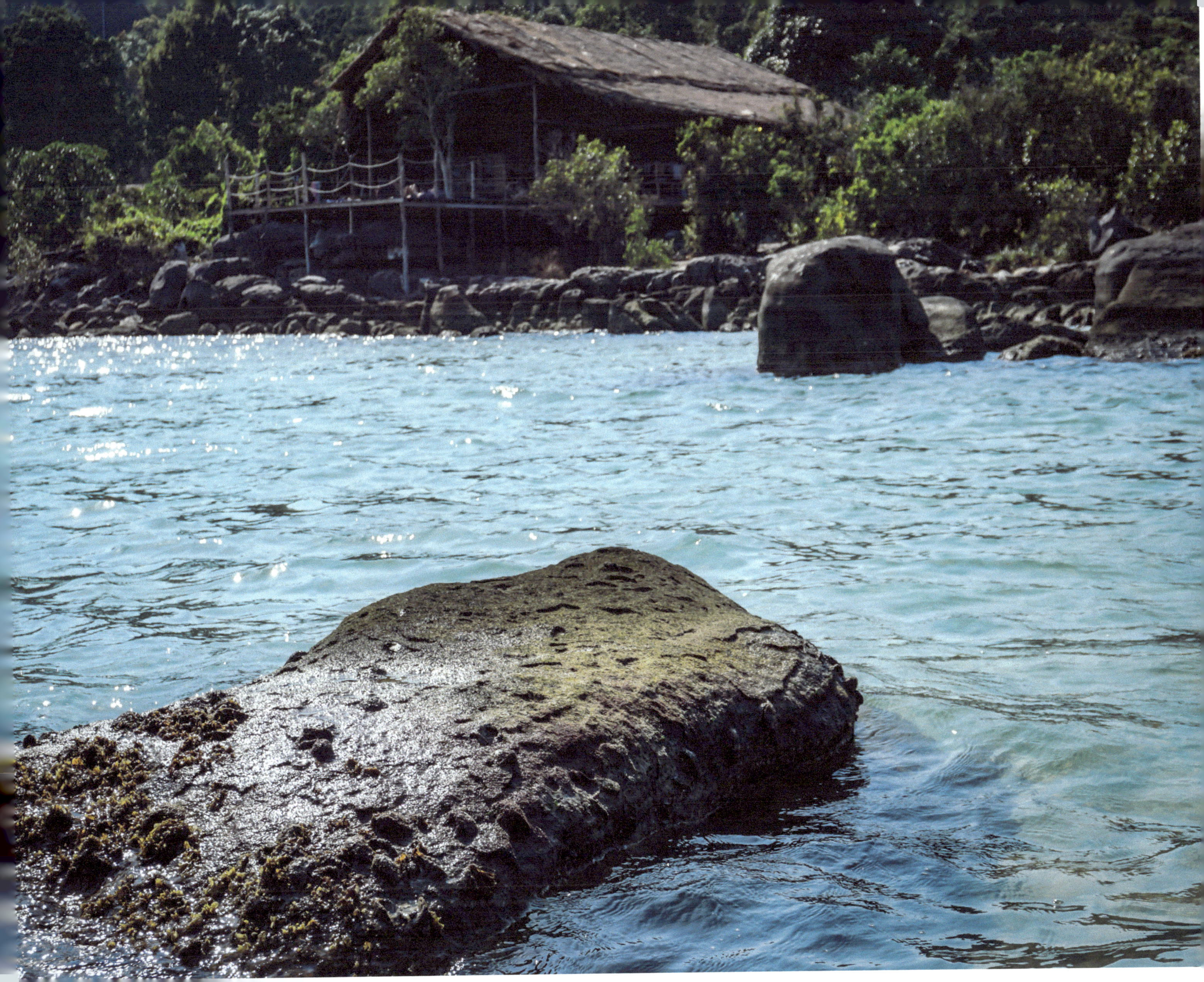

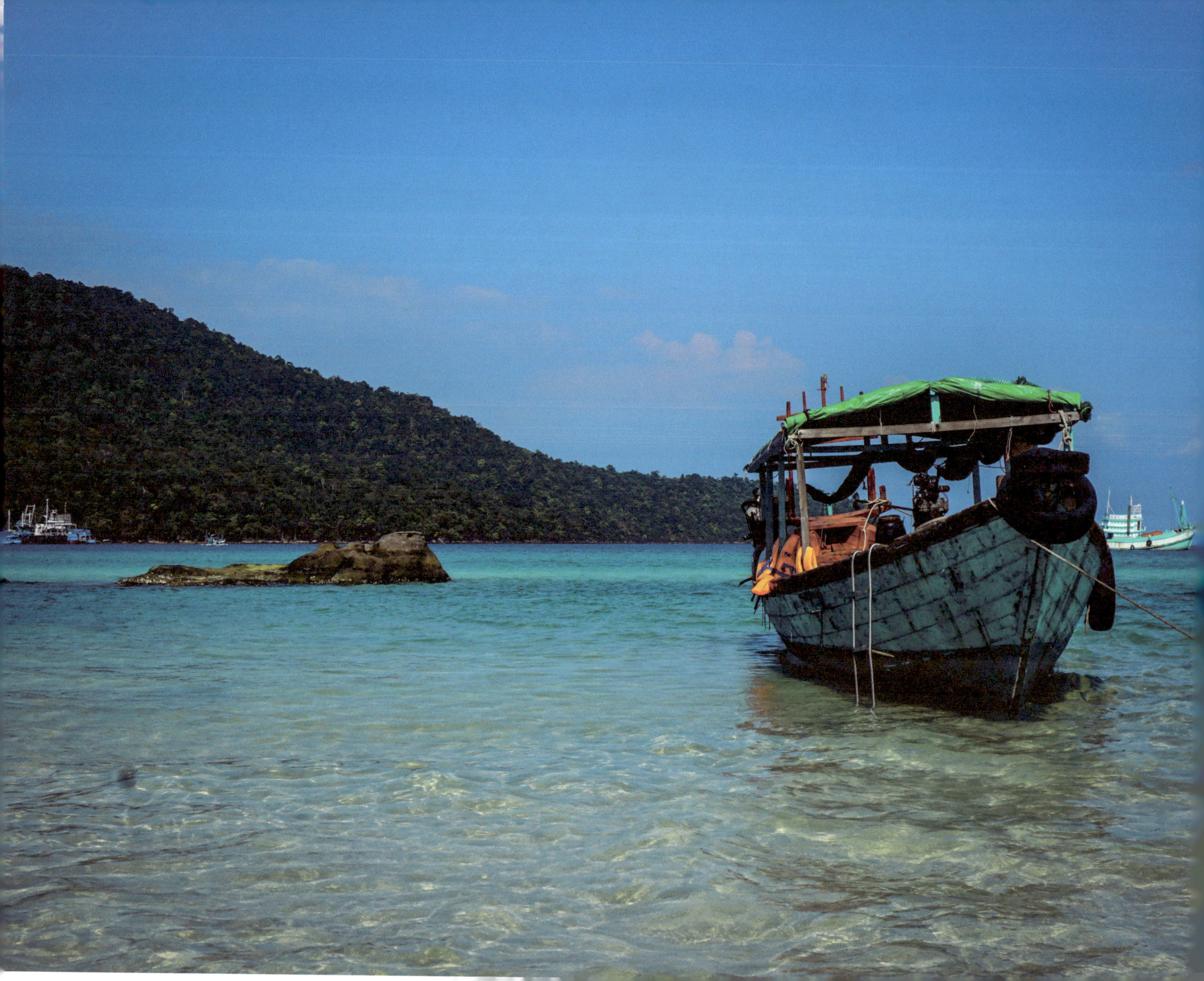

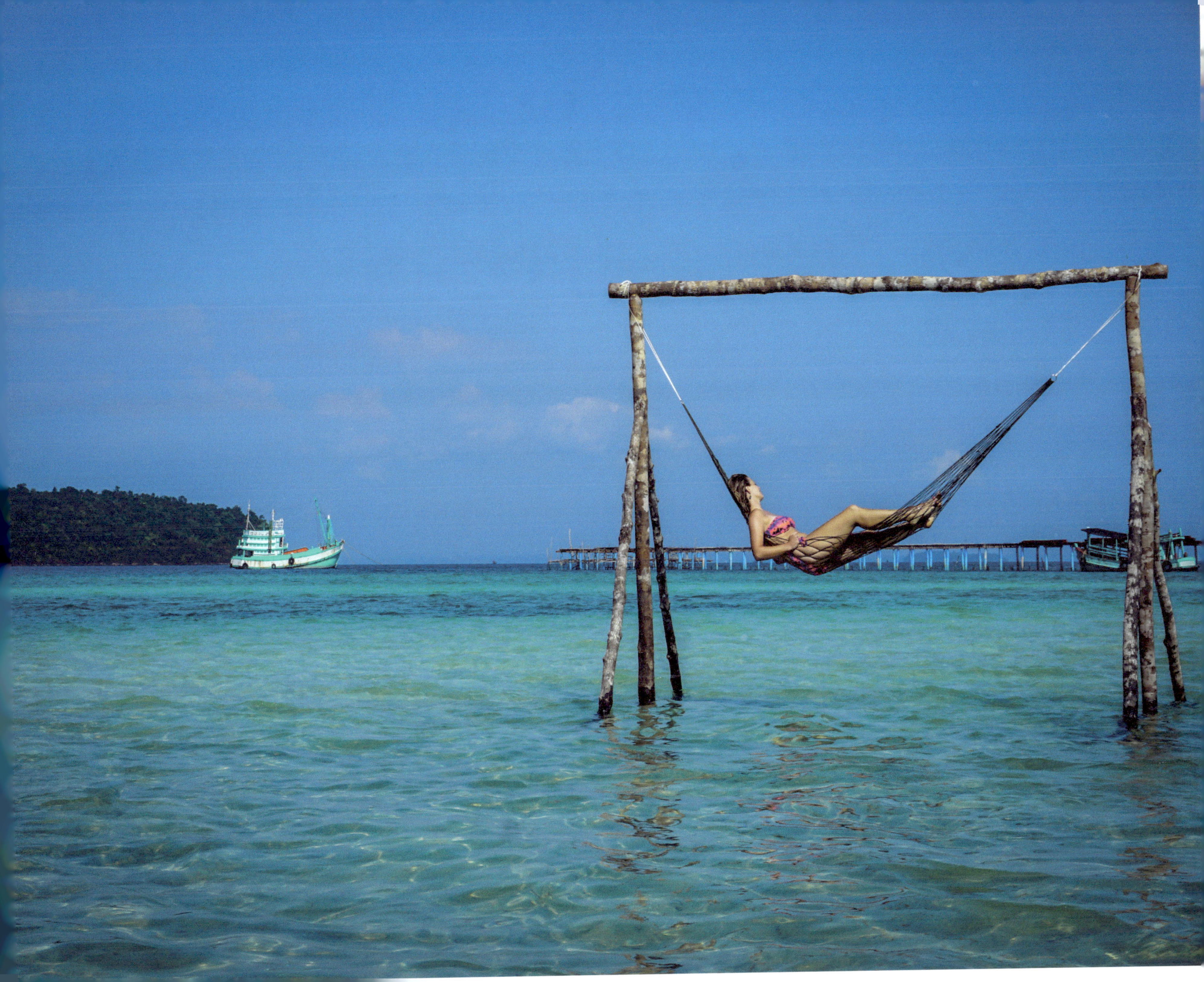

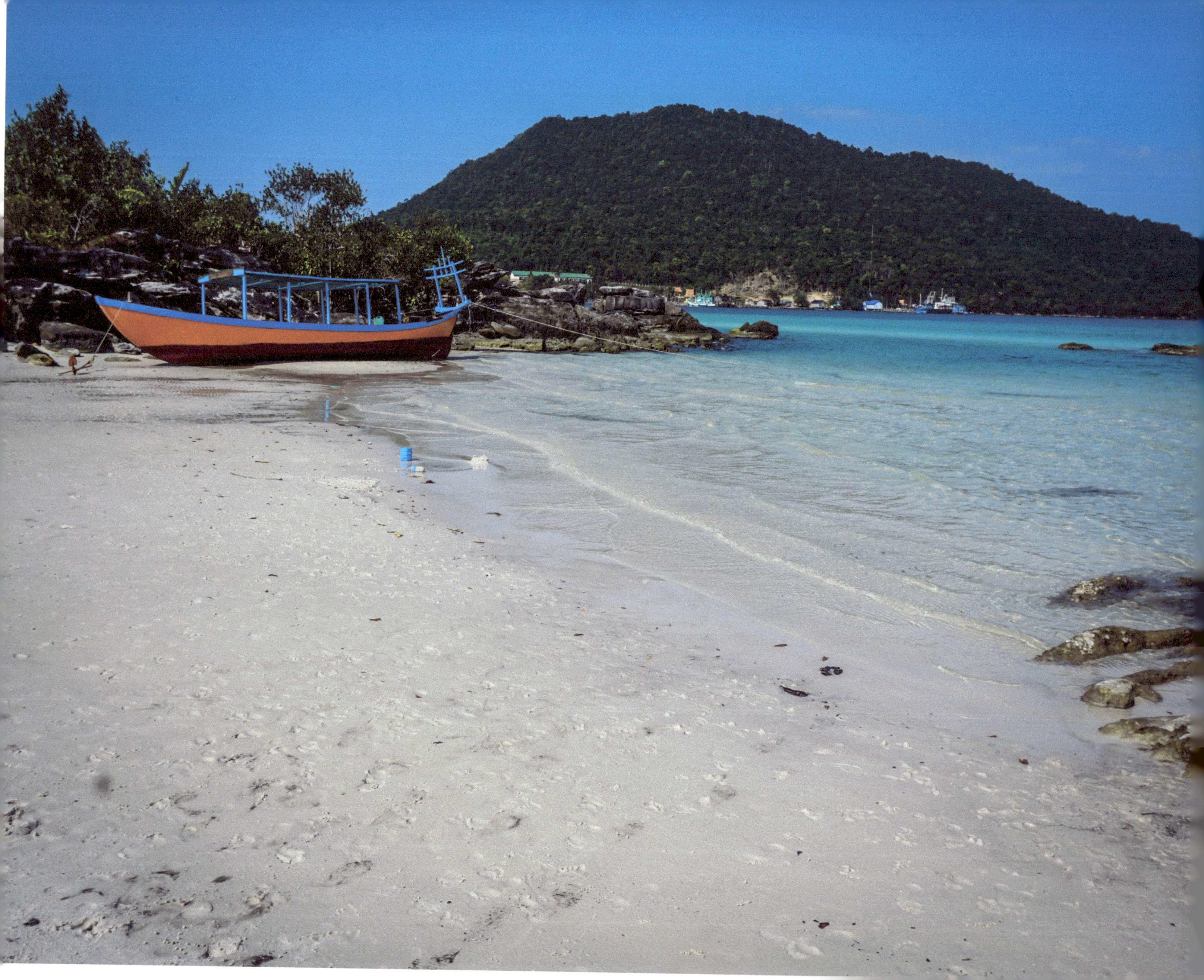

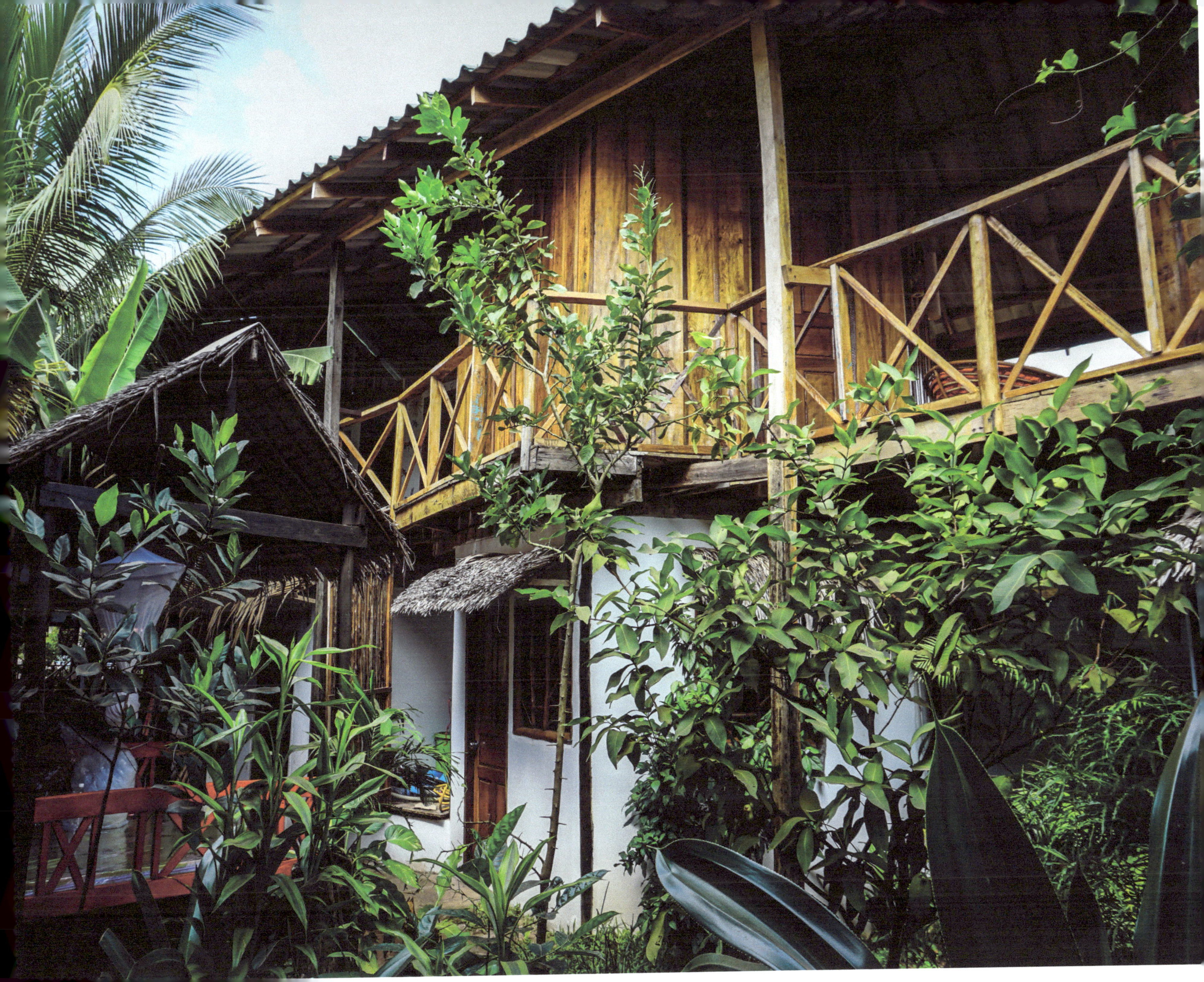

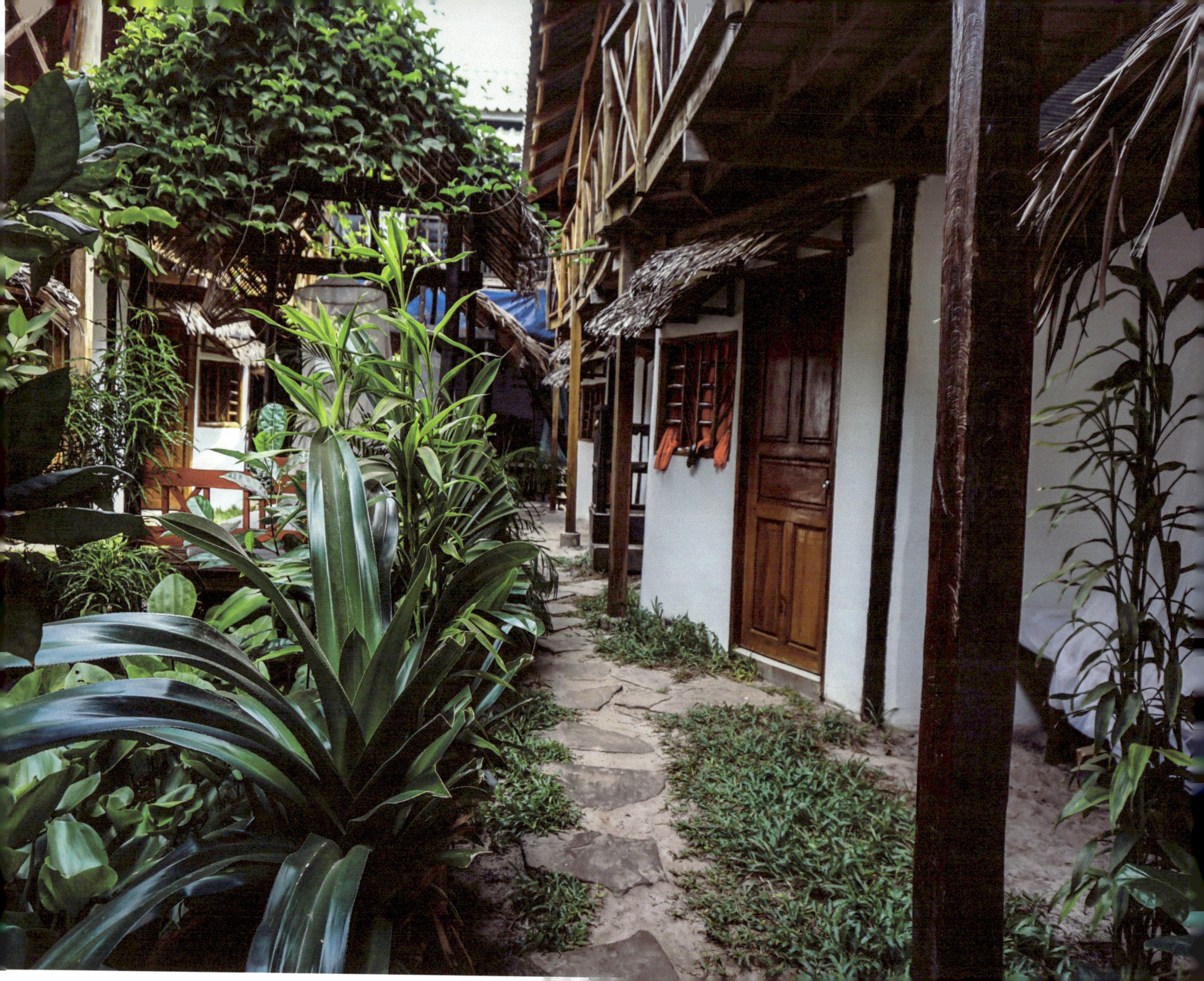

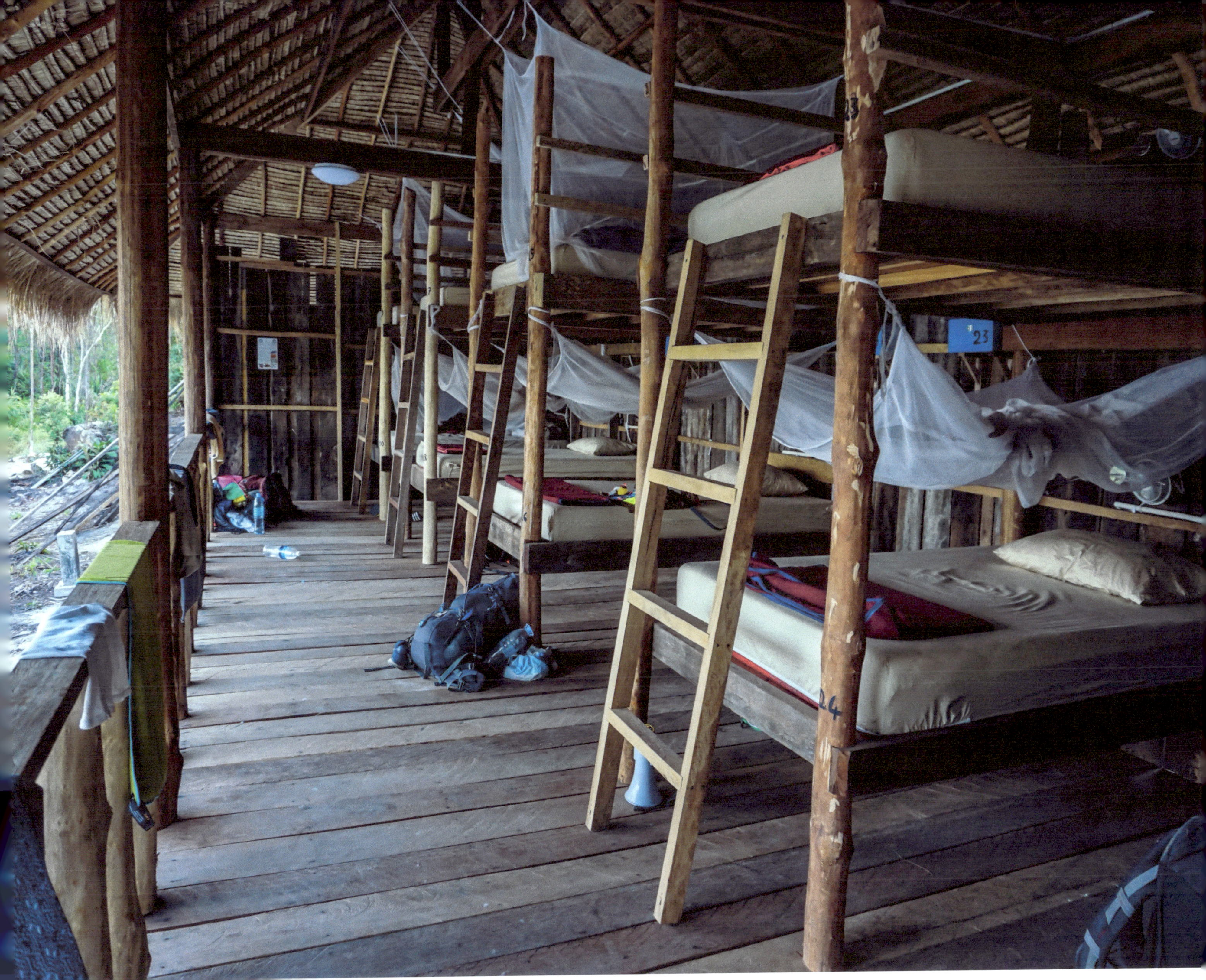

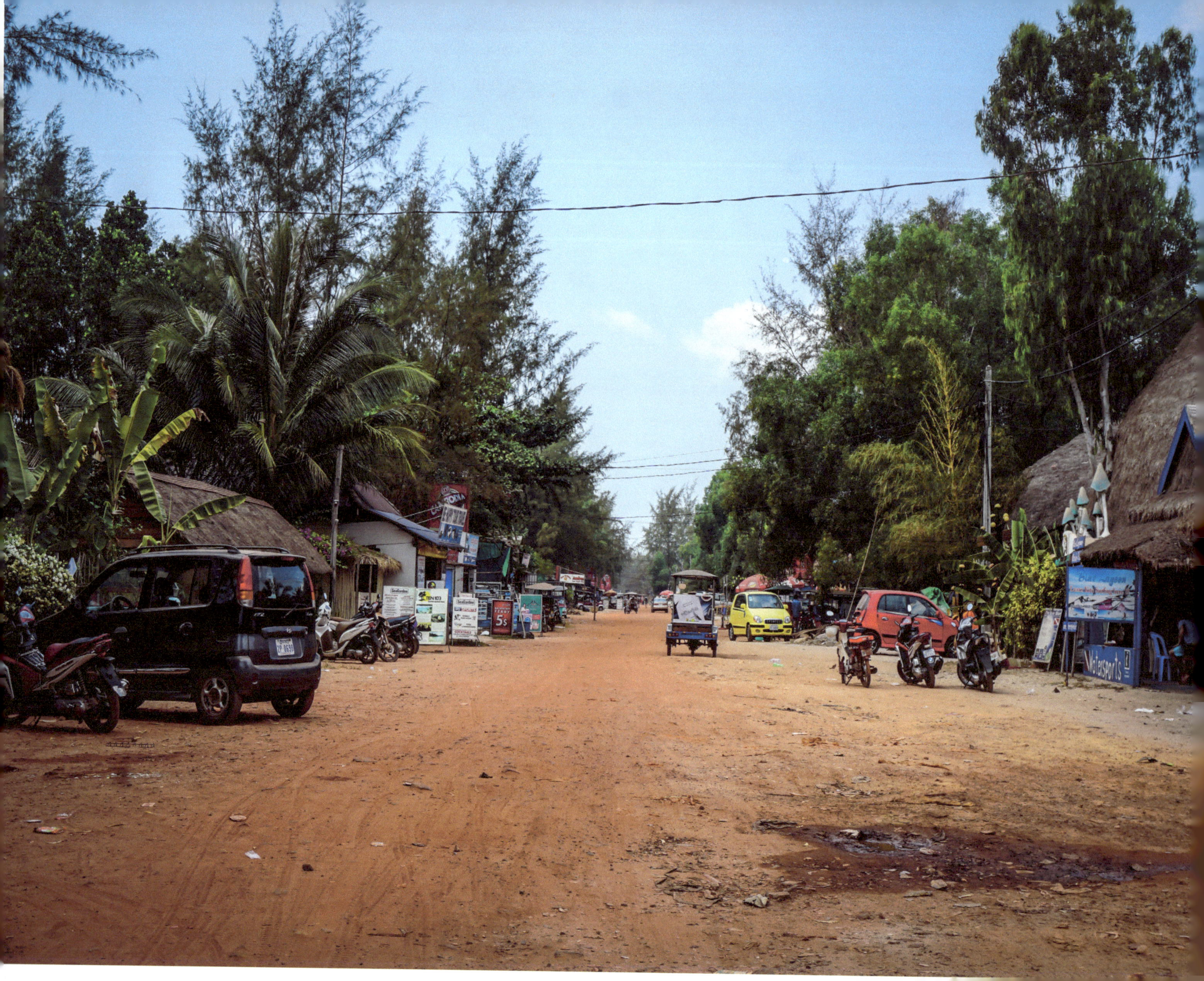

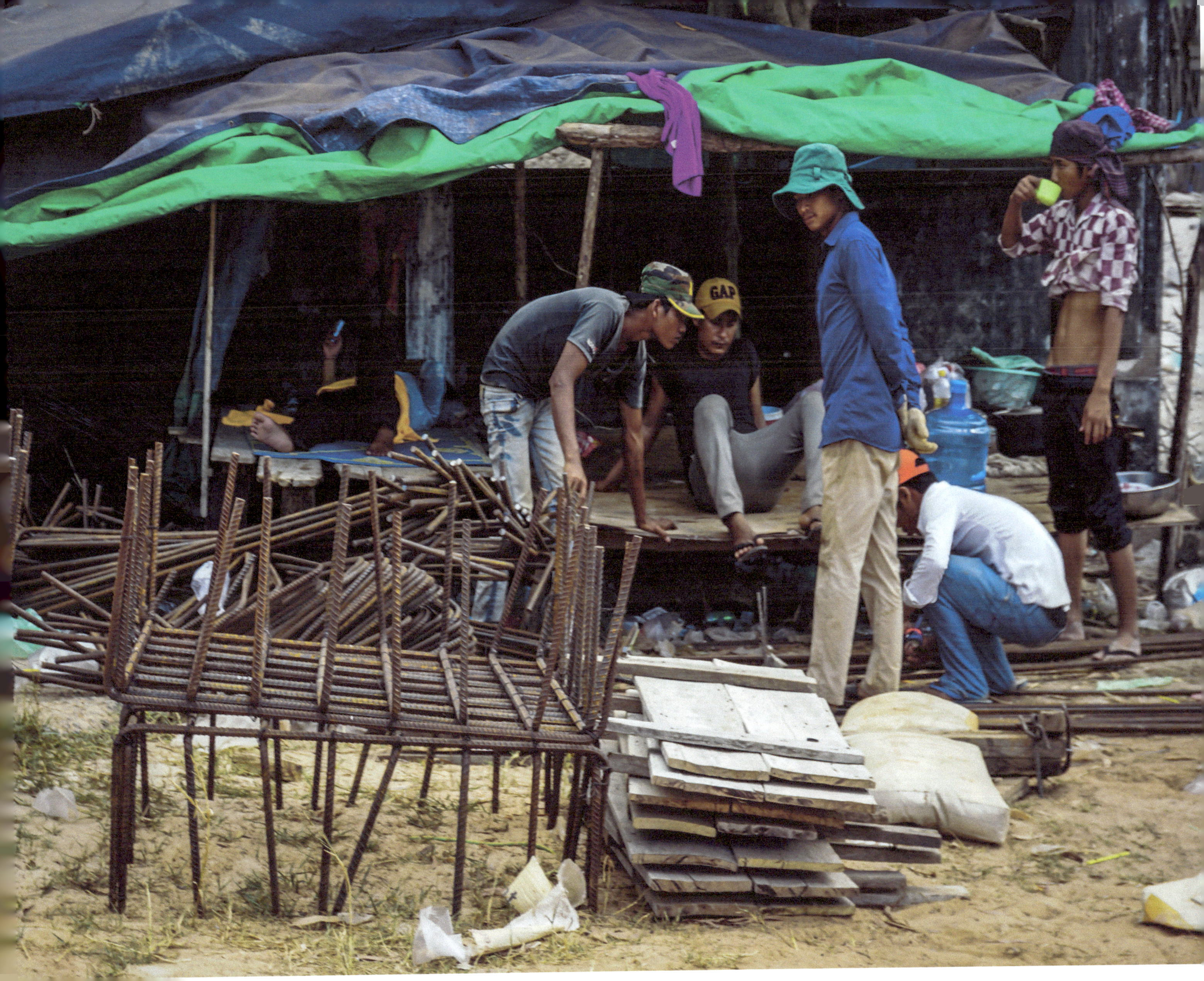

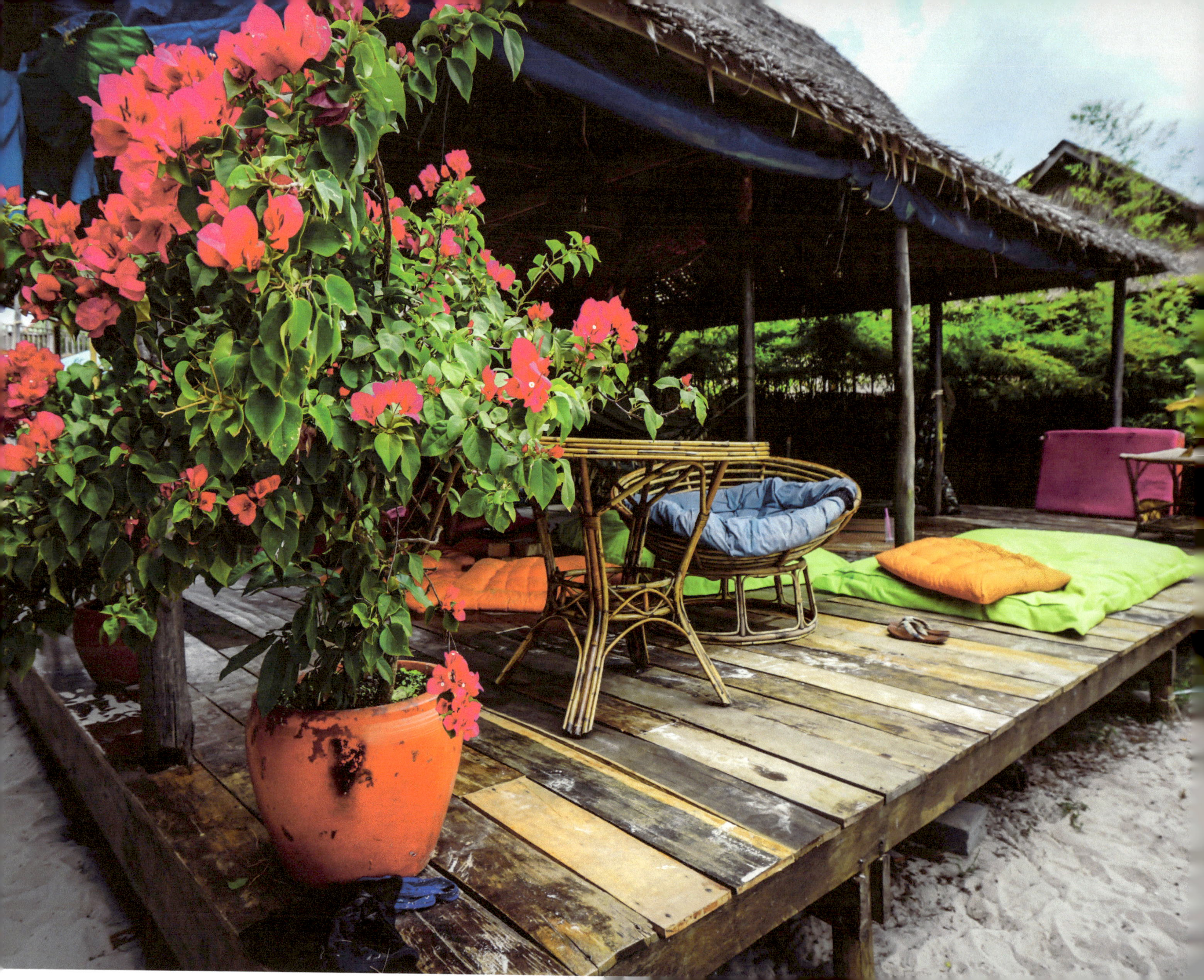

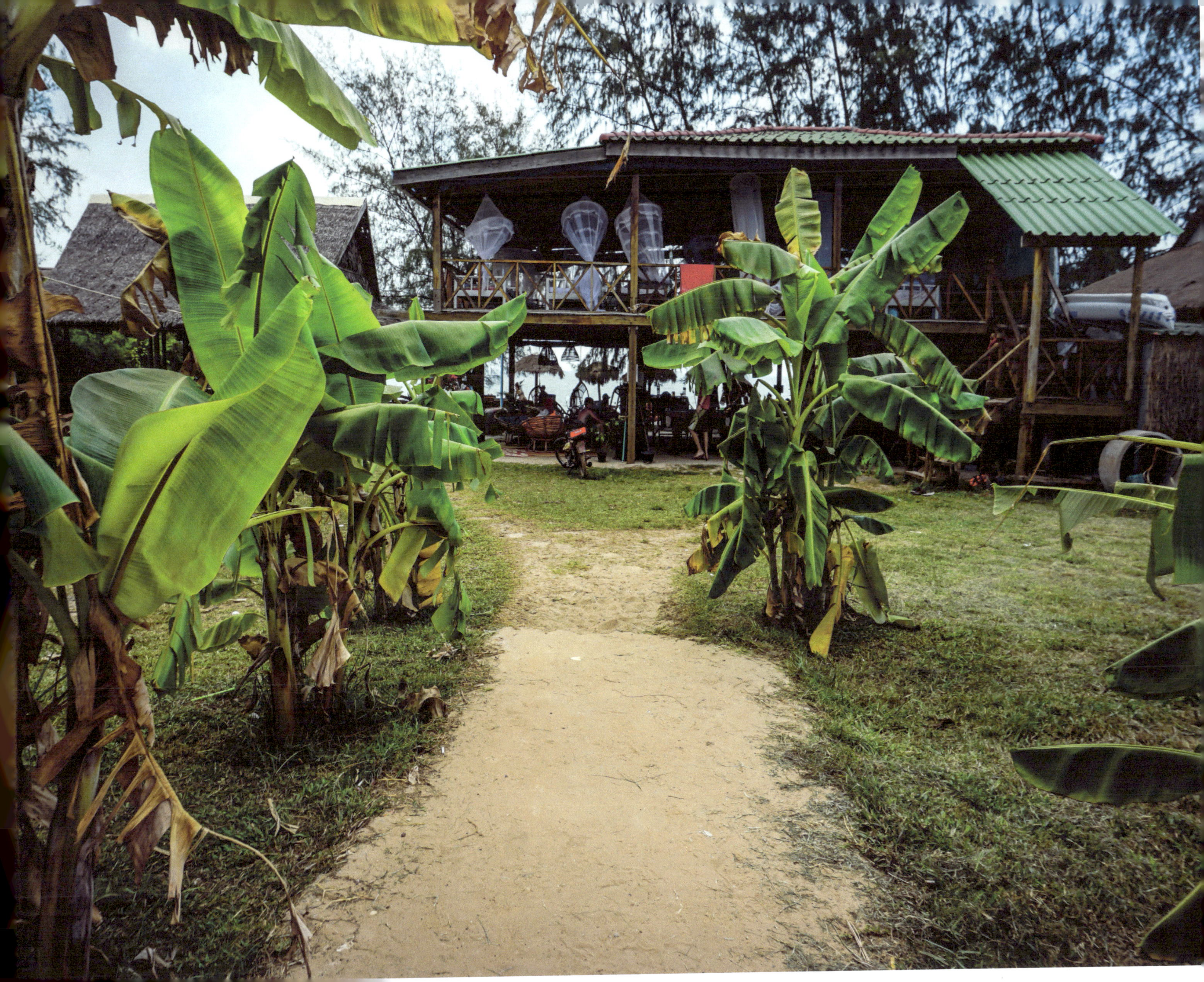

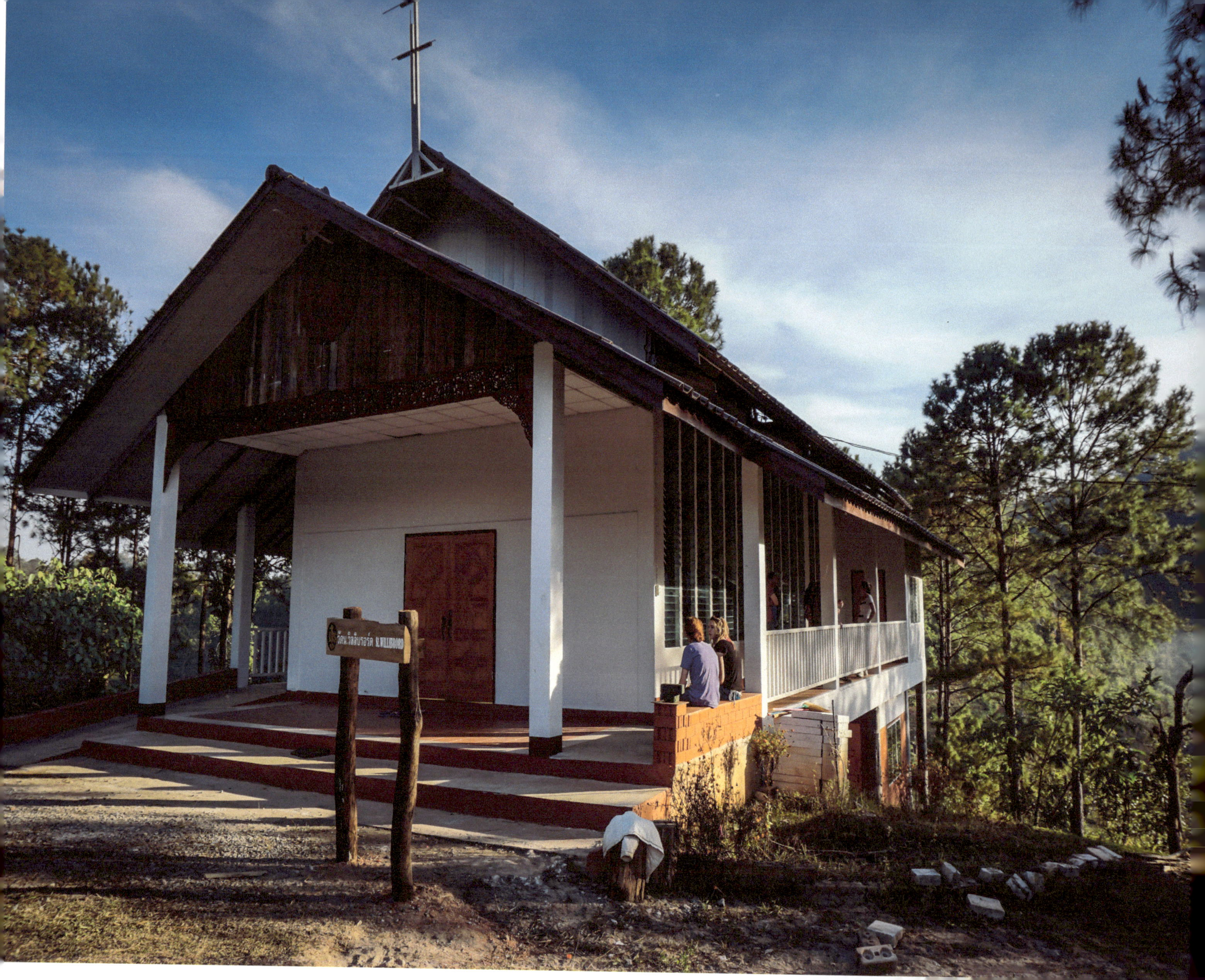
วัดน.วิลลิบรอร์ด  St.WILLIBRORD

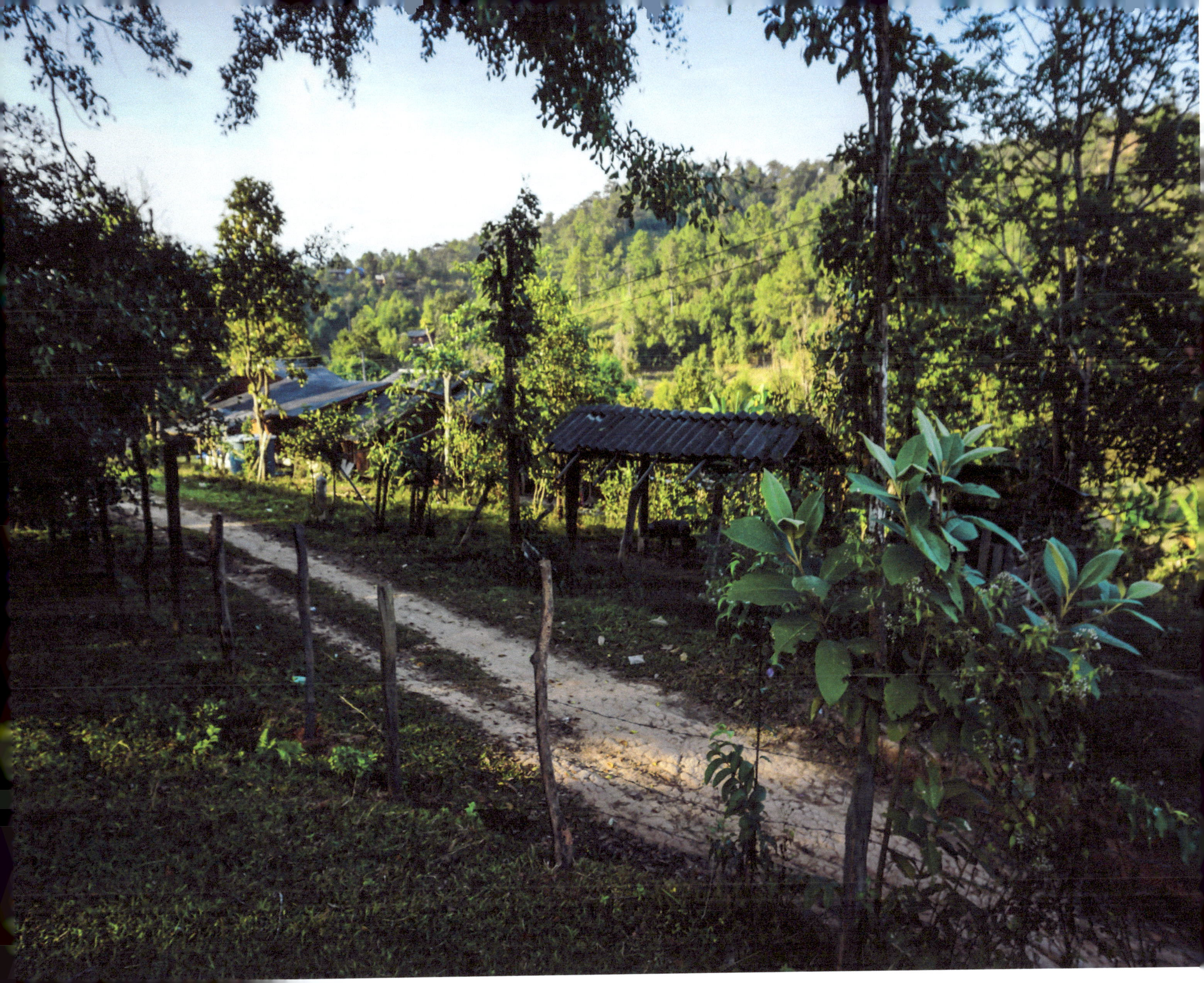

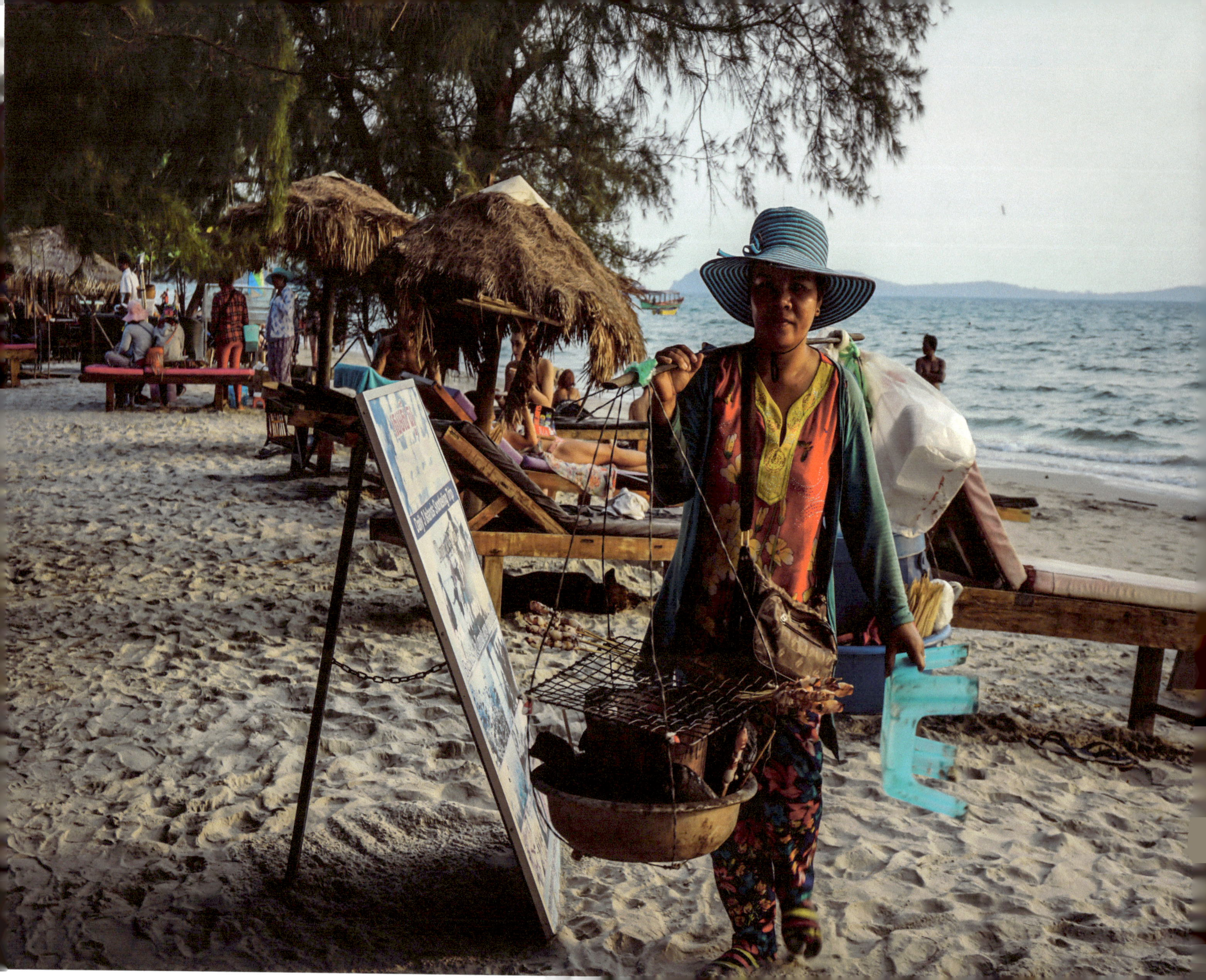

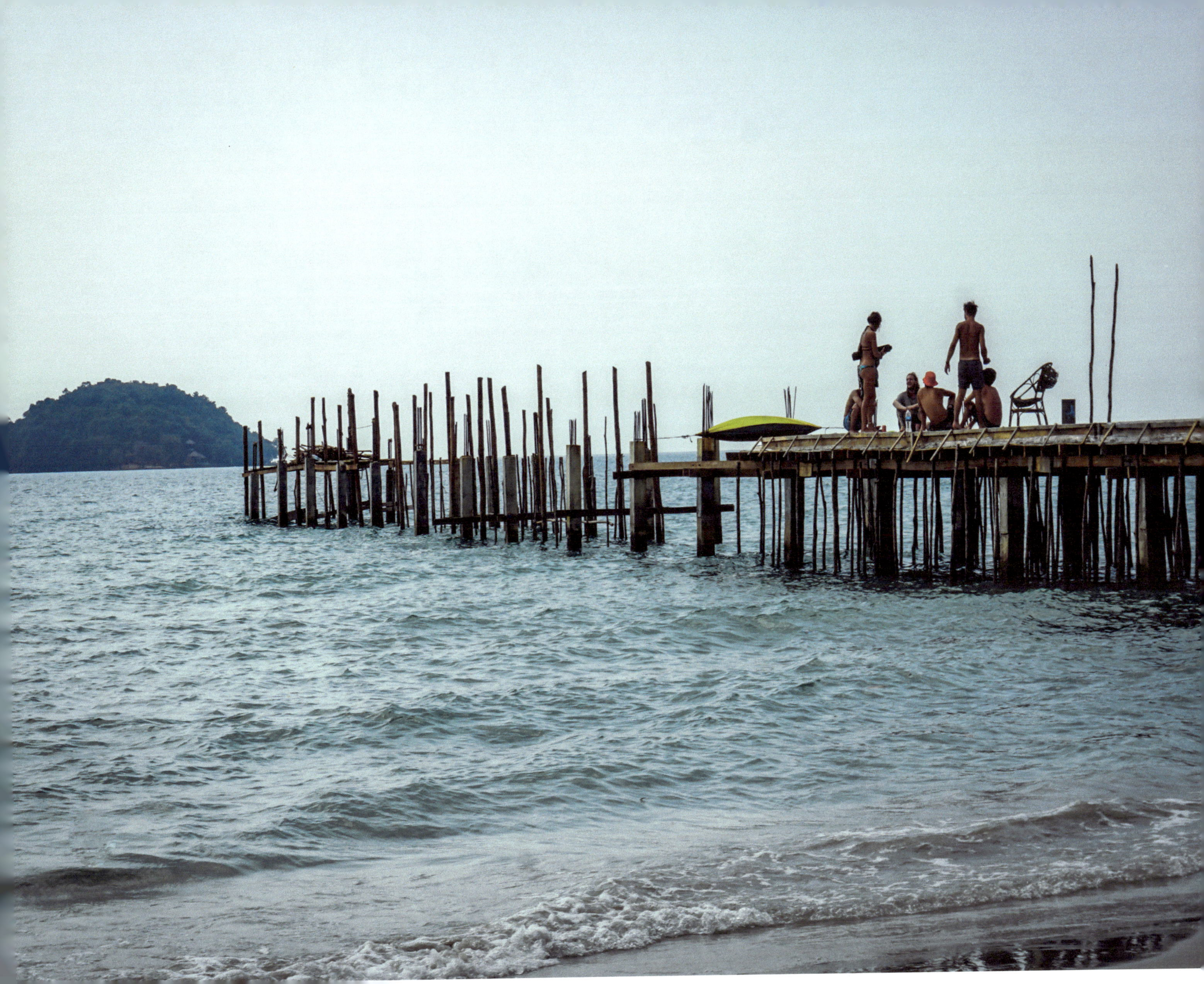

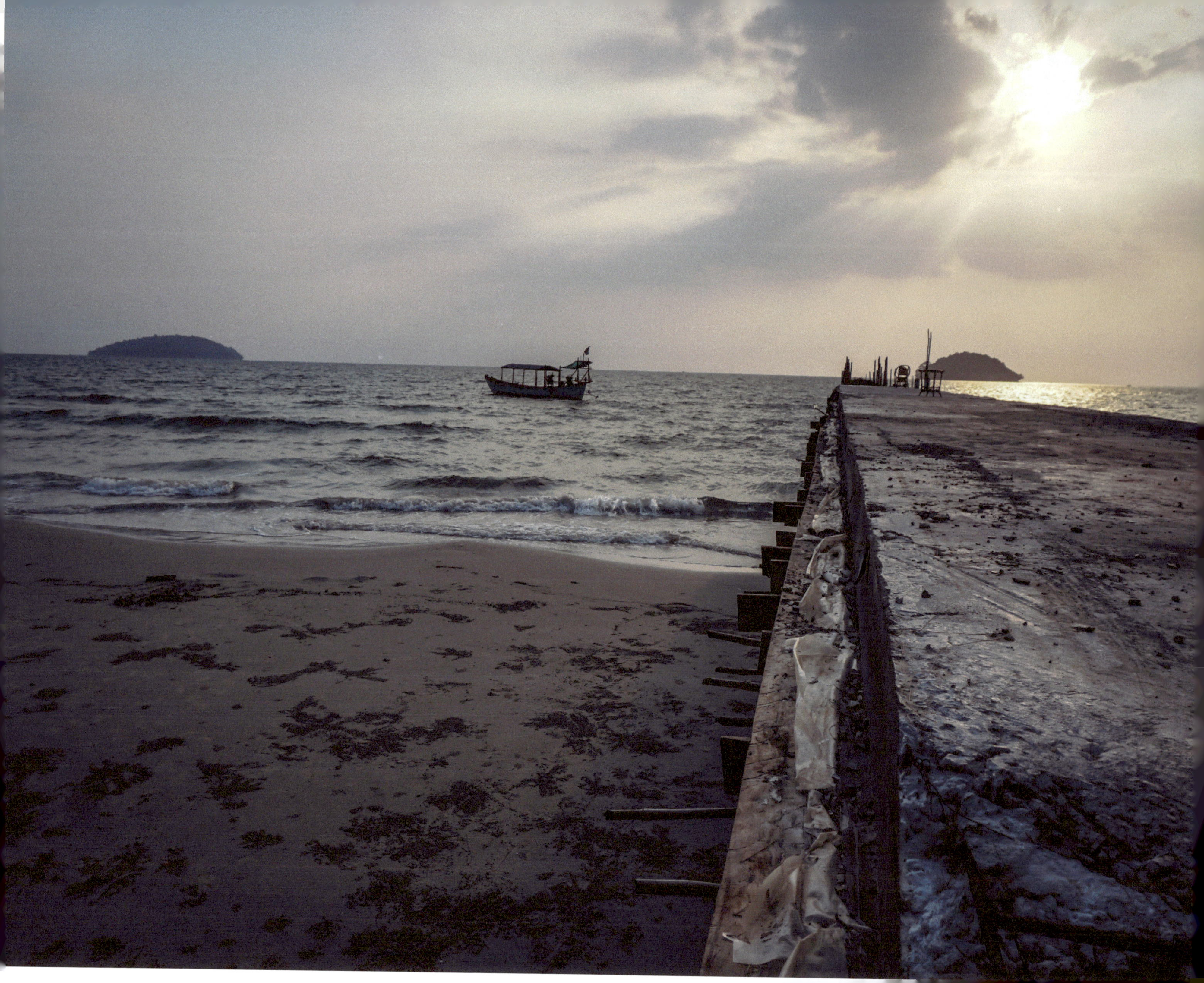

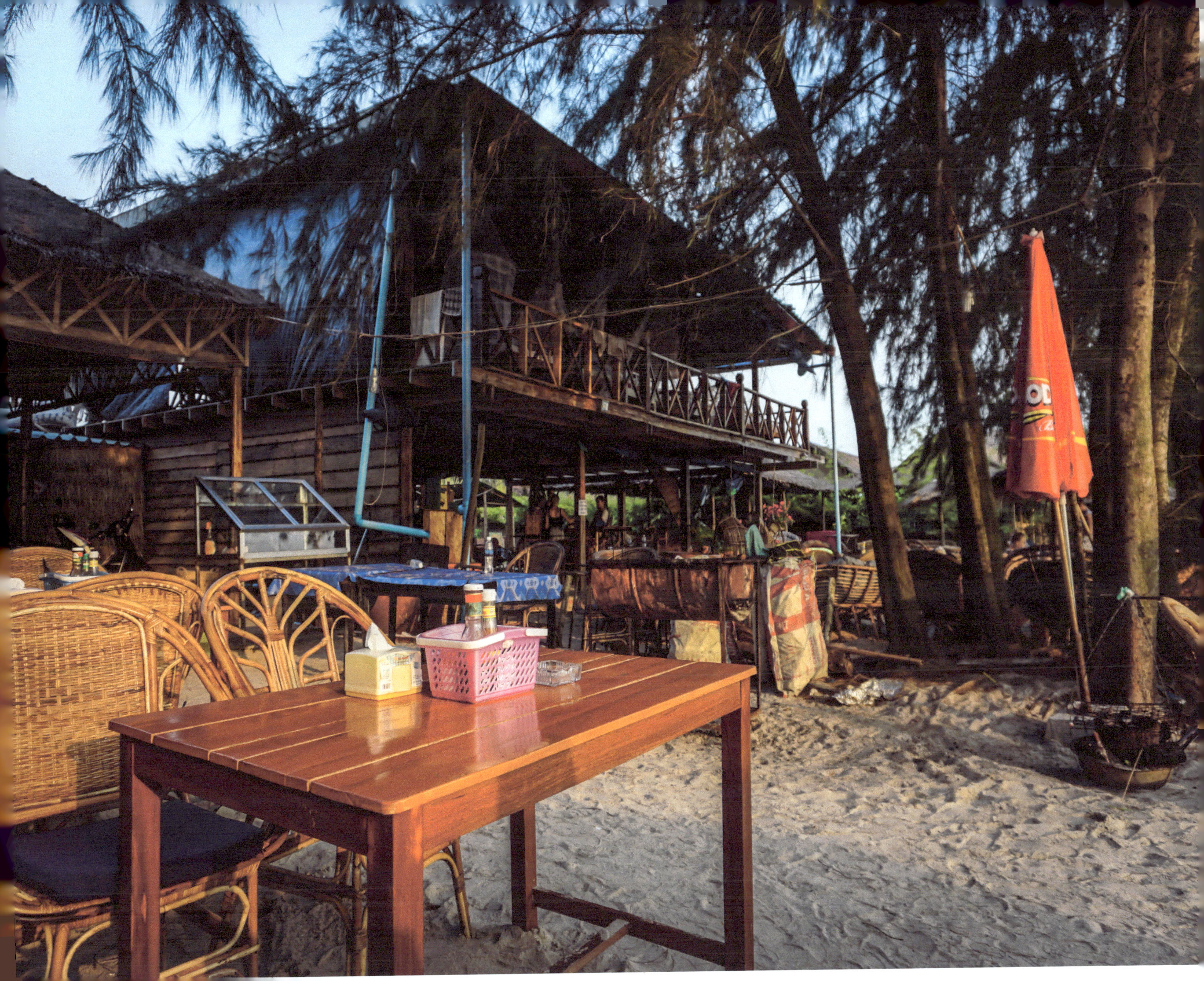

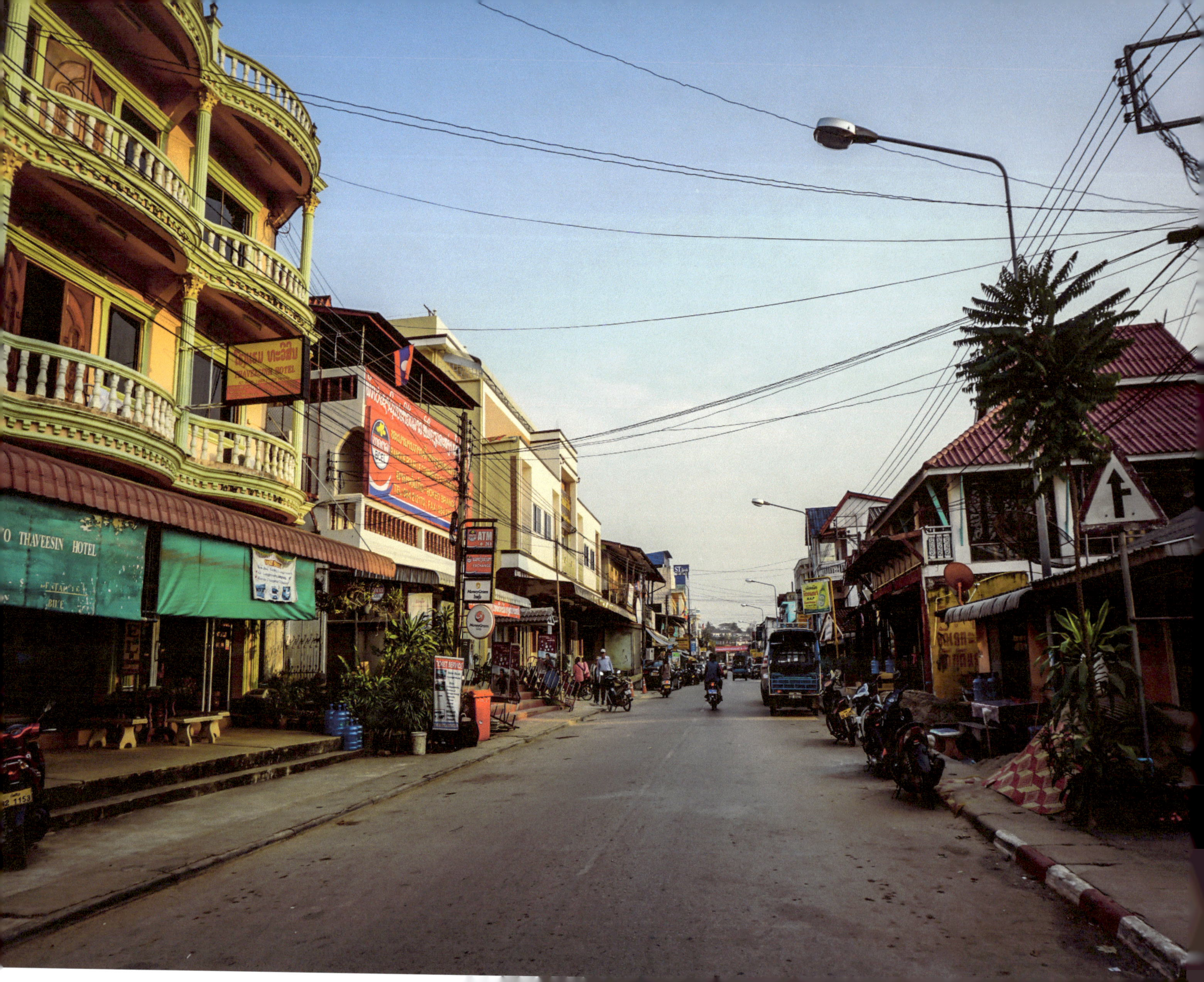

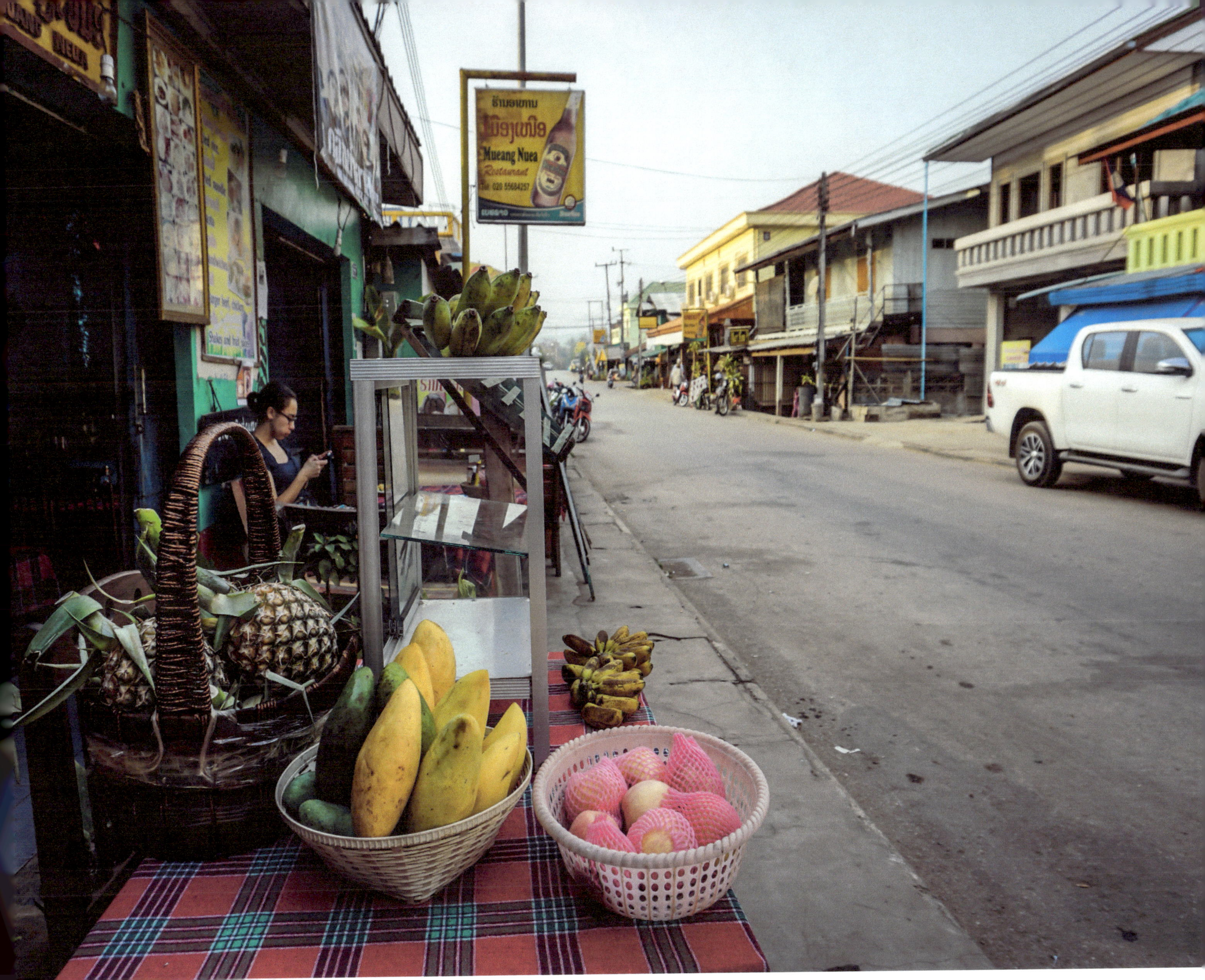
ຮ້ານອາຫານ
ເມືອງເໜືອ
Mueang Nuea
Restaurant
Tel: 020 55684257

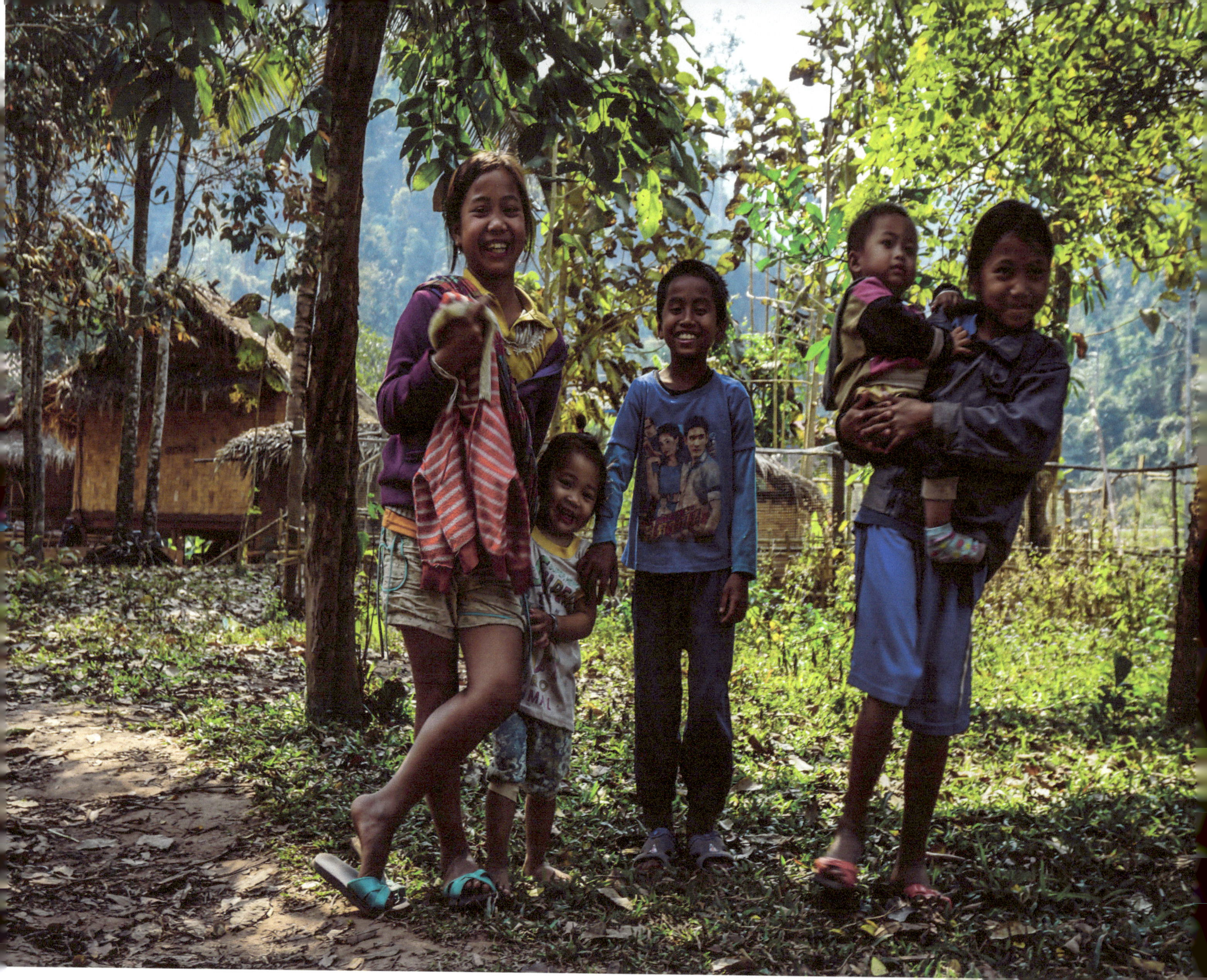

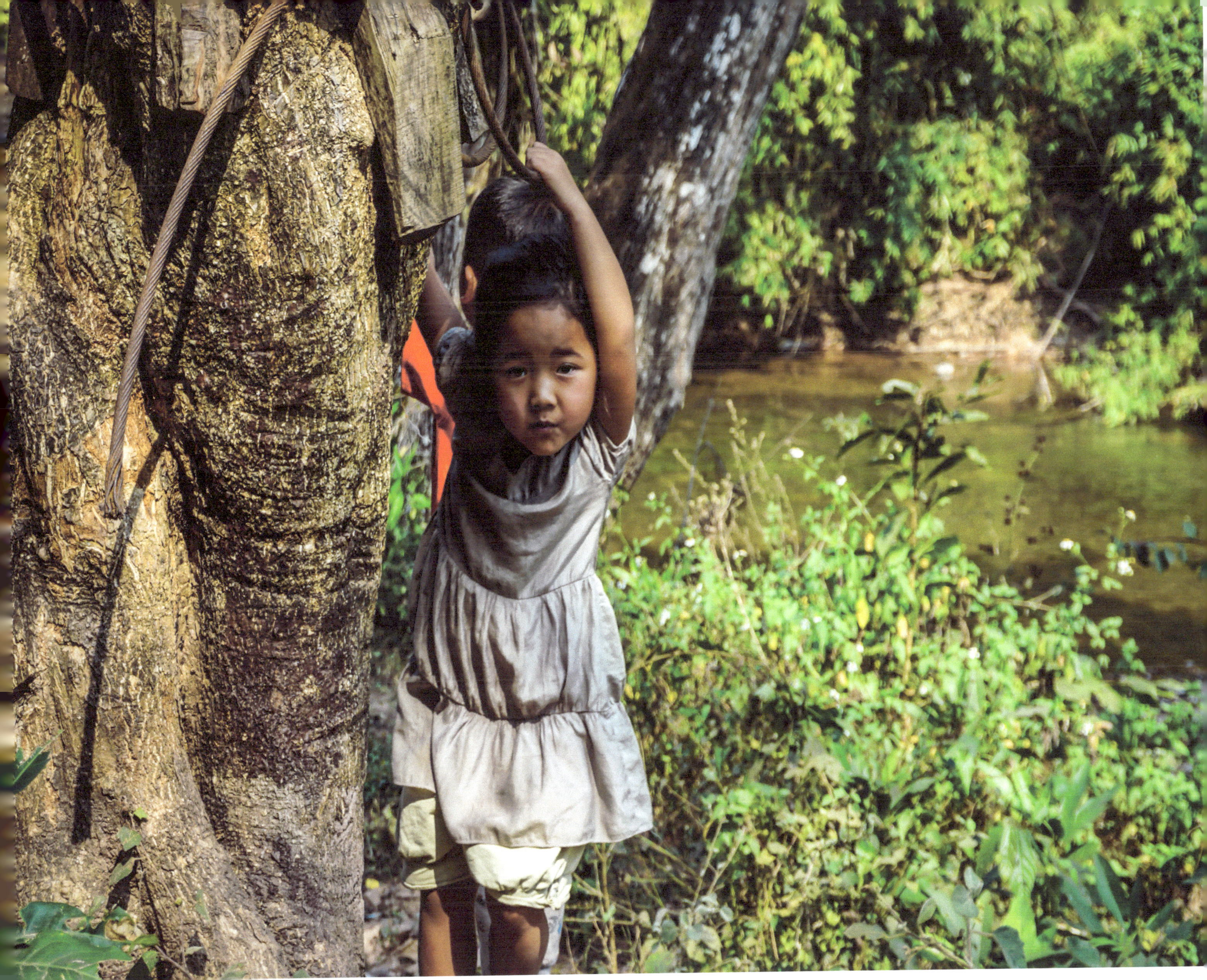

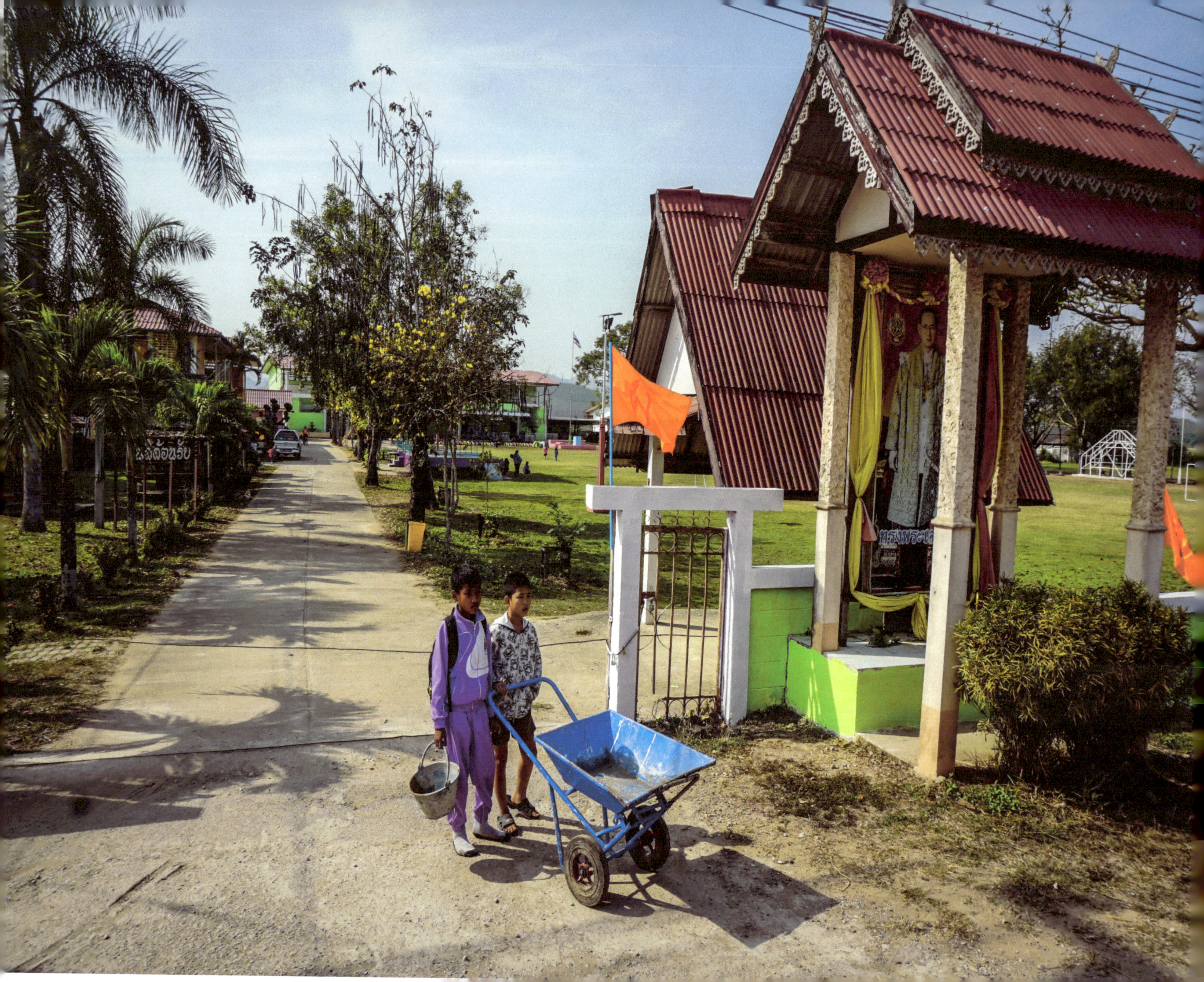

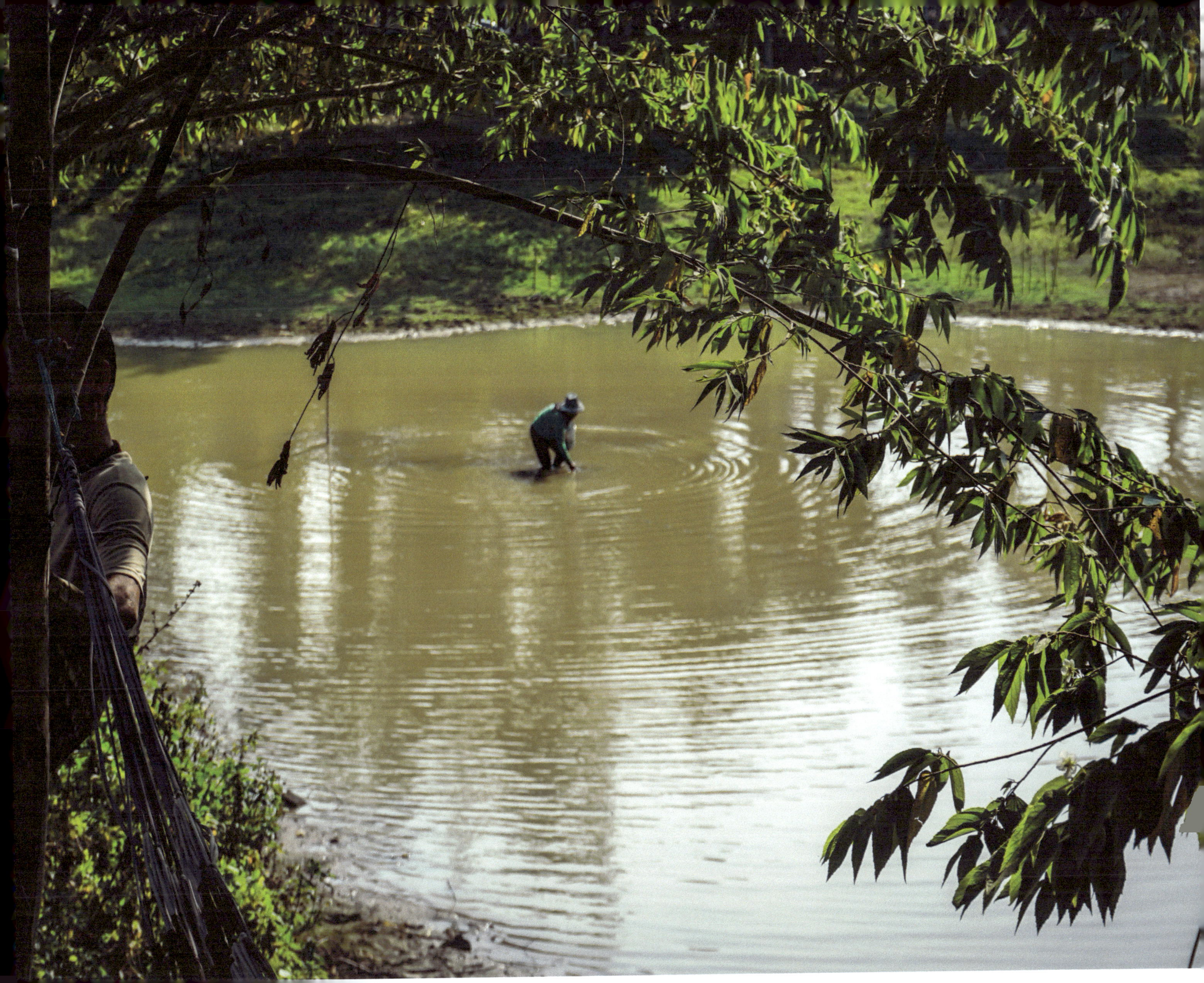

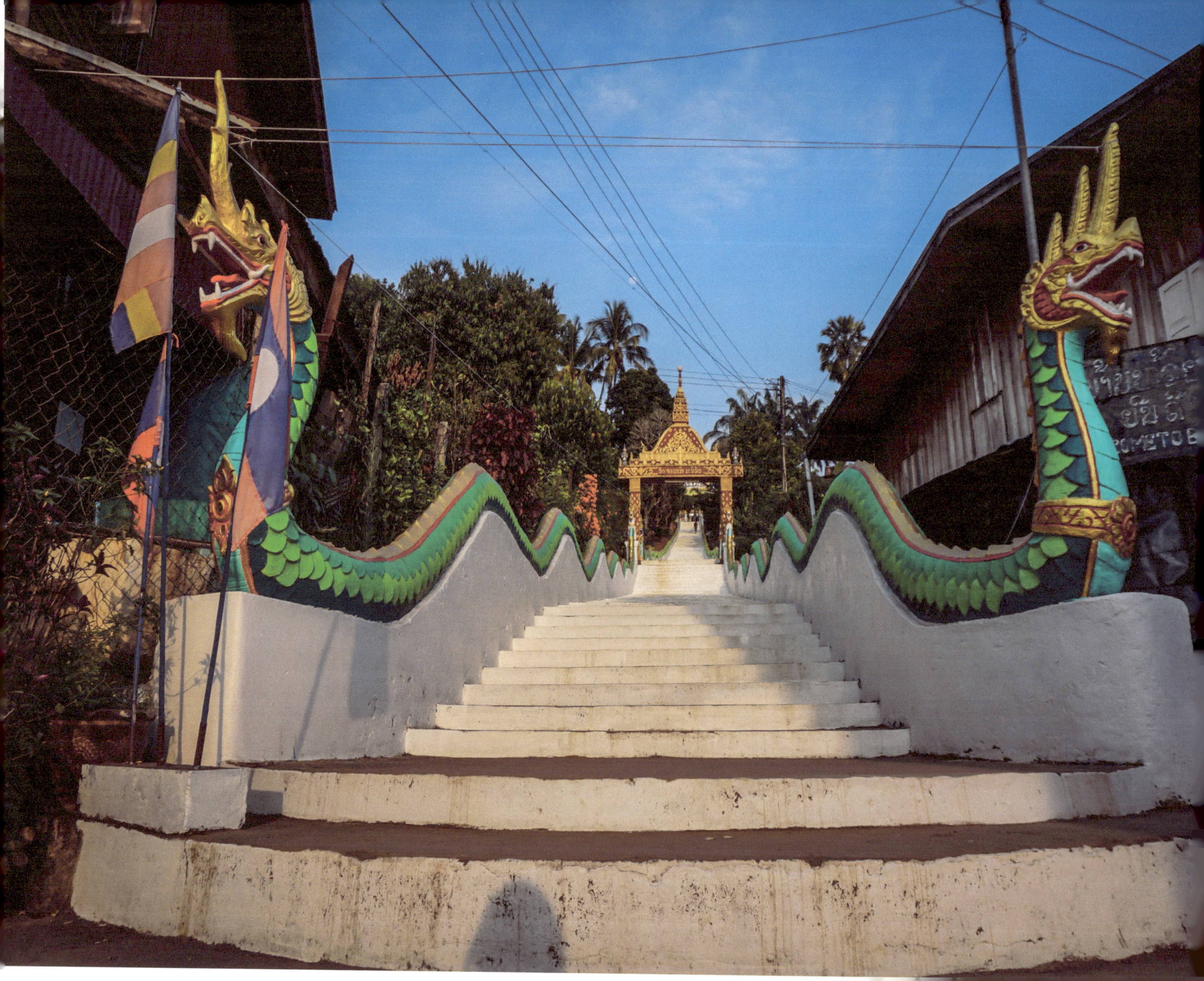

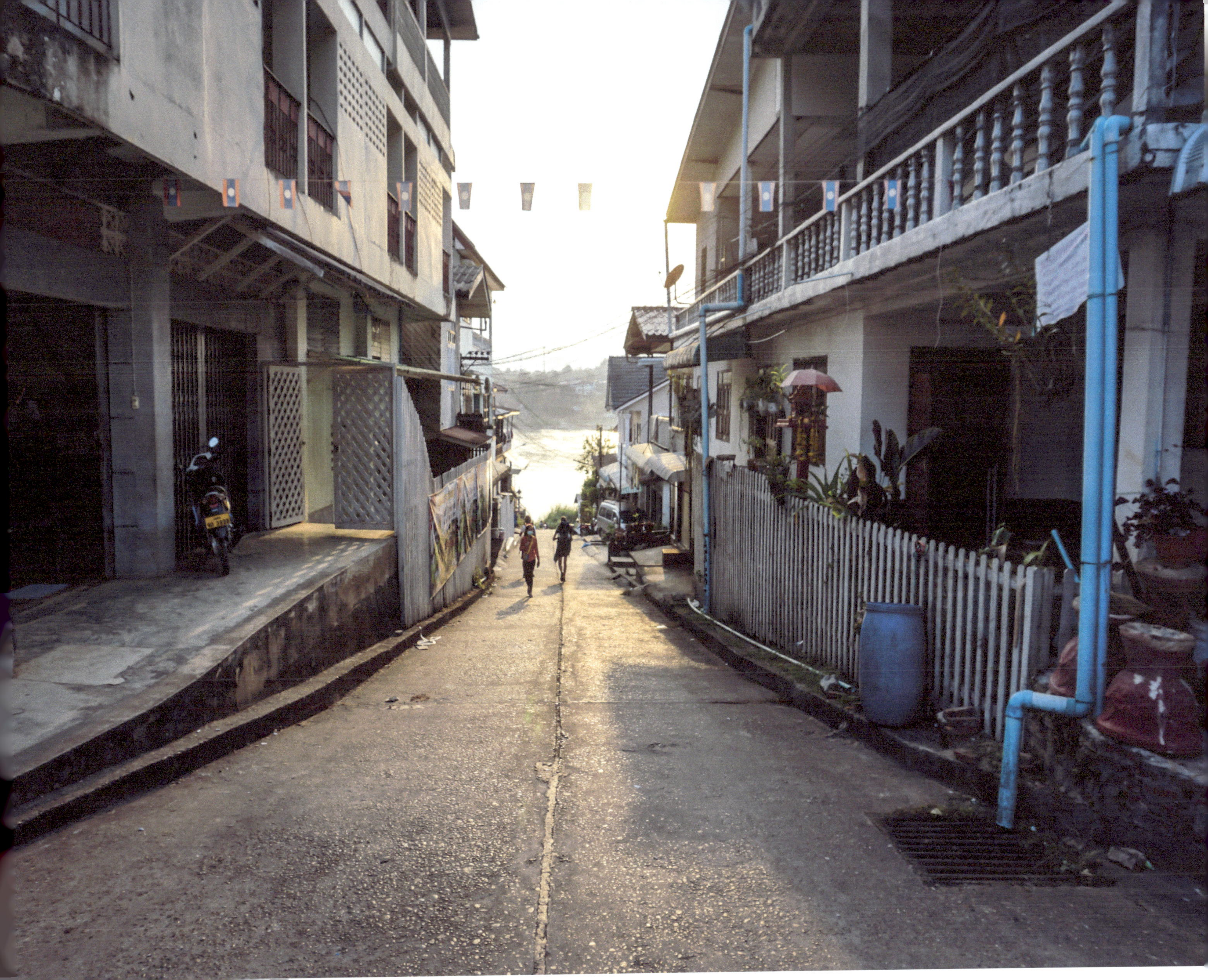

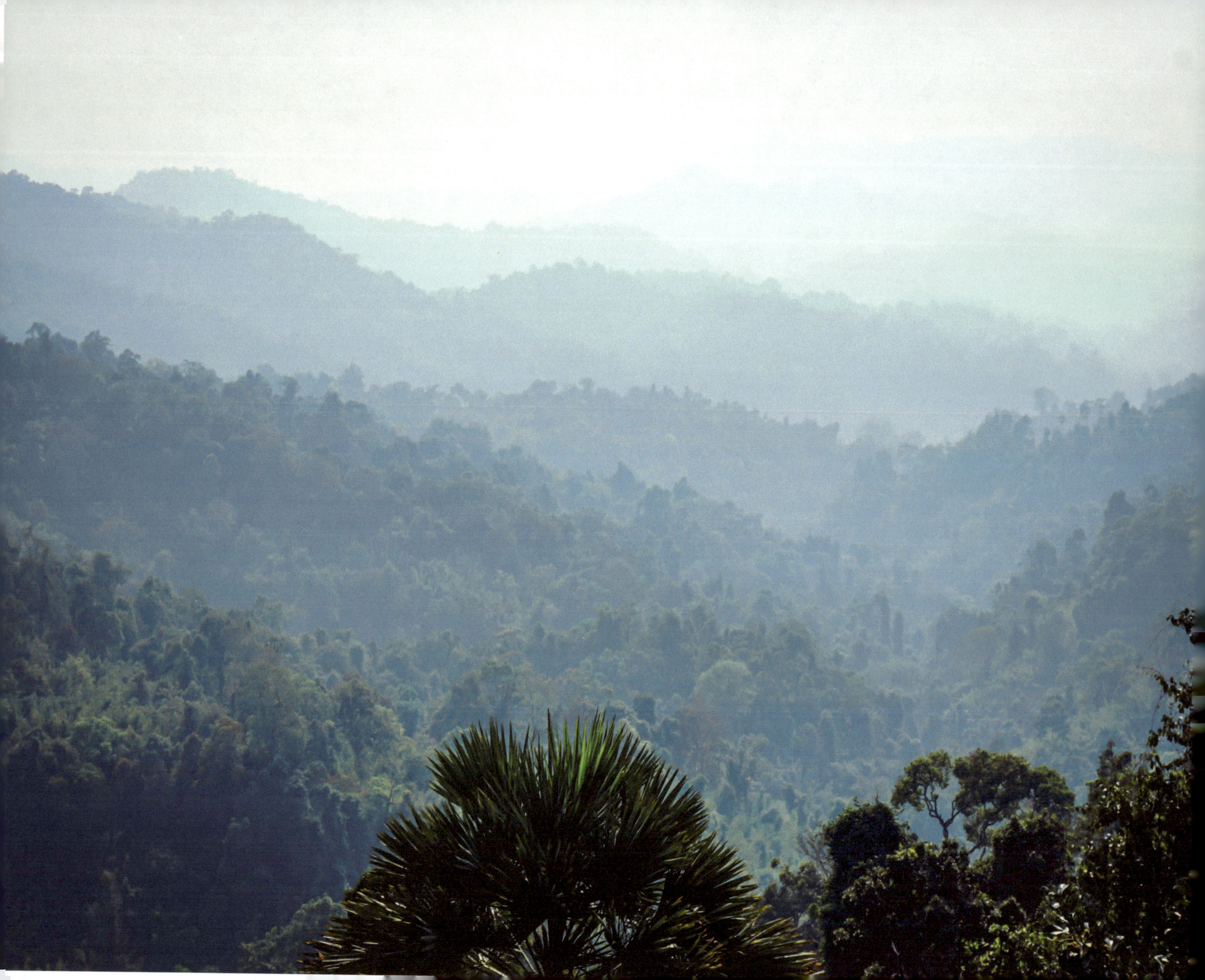

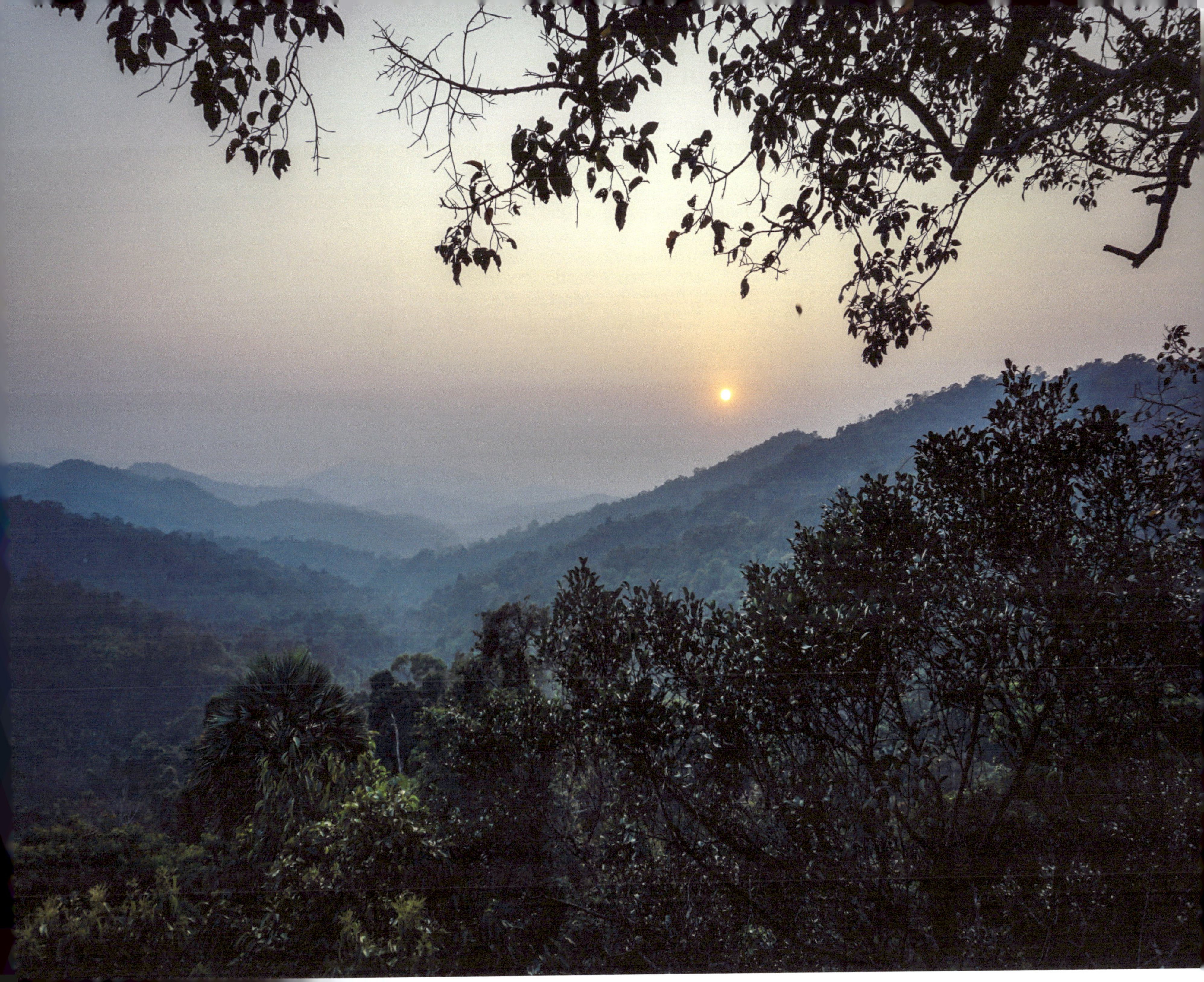

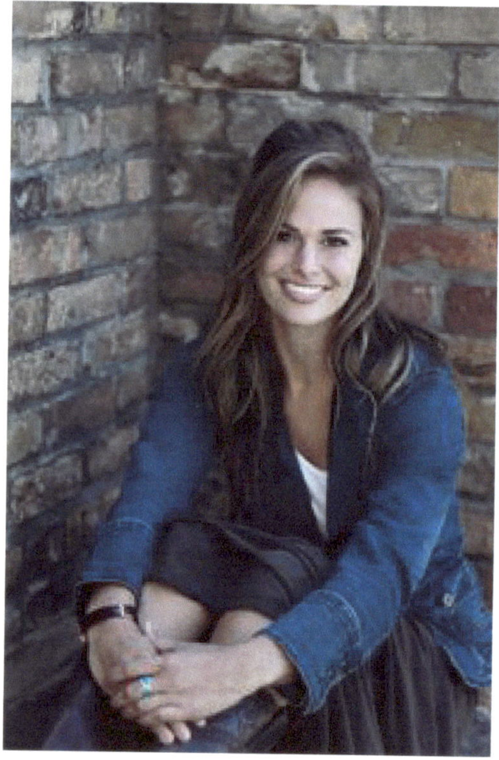

## About the Author

**Elyse Booth** is an international photographer and educator. She has travelled around the world photographing nature, people, culture, architectural icons, animals and lifestyle content. A few of the places she has travelled to include: Hawaii, Iceland, Thailand, Cambodia, Malaysia, Laos, Italy, France, Ireland, Croatia, Hungary, Czech Republic, England, Scotland, Costa Rica, Bermuda and Mexico.

Elyse is an award winning Google trusted photographer. She builds virtual tours for Google Maps through her business Shutter Fotos, www.shutter-fotos.ca. Elyse has been recognized as a top performer for Google and top five in North America for her tours.

Elyse has a passion for lifelong learning. In addition to her love for travel and photography, she teaches Communications Technology in the private and public educational systems.

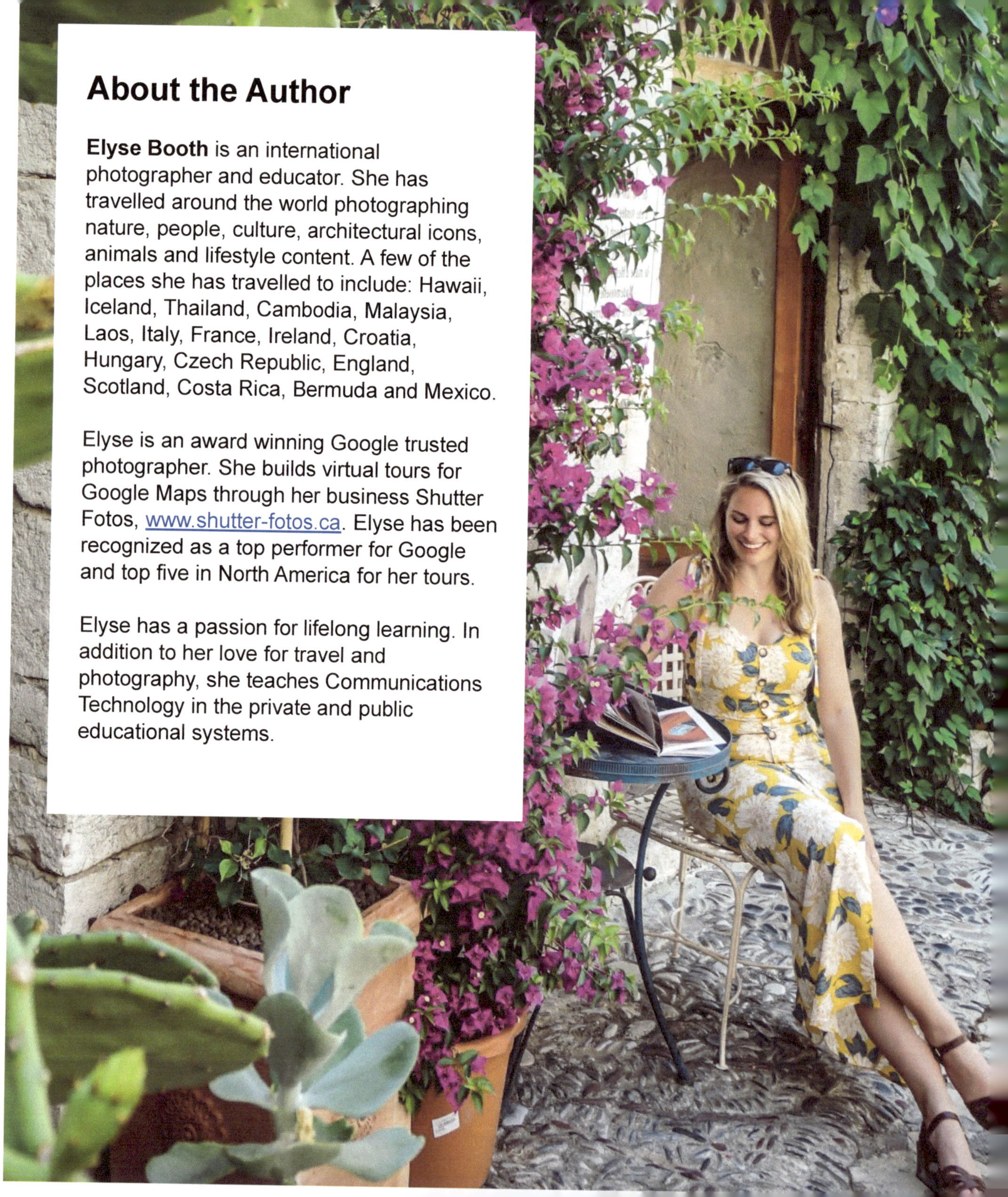

## Social Media & Contact

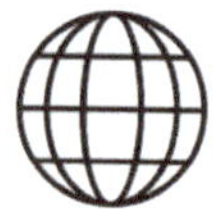 www.shutter-fotos.ca

 elyse@shutter-fotos.ca

 @shutter_fotos

 @ShutterFotos

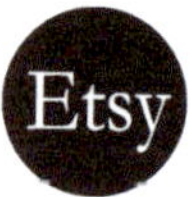 @FotoBoothphotography